The Economics of Financial Markets and Institutions

The Economics of Financial Markets and Institutions

from First Principles

OREN SUSSMAN

OXFORD
UNIVERSITY PRESS

OXFORD
UNIVERSITY PRESS

Great Clarendon Street, Oxford, OX2 6DP,
United Kingdom

Oxford University Press is a department of the University of Oxford.
It furthers the University's objective of excellence in research, scholarship,
and education by publishing worldwide. Oxford is a registered trade mark of
Oxford University Press in the UK and in certain other countries

Published in the United States of America by Oxford University Press
198 Madison Avenue, New York, NY 10016, United States of America

British Library Cataloguing in Publication Data
Data available

Library of Congress Control Number: 2023930672

ISBN 978–0–19–286973–9

DOI: 10.1093/oso/9780192869739.001.0001

Pod

לבילה

Preface

This book is based on introductory lectures on financial economics that I delivered to masters students in the Faculty of Law at the University of Oxford. Most of the students, smart and hard working (as many lawyers are), had no background in economics. Worse, some were mathsphobs; others, did not take any mathematics classes beyond the age of 16, nor did they practise their pre-16 skills since. Hence, the challenge was to deliver the basic ideas that lawyers working in financial markets need in their dealing with practitioners and regulators with the minimum use of mathematics. That, of course, required drastic simplification of the material as well as 'cutting corners'—here and there. The corners that I have decided to cut away may not be to everyone's taste. Nevertheless, I believe that the experience that I have gained while delivering these lectures is worth sharing with others.

Like many economists, following the 2008 financial crisis, I felt that finance training has become too 'engineering minded', losing touch with fundamental economic analysis. This manuscript attempts to provide the economic foundations and their application to finance—jointly. Needless to say, that limits the depth and breadth that I can provide, on both the conceptual as well as the application side. This book does not intend to replace some excellent economic textbooks on game theory, consumer theory, or contract theory, nor does it intend to replace equally good textbooks in corporate finance, banking, or asset pricing. Only to provide a foundation from which students can expand in both directions.

I am grateful to Luca Enriques who read the entire manuscript and provided me with most helpful comments. Alexander Guembel and Dan Awrey have done so on Chapters 5 and 6, respectively. I am also grateful to Carlo Sushant-Chari and Wande McCunn who commented on the first two chapters. Numerous class participants made comments that helped me to sharpen and clarify certain points. Needless to say, I am the only one to blame for the remaining faults in this book.

Contents

Introduction

Financial economics is an application of general economics to the study of the financial system.

The financial system presents examples of some of the most competitive markets in the world; for example treasury bonds or foreign-exchange markets. At the same time, the system also presents some complex non-market organizations, such as limited companies or banks. This diversity of organizational form makes clear, right from the start, that beyond the understanding of prices and trading volumes, the business of financial economics is to understand what purpose is served by this diversity of organizational form.

It is worth noting that the typical object that is traded in financial markets is not a 'thing'—a potato or an automobile but, rather, a *title*[1] to a 'thing': a promise to deliver, at some point in the future, the 'thing', contingent on certain eventualities. Debt, equity, insurance contracts, or stock options (the right to buy or sell a stock at a pre-specified price) are typical examples. Clearly, while it is important to understand prices and quantities, it is equally important to understand why these contracts are structured the way they are.

The Taoist sage Chuang Tzu (369–286 BC) held the view that 'good order [i.e. organization] results spontaneously when things are let alone'. He argued that regulations, which tend to become 'more numerous than the hairs of an ox', are inherently complicated and ineffective; the more regulation there is 'the more the people are impoverished'.[2] Friedrich August von Hayek, winner of the 1974 Nobel Prize in Economics, is often credited with the application of the concept to economics; see Sugden (1989).[3] It is important to distinguish two parts of the thesis. First, that although markets undoubtedly require rules, norms and institutions in order to function effectively, these can be devised by the traders who operate in the same markets, without any 'top down' supervision. Second, that when traders get together in order to execute certain business to their own benefit, they don't do so to the determent of others, who are not party to the business.

To put it more technically, we make a distinction between *positive* and *normative* analysis. The former aims at understanding economic reality as it *is*, the latter

[1] Words used in a technical-economics sense are presented, first time, in italics font.
[2] Cited by Rothbard (1990).
[3] Adam Smith used the better-known concept of the invisible hand. 'Spontaneous order' emphasizes that 'order' includes both market and non-market institutional arrangements.

The Economics of Financial Markets and Institutions. Oren Sussman, Oxford University Press. © Oren Sussman (2023).
DOI: 10.1093/oso/9780192869739.003.0001

aims at suggesting how it *ought* to be.[4] Clearly, normative analysis requires a more accurate criterion of evaluation. As we shall see, economists focus their analysis on one special aspect of such evaluation, which is *economic efficiency*, a concept that is, hopefully, independent of anyone's value judgement, moral or political persuasion and, in particular, of the value judgement of the economist who executes the analysis. We can thus rephrase the statement above: while positive analysis aims at understanding the modus operandi of a given market or institution, normative analysis tries to establish whether it is possible to make it operate more efficiently, possibly by regulation. Evidently, the (extreme) position of some followers of Tzu and Hayek is that the best way to achieve economic efficiency is by avoiding regulation all together.

The concept of spontaneous order has an interesting biological connotation: that the economic system is self-organizing, like a group of cells that evolves, first to a cluster, then to a colony where some cells specialize in certain tasks and, ultimately, to a complex organism, one that can adapt and survive in a changing environment. No external force shapes or directs the process, and the cells that initiate the process have no awareness or understanding of the end result. A more relevant example is a common law system, which evolves through the accumulation of court cases, with each case decided on its on merit. To a large extent, this was the approach that English law adopted towards Corporate law: once the stakeholders write their preferred rules into their business contracts (broadly defined, including charters and articles of association), and once the courts enforce these contracts as intended by the parties, a standardized body of law emerges.[5] Neither the contracting parties nor the judges that rule on a disputed interpretation of a contract have the obligation, (or, indeed, the capacity) to exercise any judgement beyond the facts of the case in front of them.

It is important to emphasize that the analysis that we present in subsequent chapters does not take it for granted that spontaneous order is the best economic arrangement; in fact, we demonstrate that in some cases it is not. Rather, our purpose is to operationalize the idea of spontaneous order by building mathematical models of individual behaviour and social interaction, and test these models against the data so as to evaluate the outcomes in terms of economic efficiency. While we do not wish to impose any prior judgement upon the analysis, we do find that spontaneous order is a very useful benchmark; an option to be considered and tested, not a foregone conclusion, dictated in advance. Perhaps we should also make clear that our analysis is not conclusive. Rather, we suggest a line that separates settings where spontaneous order yields efficient outcomes from settings where it does not. That line should be reexamined and redrawn according

[4] The distinction between is and aught statements is due to the great Scottish philosopher David Hume (1711–1776).

[5] The above is a somewhat idealized view of nineteenth-century English commercial law, rather than present-day English law.

to changing circumstances such as new technologies, conceptual innovations in economic analysis, as well as by the availability of new data.

On Mathematical Modelling

Much of economics is about quantifiable phenomena: prices, volumes of funding, profit, and loss. We use mathematics in order to build models that mimic the forces that drive these magnitudes so as to guide the statistical analysis that tests these models against actual data.

Crucially, 'mathematics' does not mean complicated mathematics. In fact, the reader of this book is not required to perform any algebraic operation above the level that a 16-year-old high-school student is expected to achieve. Wherever possible, we progress the argument using diagrams, saving the reader the effort of algebra. The appendix to the book reviews the little mathematics that is required.

Nevertheless, following the arguments in this book requires a capacity that high-school students, drilled to follow certain steps in order to solve standardized problems, are not trained for: to express an argument about the operation of a certain economic system in terms of mathematical functions and then to relate the solution of the model back to the reality that has motivated the analysis. The reader is therefore advised not to worry too much about algebraic detail, but to pay much attention to the structure of the models, their assumptions, and the way assumptions are followed by conclusions.

On Abstraction

By their very nature, economic models are abstract. Many readers are likely to ask the question: why should it be so? Why can't we have an analysis that looks, right from the start, more realistic? The simple answer is that such an analysis would be far too complicated. The argument is brilliantly articulated by the great Argentinian writer, Jorge Luis Borges (1899–1986), in a short story called "On Exactitude in Science", narrated by a fictional seventeenth-century traveller. The story is brought, below, in its entirety:

> In that empire, the art of cartography attained such perfection that the map of a single province occupied the entirety of a city, and the map of the empire, the entirety of a province. In time, those unconscionable maps no longer satisfied, and the Cartographers Guilds struck a map of the empire whose size was that of the empire, and which coincided point for point with it. The following generations, who were not so fond of the study of cartography as their forebears had been, saw that vast map was useless, and not without some pitilessness was it, that they delivered it up to the inclemencies of sun and winters. In the deserts of the

> west, still today, there are tattered ruins of that map, inhabited by animals and beggars; in all the land there is no other relic of the disciplines of geography.
>
> *Suarez Miranda,Viajes de varones prudentes, Libro IV,Cap. XLV, Lerida, 1658*

Hence, our purpose here is to identify the main forces that drive the financial system, abstracting from detail that is either irrelevant or has an effect that is too small to justify the cost, in terms of extra complexity, of its inclusion.

On First Principles

By first principles we mean that we build our financial models on general economic principles. We do not mean that all the models in this book add up to a unified and cohesive body of theory that answers, unambiguously, any question that a practitioner or a policy maker might seek to answer. Rather, to apply the ideas in this book to a problem, the reader may have to apply different models to different aspects of the problem with, sometimes, conflicting implications. Which might raise the question whether the effort of studying financial economics is worth making. Ben Bernanke, Chair of the Federal Reserve (the central bank of the United States) between 2006 and 2014 and winner of the 2022 Nobel Prize in Economics, in a speech delivered at the Baccalaureate Ceremony at Princeton University[6] on 2 June 2013, provides a possible answer:

> Economics is a highly sophisticated field of thought that is superb at explaining to policymakers precisely why the choices they made in the past were wrong. About the future, not so much. However, careful economic analysis does have one important benefit, which is that it can help kill ideas that are completely logically inconsistent or wildly at variance with the data. This insight covers at least 90 percent of proposed economic policies.

The Structure of This Book

Chapter 1: we study the decision-making process of a *rational* individual, acting in isolation from other decision makers. Since financial markets trade claims against future deliveries, we focus the analysis on decisions that have a time and *uncertainty* dimension.

Chapter 2: we analyse the simplest possible economic interaction, which is trade between two individuals, where the terms of trade are decided through a

[6] See: https://www.federalreserve.gov/newsevents/speech/bernanke20130602a.htm

process of *bargaining*. The concept of equilibrium is introduced. We provide a precise definition of economic efficiency. We introduce the *Coase Theorem*, namely that in a *frictionless* world, spontaneous interaction yields efficient outcomes. The analysis is applied to an important real world problem: the resolution of *financial distress*.

Chapter 3: we analyse the concept of *property rights*. Since companies may be defined by the assets that they own, the analysis is intimately related to the analysis of the *nature of the firm*. We introduce the idea that in order to overcome certain frictions, some economic activity is internalized into non-market institutions. We also introduce the idea that imperfect information may be a major source of frictions.

Chapter 4: we analyse the concept of a *competitive market*, where a relatively large number of individuals trade identical objects, simultaneously. Competitive markets are the paradigmatic example in economics of *decentralization*, a more accurate representation of spontaneous order. We present the two *Welfare Theorems* regarding the economic efficiency of competitive markets.

Chapter 5: we apply the analysis of Chapter 4 to the market for risk and to the pricing of *risky securities* such as equities or options. We derive the *Capital Assets Pricing Model* (CAPM), a major tool used by financial-markets participants.

Chapter 6: we provide an analysis of *market failures*, where decentralized markets do not achieve economic efficiency. We elaborate on the idea that non-market organizations emerge so as to overcome frictions in trading.

Chapter 7: we present a rigorous analysis of frictions in the form of *asymmetric information*, where one party to a deal is better informed than the other. We elaborate on the efficiency implications of *adverse selection* and *moral hazard*.

Chapter 8: we analyse how, in certain cases, asymmetric information is revealed through the process of trading and how that information is *aggregated* into market prices through several variations of the *rational expectations* model.

References

[1] Rothbard, Murray, N. (1990). 'Concepts of the Role of Intellectuals in Social Change Towards Laissez Faire'. *Journal of Libertarian Studies*, Vol. 9, No. 2, 43–67.

[2] Sugden, Robert (1989). 'Spontaneous Order', *The Journal of Economic Perspectives*, Vol. 3, No. 4, pp. 85–97.

1
Making (Rational) Decisions

1.1 Introduction

The main business of economics is the study of interaction between decision makers such as managers, workers, traders, consumers, or politicians; we will call them *players* from now on. That is, modelling one player's decision-making in relation to the decisions made by others. Since such modelling is complicated we take, in this chapter, a preliminary step of understanding how players make decisions when they are isolated from other players—a somewhat easier task. More specifically, we analyse how players make *rational* decisions. Some readers may lose interest at this point: for how can the behaviour of ordinary humans, some with dubious character, some with only modest intelligence, others poorly educated, all facing a complex circumstance, be investigated on the assumption that they make decisions in the manner usually associated with philosophers or scientists? We beg readers to be patient while demonstrating that the concept of rationality, in its narrow technical-economics sense, can accommodate most of the characteristics commonly attributed to ordinary humans. Moreover, we argue that it is hard to see how an empirical (positive) study can be executed without the use of the rationality assumption. We shall also argue that most policy (normative) analyses actually make the rationality assumption, often implicitly.

Definition 1.1. A rational player selects actions so as to advance outcomes that satisfy her own motives and objectives, the way she feels about these objectives, to the best of her understanding of the causal relationship between the action that she takes and the outcome that results.

A few points are worth emphasizing:

- Rationality is a property of individual players. It is not applicable to groups of players. Hence, proposition such as 'country X (or company Y) is irrational' or 'the stock market is irrational' are, simply, meaningless. In Chapter 2 we provide an accurate definition of economic efficiency that allows us to evaluate the performance of groups of players. As we shall see, the rationality of each and every member of the group is not sufficient to guarantee that the outcome of the interaction is efficient.
- By 'motives and objectives' we mean the gratification of certain sentiments; these are, simply, what players 'feellike' getting or achieving. No restrictions

The Economics of Financial Markets and Institutions. Oren Sussman, Oxford University Press. © Oren Sussman (2023).
DOI: 10.1093/oso/9780192869739.003.0002

are imposed on the sentiments that drive players towards one objective or another. Players may be vulgar or gentile, materialistic or spiritual, selfish or altruistic, far sighted or short sighted, clever or foolish, well-calculated or hot-headed. The rationality assumption does not exclude any of these characteristics.

- Rationality does not imply that a player who makes a decision knows all that there is to know about the problem at hand. Often, players are forced to make decisions with very little information. As a result, it is possible that they make costly mistakes on the way to achieve their objectives. At the same time, the definition implies that players do their best in order to avoid such mistakes.
- The definition above is incomplete. The words 'satisfy', 'motives', or even 'understanding' have no precise technical meaning. Nevertheless, the definition is sufficient for our purpose—at least for the time being.

1.2 From Sentiment to Quantified Subjective Valuation

The sentiment that motivates an individual player cannot be objectively assessed, let alone quantified, by an impartial observer. But the actions that the player takes in an attempt to satisfy this sentiment are observable, so that they can be objectively documented. In particular, the player's valuation of a 'thing', a commodity that she desires, is observable and even quantifiable according to the highest price that she is willing to pay for that commodity. Since valuations are driven by subjective sentiment, they are specific to the player who acts upon them. One player's vanity may be satisfied by the acquisition of an expensive sports car, another player derives aesthetic comfort from listening to classical music, yet another player derives a sense of fulfilment from a charitable donation. Payments may be denominated in terms of money or in kind (namely in terms of other commodities). It follows that a player that *subjectively values* a commodity at £10/*unit*, but buys the commodity for a price less than £10/*unit*, is made better off by 'cutting such a deal'. At the same time, the player declines an offer to buy the commodity at a price higher than £10/*unit*. (Offered the commodity for exactly £10/*unit*, the player is indifferent between acquiring it or not.) Since the valuation is subjective, it is likely to trigger different reactions in different players: for example, if player *A* values a certain commodity at £10/*unit* and player *B* values the same commodity at £8/*unit*, and if both players face the same market price of £9/*unit*, then player *A* would buy the commodity while player *B* would decline such an offer; indeed, in case player *B* already has the commodity, she should sell it. The *surplus* for player *A* (*B*) from buying (selling) the commodity is £1.

The examples above highlight the distinction between subjective valuations and market prices. The former is an expression of a sentiment that is hard-wired into a player's psyche, the latter is an objective economic fact. When a large number of players come together in order to trade, a market is formed and a uniform price tends to emerge. (The price is likely to be uniform across transactions at each point of time but may change over time.) Economists try to explain market prices, taking the subjective valuations as given. For example, suppose that the subjective valuations of players in a certain market are either £10/*unit* or £8/*unit*. We would not expect to observe a market price above £10/*unit* for then, all market participants would like to sell the commodity, with no one willing to buy. For a similar reason, we would not expect to observe a price below £8/*unit*. Benign as these observations are, the central role that they play in subsequent chapters justifies emphasizing them as follows:

Proposition 1.1. *A player benefits from buying (selling) a commodity that is available at a price lower (higher) than her own subjective valuation.*

1.3 The Subjective Value of Time

It is popularly argued that greed and fear are two basic sentiments that drive financial markets. We can capture these sentiments by applying the notion of a subjective valuation a bit more imaginatively. We therefore model 'greed' as a desire for quick satisfaction while 'fear' relates to the anguish that a player feels while he faces the prospect of losses even when, at the same time, he also faces the prospect of similar magnitude gains. The technical-economics terms are *impatience* and *risk aversion*, respectively (see Section 1.9.2 below).

It is easier to conceive time as a sequence of *discrete* points, $t = 0, 1, 2, 3...$, rather than a flux, and to assume that decisions and actions take place at these points alone rather than in the continuum between them. Let $0 < \beta < 1$ (the Greek letter beta[1]) be the subjective valuation of a commodity delivered at $t + 1$ in terms of another commodity, which has the same physical characteristics, but is delivered at period t.[2] Hence, a player with $\beta = 0.8$ is indifferent between receiving one unit of income next period or 0.8 units of income, presently. A lower β is interpreted as a stronger desire for quick satisfaction or a higher level of impatience. We call objects, like β, that capture a player's sentiment: *behavioural parameters*.

Notice that, economically speaking, the t-delivered object and the $t + 1$-delivered object are two different commodities even though they have the same physical characteristics; otherwise, they would have the same subjective valuations. Hence, a commodity's subjective valuation is not dictated by its physical properties. The present-delivered object and the future-delivered object are identical in their engineering and chemical properties, though differences in the timing

[1] To be distinguished from the famous 'finance beta' that we discuss in Chapter 5. The use of the same symbol for two different objects is awkward but unavoidable.

[2] Free storage implies that βs above 1 are 'not interesting'.

of delivery affect a different subjective valuation. A patient player may feel that a delay in delivery hardly affects her while an impatient player may feel that deferring satisfaction causes him much irritation. As a result, the former is willing to give up only a small fraction of the present commodity in order to avoid delay, while the latter is willing to give up a large fraction of the present commodity in order to avoid delay.

As noted, we should make a sharp distinction between the subjective value of a commodity and its market price. In practice, the trade in future deliveries is carried out through *future contracts*. That is a binding contract, by the issuer, to deliver, on a certain day, to the bearer, a certain object. For the time being, we abstract from the possibility that the issuer *defaults* on his obligation to deliver the object when the time comes. The closest real-world example of future contracts with no default risk is a treasury bond.

1.3.1 Arbitrage

The price of a future contract is closely related to the rate of interest, through an important concept in financial economics: *arbitrage*.

Let R be the market price of a contract that delivers one unit of income in the next period. Suppose that, at the same time, the economy also has a market for riskless loans that pay an interest rate, r, per period. That is, investing £1 in a 5% bond or a bank account, a player will be paid back, next period, £1.05.

Proposition 1.2. *By arbitrage, the only conceivable relationship between R and r is*

$$R = \frac{1}{1+r}.$$

The argument is straightforward. Suppose, by way of contradiction, that

$$R > \frac{1}{1+r}. \tag{1.1}$$

By presently selling one future contract and lending the proceeds, R, at the market interest rate, r, a player can generate a next-period profit—after collecting the interest and redeeming the future contract, of

$$R(1+r) - 1 > 0.$$

It follows that in a *counterfactual* world where the inequality (1.1) holds, players can make a profit without making any effort, bearing any cost or exposing themselves to any risk. Moreover, it is hard to see why a player who faces such an opportunity would not scale it up to £10, £100, £1000..., making astronomical profits. And, in addition, every player in the market would like to exploit such an opportunity. However, a state of affairs where all players would like to sell future contracts and lend the proceeds, with no buyers or borrowers on the other side, is inconceivable.

In case:

$$R < \frac{1}{1+r},$$

the opposite trade, namely borrowing one unit to buy $1/R$ units of future contract, would leave the trader with a future profit of

$$\frac{1}{R} - (1+r) > 0.$$

1.3.1.1 Discounting

The following terminology is both common and convenient. Instead of saying 'the value of a next-period-delivered commodity in terms of a present-delivered commodity is R', we say that the *present value* or the *discounted value* of a next-period delivery is R.

In a multi-period setting, the $t = 1$ value of £1 delivered in $t = 3$ is R^2. That is because the $t = 2$ value of the $t = 3$ delivery is R; discounting $t = 2$ delivery of R to $t = 1$ yields $R \cdot R$. Obviously,

$$R^2 = \frac{1}{(1+r)^2}$$

(assuming that both R and r are fixed over time).

We can also apply the formula of a converging geometric series to calculate the market value of a *console*, a bond that delivers £1 in perpetuity,

$$\frac{1}{(1+r)} + \frac{1}{(1+r)^2} + \frac{1}{(1+r)^3} \cdots = \frac{1}{r}$$

(see Mathematical Appendix, Section A.1 for the derivation of a geometric series and substitute in $\frac{1}{1+r}$ instead of q, there).

By a similar argument, we derive the current subjective valuation of a bundle of deliveries using the subjective discount factor. Consider such a bundle, delivering objects subjectively valued v_1 and v_2 at $t = 1$ and $t = 2$, respectively. Then, the $t = 1$ subjective valuation of the $t = 2$ delivery is βv_2 and the present ($t = 1$) valuation of the entire bundle is

$$V = v_1 + \beta v_2.$$

Notice that the *v*s denote the subjective values of *instantaneous* deliveries, namely valuations at the time of the delivery, while V denotes the discounted subjective value of a flow of such instantaneous subjective valuations. To complete the parallel (though conceptually distinct) treatment of market valuations and subjective valuations we define the subjective discount rate, ρ (the Greek letter rho), such that

$$\frac{1}{1+\rho} = \beta.$$

To summarize:

R is the market discount factor,
r is the market interest rate,
β is the subjective discount factor,
ρ is the subjective discount rate.

1.3.2 The Net-Present-Value (NPV) Formula

By a well-known decision rule, a *project* that costs I to start up and generates a certain cash flow, y_t, $t = 1, 2, \ldots, T$, is profitable if (and only if)

$$\frac{y_1}{(1+r)} + \frac{y_2}{(1+r)^2} + \ldots + \frac{y_T}{(1+r)^T} - I > 0$$

(provided that the interest rate remains constant). It is easy to see that the NPV rule is just an application of the above principles. That is, if the market value of a bundle of future cash flows exceeds the cost of producing it then, by arbitrage, this is an opportunity worth exploiting. In principle, the statement is no different from: if one can produce a basket with one x commodity and two y commodities for a sum lower than $p_x + 2p_y$, where p_x and p_y are the market prices of x and y, respectively, she would profit from doing so.

1.4 An Application: Rational Drug Addiction

Gary Becker, winner of the 1992 Nobel Prize in Economics, has demonstrated, through many publish papers, that the concept of rationality can accommodate surprisingly rich and varied sorts of attitudes and behaviours. One of the most dramatic examples of this effort is a 1977 paper, co-authored with George Stigler, winner of the 1982 Nobel Prize in Economics, which analyses rational drug addiction. The paper demonstrates that even if we think that drug addiction is a 'horrible thing', it does not follow that addicts are irrational. A player may behave in a manner that others consider foolish, irresponsible, self-harming, or socially unacceptable and, yet, qualify as rational as far as technical economics is concerned. The following is a much simplified exposition of the Becker–Stigler argument.

1.4.1 The Decision Tree of a Potential Drug Addict

Figure 1.1 describes the decision problem facing a potential drug addict. The problem is *dynamic*, in the sense that several interrelated decisions need to take place at different points in time. We stick to a discrete-time representation and limit the number of periods to just two: $t = 1, 2$, present and future, with no horizon beyond the second period, as if the 'world ends' thereafter. The problem is modelled using a *decision tree*: a set of nodes, each representing a point in time where the player has to select an action out of several alternatives. Each node (save the terminal ones) is connected to subsequent nodes, showing how one decision gives rise to another. A sequence of actions lead to an outcome, which is evaluated subjectively. Using the subjective discount factor, β, the subjective valuations of future outcomes can be discounted, so that all 'lines of actions' can are valued (see on the right-hand side of Figure 1.1).

The two-period modelling is obviously coarse and may seem contrived at first glance. A more realistic modelling that would add many more periods is possible, but the cost in terms of technical complexity is not sufficiently rewarded in terms of extra economic insight. In general, two-period settings prove sufficient in capturing the essence of many dynamic problems in economics.

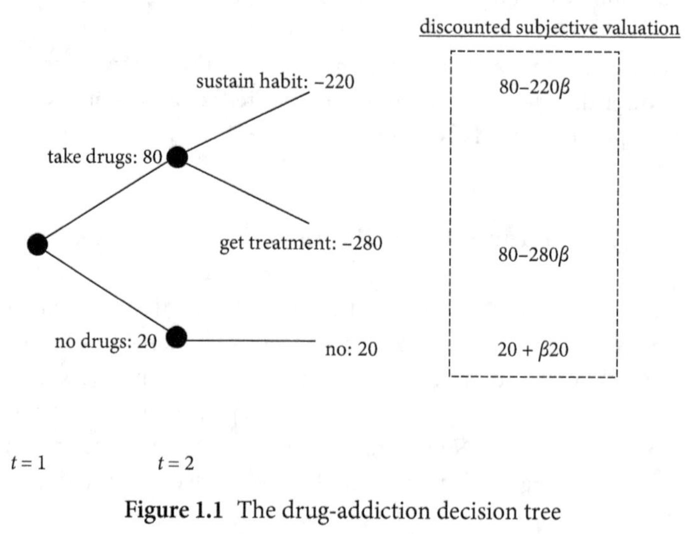

Figure 1.1 The drug-addiction decision tree

At $t = 1$ the player faces the decision whether to take drugs or not. Taking drugs would make him 'high', a sentiment that he values, subjectively, as equivalent to receiving 80 units of income (netting out the cost of buying drugs). Avoiding drugs generates a subjective value of only 20. If the player takes drugs he will become, at $t = 2$, an addict. In such a case, drugs will no longer give him the initial high, although he will have to spend a considerable amount of money on buying them. In addition there are indirect costs: loss of job opportunities, relationships, and health. The direct costs, together with the subjectively valued loss of well-being, are equivalent to *paying out* 220, at $t = 2$. Alternatively he can take painful treatment that has a subjective value of –280, i.e. inflicts pain equivalent to paying out 280 units of income. If he does not take drugs at $t = 1$, he stays with the same level of subjective valuation of 20. (We assume, for simplicity, that the option of taking drugs is no longer available at $t = 2$.)

1.4.2 Rational Decisions

A rational player is forward looking. Already at $t = 1$ he must ask himself what his next ($t = 2$) move will be if he decides to take drugs—presently. The answer is obvious: he will have to decide whether to take treatment or sustain his addiction. It should be clear to him, already at $t = 1$, what that decision would be: the pain of treatment is too high to bear (as 280 > 220) and should be avoided, regardless of β. If so, the player can eliminate the option of treatment, and replace the $t = 2$ decision problem with the value of the preferred action, that is –220, which discounted to period 1 has a subjective value of -220β. Doing so simplifies the $t = 1$ decision to selecting one of the following options: either enjoy the present high and the future pain of sustaining the habit with a joint discounted value $80 - 220\beta$, or avoid both, a line of action that is valued at $20 + 20\beta$. Hence, the $t = 1$ decision is to avoid drugs if and only if

$$20 + \beta 20 > 80 - 220\beta. \tag{1.2}$$

Solving out for the inequality (1.2) we derive the following result:

Proposition 1.3. *Patient players, i.e. players characterized by a relatively high subjective discount factor, $\beta > 0.25$, would avoid drugs.*

1.4.3 Practical Implications

No deep insight about human nature is revealed by the conclusion that drug addicts have a personality that is highly attracted to immediate satisfactions and, at the same time, tend to be relatively indifferent to future pain. Yet, Proposition 1.3

still serves a purpose: to demonstrate that the rationality assumption is, actually, quite benign.

But then, is the rationality assumption interesting at all? Proposition 4 derives another benign result regarding the effect of a policy that offers drug addicts subsidized treatment:

Proposition 1.4. *Subsidizing treatment for drugaddicts by an amount of 120 (so that the subjective valuation of treatment, net of the subsidy, drops to 160) would switch addicts' decision from sustaining their habit to getting treatment but, also, would tempt more patient players, with* $0.25 < \beta < \frac{1}{3}$, *who hitherto stayed clean, to experiment with drugs at* t = *1.*

While it might be argued that we do not need a formal theory in order to make such a statement, our purpose here is different: to demonstrate that most (normative) policy analysis makes the rationality assumption, often implicitly. For only rational agents respond to material incentives in the form of 'carrots and sticks'. It is only because players have well-defined objectives and operate rationally in order to achieve them, that their behaviour can be affected by policy in a predictable manner.

1.4.4 Backward Induction

The method, above, for finding a best line of action on a decision tree is called *backward induction*. Generally, it can be described as follows: *i*) in a decision tree T-periods long, for each terminal node, select the option with the highest *payoff*; discount and add the result to the payoff generated by the $T-1$ action that gives rise to the respective node. Replace that terminal nodes by the sums. Notice that the result is a new decision tree of length $T-1$. *ii*) Repeat the previous step until only the $t=1$ node is left. *iii*) Spanning the tree forward, marking each node's selected action shows the best line of action.

1.5 Opportunity Costs

We have stated, above, that sustaining drug addiction should be valued not just according to the direct, 'out-of-pocket', cost of buying drugs but, also, according to missed professional and personal opportunities, such as suffering inflicted on family members and friends. The concept of an *opportunity cost* accounts for costs, in cash and in kind, resulting from a certain action, including opportunities lost due to the action that was taken. For example: the economic cost of a university degree should include both out-of-pocket tuition fees and the income foregone by being out of a job. At the same time, out-of-pocket costs on food and accommodation should not be included because these would have been borne even out of university.

1.6 Revealed Preferences

It should be clear, by now, that the rationality assumption plays a pivotal role in both positive and normative economic analysis. It allows us to identify players' motives and, then, to design policies that affect their behaviour. The doctrine of *revealed preferences* demonstrates that some of these results can be derived, directly, using the rationality assumption alone, without drawing on behavioural parameters, such as the subjective discount factor, β. The theory was developed by Paul Samuelson, the winner of the 1970 Nobel Prize in Economics. The following is a much simplified exposition of the argument, in the context of spending and saving decisions—by themselves decisions that are important in the analysis of financial markets. We start with the basic framework, still using the β, parameter.

1.6.1 Lending and Borrowing Decisions

Consider a player who lives for just two periods, $t = 1, 2$, present and future, young age and old age; the 'world ends' thereafter. In each period, the player earns y_t units of income, so that the combination of her present and future income can be described, diagrammatically, by the point, $y = (y_1, y_2)$, on a graph with period-t magnitudes on the axes; see Figure 1.2.[3] The player has to decide her *consumption plan*, represented, similarly, by point $c = (c_1, c_2)$. There is a $t = 1$ market for future contracts; each contract delivers one unit of income at $t = 2$. The market is perfect in the sense that the player can buy and sell them at the same price, R. Clearly, buying a contract, whereby the player pays out presently in order to receive future payments, is just a different way of saying that the player is lending, so as to defer consumption from the present to the future: $c_1 < y_1$ where $c_2 > y_2$. Notice also that $y_1 - c_1$ is the player's savings. In everyday parlance it is common to apply the word 'saving' only to a positive $y_1 - c_1$, but the distinction between positive and negative savings serves no purpose here. The arbitrage condition of Proposition 1.2 holds.

[3] See Mathematical Appendix for a brief introduction to functions and graphs. In Figure 1.2, in order to make a clearer distinction between the level and the variable 'period-one income', we use a bold font for the latter, so that that y_1 is the actual level of period-1 income, and $\boldsymbol{y_1}$ is a variable that can take on any such level. A more precise distinction between the variable and the level could be adopted at the cost of a more cumbersome notation. In general in this book, in the tradeoff between precision and simplicity, we lean for the latter.

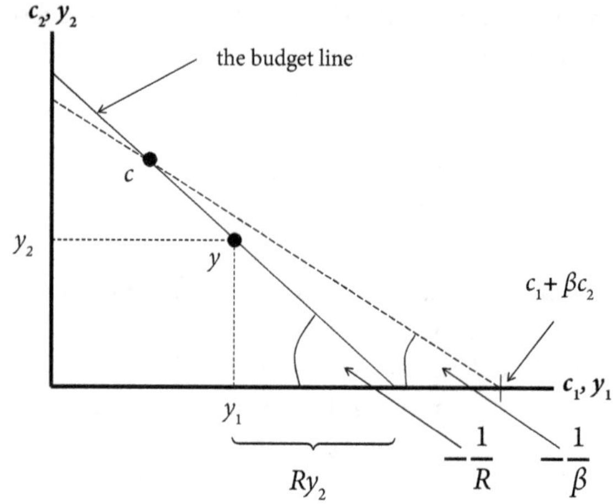

Figure 1.2 The lending/borrowing problem

Let x be the number of future contracts that the player sells at $t = 1$. A negative x means that the player buys future contracts, as is the case in Figure 1.2. Then,

$$c_1 = y_1 + Rx, \tag{1.3}$$

$$c_2 = y_2 - x. \tag{1.4}$$

Solving $x = y_2 - c_2$ from Equation (1.4), substituting the result into Equation (1.4) and re-arranging, we get the player's *life-time budget constraint*:

$$c_1 + Rc_2 = y_1 + Ry_2,$$

which has an intuitive interpretation: the discounted value of the player's life-time income must equal the present value of his life-time consumption.

The (downwards sloping) straight line with a slope of $-\frac{1}{R}$, drawn through point y, is called the *budget line*. To see why, consider the triangle that is formed between the budget line and the horizontal axis, to the right and below point y. Since the height/base ratio of that triangle equals $\frac{1}{R}$, and since the height is y_2, the length of that triangle's base must be Ry_2. It follows that the horizontal distance from the origin to the point where the budget line intersects with the horizontal axis represents the discounted value of the player's life-time income, $y_1 + Ry_2$. Now consider any consumption point that lies on that straight line; the present value of that consumption plan is also represented by the intersection of the budget line with the horizontal axis. It follows that any consumption plan that lies on the budget line is affordable, just. Consumption points above the budget lines are not affordable while consumption points below the budget line are affordable but leave behind some unspent income. Since the 'world ends' at $t = 2$, it is in the player's best interest to spend all his resources on consumption.

Next, we consider the subjective value of alternative, affordable, consumption plans; consider, for example point c in Figure 1.2. We follow the same steps as in the previous paragraph, only that this time a (broken) line with a $-\frac{1}{\beta}$ slope is drawn via point c. The subjective value of that plan is represented by the horizontal distance between the origin and the point where that broken line intersects with the horizontal axis. Clearly, lending has benefited the player, for the broken line in the figure lies above a (hypothetical) line drawn through point y, indicating that the player is better off executing the affordable consumption plan (c_1, c_2), relative to avoiding trade in future contracts that would leave her at point (y_1, y_2). But then, lending even more would benefit her to an even greater extent. It follows that:

Proposition 1.5. *Players whose subjective valuation of future consumption is higher than the market's valuation of future consumption, namely $\beta > R$, will buy future consumption (i.e. lend) all the way through to the corner where $c_1 = 0$. Players with $\beta < R$ will borrow up to the point where $c_2 = 0$.*

Proposition 1.5, which is just an instance of Proposition 1.1 above, demonstrates how to model lending and borrowing (saving and spending) decisions using the β behavioural parameter. That is, lenders are patient players, characterized by high βs, while borrowers are impatient players, characterized by low βs—relative to R. Evidently, the procedure does not identify the exact magnitude of players' βs, only sorts them to high/low patience groups—relative to R. Yet, more data, such as observing environments with changing Rs, may allow us to obtain more refined estimates.

1.6.2 The Revealed-Preference Principle

Consider a rational player with income y who opts to become a lender at point c in Figure 1.3. Suppose that the interest rate increases from r to r' (remember that $\frac{1}{R} = 1 + r$). Might the player switch from lending to borrowing as a result? The answer is, clearly, no. His previous selection of point c' when point c'' was already available revealed a preference for the former over the latter. If so, there is no reason to reverse the decision when a higher interest rate, r', still leaves both c' and c'' as affordable options. Nor is there a reason to switch to any point on the segment between points y and c'', i.e. become a borrower.

Moreover, we can also infer that the above player is made better off by the higher interest rate:

Proposition 1.6. *By the rationality assumption alone, a lending (borrowing) player would benefit from a higher (lower) interest rate.*

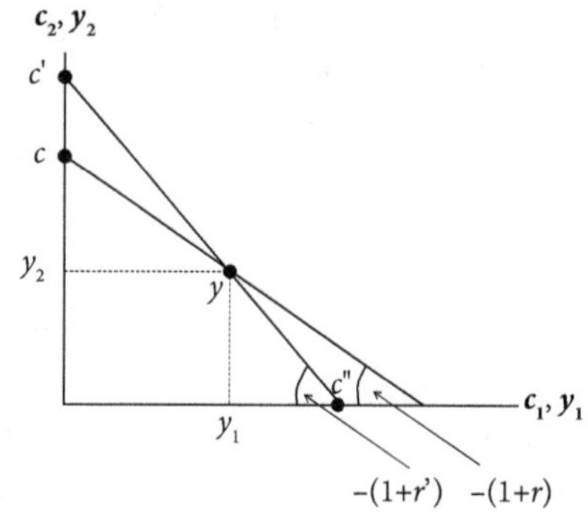

Figure 1.3 The effect of an increase in interest rates

The reader may notice that analysing the effect of a lower interest rate for a lending player is not that obvious for, then, some attractive trading opportunities are lost, while others are introduced. Without knowing his subjective discount factor it is not possible to predict whether the player will keep on lending or would start borrowing, and whether he is better or worse off due to the lower interest rate.[4]

As for Proposition 1.6 itself, the reader may feel, again, that no elaborate theoretical argument is required in order to conclude that a player who lends money in order to benefit from higher consumption later in life would become better off when he faces a higher interest rate. However, the point here is to demonstrate that an intuitive statement to that effect actually makes the rationality assumption—implicitly. For had the player been a lender just by mindless coincidence rather than by rational choice, there is no guarantee that a higher interest rate actually makes him better off.

Figure 1.4 highlights the structure of the revealed-preference argument even more generally. Consider a rational player who selected option *B* from a choice set of five feasible options, *A* to *E*. Could he be worse off if we eliminate option *E* from his choice set? Definitely not, if he is rational. Through his choice the player had already revealed that option *B* is preferable to option *E*. Since he can still select option *B*, he cannot be harmed by the removal of an inferior option, *E*, from the set of available options. At the same time, expanding his choice set by adding option *F* cannot harm the player but could make him better off. Hence:

Proposition 1.7. *A player cannot benefit from a truncation of a set of his feasible options. He is likely to become worse off if the truncation eliminates an option that was preferable to all others. Likewise, the player will never be harmed by an expansion of the set of feasible options.*

[4] More advanced analysis relates these considerations to income and substitution effects.

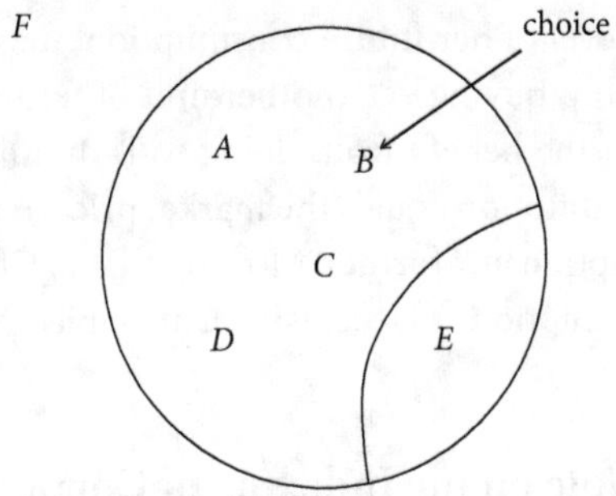

Figure 1.4 Revealed preferences

1.7 Decreasing Unit Subjective Valuation (DUSV)

The analysis in Section 1.6 has the awkward and unrealistic prediction that players are pushed towards *corner solutions*, namely points where they either borrow or lend to the limit of their capacity. This can be easily fixed by making an additional assumption: that the subjective value of an extra unit of consumption depends, negatively, on the amount already consumed. We explain the idea with the aid of Figure 1.5. So far, we have assumed that subjective valuations are fixed and independent of the amount consumed. Hence, a player with a fixed $\beta > R$ subjectively values future consumption above its market price, regardless of how much he consumes in the future. Starting with, say, c_2 units of future consumption he benefits from buying another unit of future consumption, and then another, until he hits a corner solution where he exhausts all his life-time income.

Compare the above player to another whose subjective valuation of an extra unit of future consumption is lower at higher levels of future consumption; see Figure 1.5. Suppose that, like in the previous case, she starts with c_2 units of future consumption and, where the subjective value of an extra happens to be β. Since $\beta > R$, she is motivated to buy an extra unit. Unlike in the previous case, now that

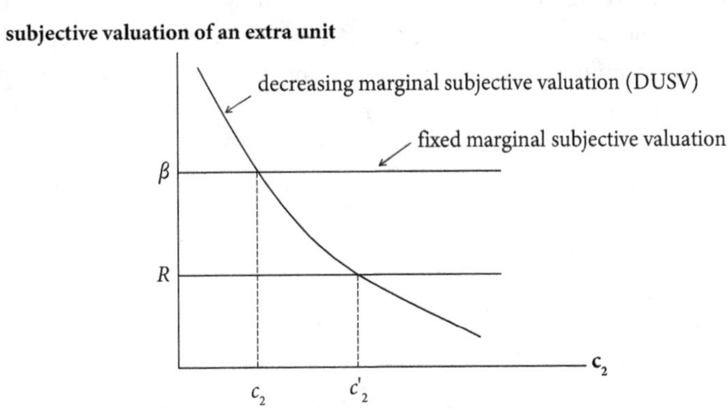

Figure 1.5 Decreasing marginal valuations

she has increased the level of her future consumption, the value of an extra unit is slightly lower. Probably, buying yet another unit of future consumption is still in her best interest, but the benefit from doing so is diminishing. At c_2' her own valuation of future consumption equals the market price, removing any motive to increase future consumption any further. More on that in Chapters 4 and 5, where we shall refer to this assumption as Decreasing Unit Subjective Valuation (DUSV).

1.8 A Note on the Indexing of Commodities

It is worth drawing the reader's attention, once again, to the fact that, in Section 1.6's analysis, c_1 and c_2 are denominated in units (of income or goods) that are identical in all their physical and chemical characteristics. That players feel differently about two physically identical objects, just because they are delivered at different points of time, is a good-enough reason to define these objects as different commodities. From an economic point of view, what matters is how players feel about objects, not their molecular composition or their engineering design. In Chapter 5 we shall see how a similar approach, of indexing consumption by eventualities, allows us to gain important insight into the functioning of financial markets under conditions of uncertainty.

Admittedly, such an analysis requires a certain level of abstraction. On first glance, the statement that present and future consumption differs in the same sense that chocolate and vanilla ice cream differ may seem somewhat contrived. Hopefully, the reader can appreciate the analytical gain of an approach that allows for the development of a general theory of markets, for which ice cream and bonds are just special cases.

1.9 Attitudes towards Risk

By their very nature, financial markets are risky. It is therefore essential that we apply the ideas that we have developed so far, regarding the relationship between observed behaviour and unobservable sentiment, in order to parametrize players' attitudes towards risk. However, such effort is often hampered by observations of real-world behaviour which is more difficult to reconcile with the rationality assumption. We therefore start this section with one of the most famous example of such behaviour.

1.9.1 The Allais Paradox

Maurice Allais, winner of the 1988 Nobel Prize in Economics, suggested the following experiment: allow players to choose between lotteries A and B. Lottery A

delivers a £1 million (£1m) prize with certainty; lottery B delivers a bigger prize of £5m with a probability of 10%, but involves a small 1% risk of getting nothing; see Table 1.1. Real-world subjects that participate in actual experiments typically prefer the certainty of lottery A over the bigger but riskier prize in lottery B. Next, allow players to choose between lottery C and lottery D. Similar to the A–B choice, lottery D trades off the £5m prize at a 10% probability against an extra 1% probability of getting nothing, only that now the base-level lottery-C prize of £1m has a probability of only 11%. Real-world subjects typically prefer the lottery D over lottery C. It is sometimes claimed that this is irrational.

To better understand Allais' problem we derive, for each one of the A–D lotteries, an alternative two-stage representation, where one of the prizes in the first stage is another lottery; see Figure 1.6. Denote the first and second stages by the subscripts 1 and 2, respectively. For example, the base-level lottery B_1 delivers £1m with a 89% probability and a B_2 lottery otherwise. The B_2 lottery delivers £5m with a $\frac{10}{11}$ probability, and zero otherwise. Notice that, jointly, B_1 and B_2 deliver the £5m prize with a probability of $0.11 \times \frac{0.1}{0.11} = 10\%$, exactly the same as lottery B in Table 1.1. The reader is invited to check that the same applies to lotteries A, C, and D and their (A_1, A_2), (C_1, C_2), and (D_1, D_2) counterparts. In other words, there is no material difference between the Table 1.1 representation of the four lotteries and the Figure 1.6 representation.

The irrationality argument goes as follows: A_1 and B_1 are identical. It follows that if a player prefers lottery A on lottery B it is because she prefers lottery A_2 to lottery B_2. However lotteries A_2 and C_2 are identical and, also, lotteries B_2 and D_2 are identical. It thus follows that since the player prefers lottery A_2 to lottery B_2 she also prefers lottery C_2 to lottery D_2. Lastly, notice that lotteries C_1 and D_1 are identical; it follows that the joint C_1–C_2 lottery is preferable to the joint D_1–D_2 lottery. It is therefore irrational for a player to prefer lottery A to lottery B and, at the same time, to prefer lottery D to lottery C.

Table 1.1 The Allais Paradox

		prize		
		£5m	£1m	0
		probabilities		
lotteries	*A*	0	100%	0
	B	10%	89%	1%
	C	0	11%	89%
	D	10%	0	90%

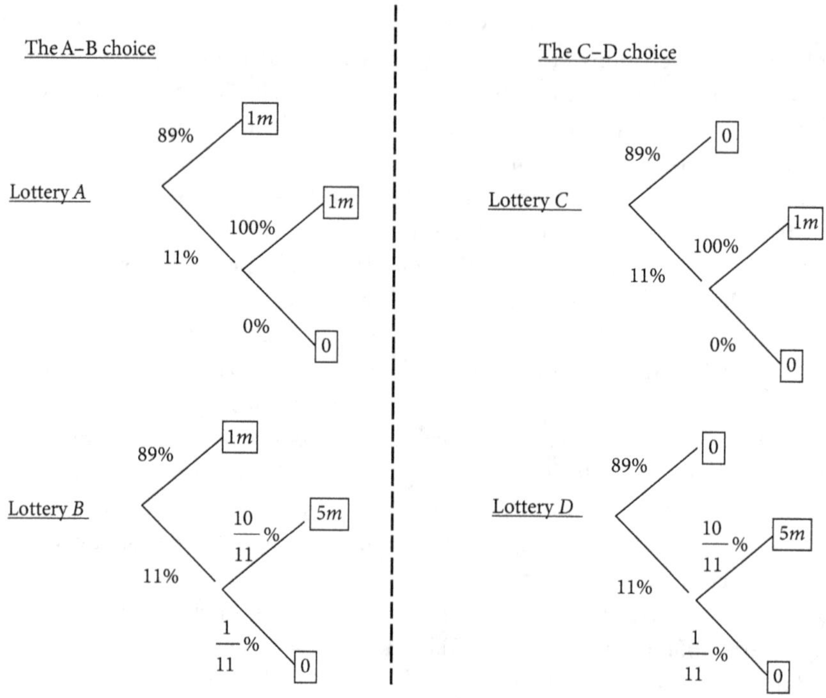

Figure 1.6 The Allais Paradox, different representation

There are two responses to this argument. The first is that, due to poor training in probability theory, many of the participants in such experiments miss the point that the lotteries in Table 1.1 have a Figure 1.6 representation. As already noted above, by themselves (even serious) errors in the decision-making process do not indicate irrationality; only the unwillingness to correct such errors does. The second response is that the argument above does not make a clear enough distinction between the statistical properties of the lotteries and their subjective valuation. Moreover, it assumes that lotteries can be subjectively valued by decomposing them in to parts, evaluating each part independently, and then calculating the subjective value of the whole by adding up the values of the parts, ignoring possible interaction between the parts.[5] For example, it can be argued that in the *A–B* choice, the player feels that he would not be able to cope, emotionally, with the disappointment of ending up with nothing being 'so close to winning a million pounds' and, therefore, prefers to 'play it safe' and settle for lottery *A*. In contrast, in the *C–D* choice, 'not expecting much in the first place' the player is 'willing to double down' at the second stage, thereby preferring lottery *D* on *C*.

[5] Such interactions are common in physical commodities: mustard and hot dogs have, jointly, a subjective value that exceeds the sum of their separate subjective values.

Given that these are legitimate sentiments, they should be incorporated into the modelling of rational risk attitudes. Capturing sentiment is what the modelling of rational decision-making is all about. Hence, both responses, while raising interesting points about human behaviour, do not necessarily undermine the notion of rationality.

1.9.2 The Subjective Valuation of Risk Attitudes

We follow our original line of analysis by modelling another sentiment into a behavioural parameter—the *coefficient of risk aversion.* To do so, conduct the following experiment: augment a player's basic (riskless) level of income and consumption, $\bar{c}$, with some risk exposure, on top. The risk is modelled as a random variable, $\tilde{\varepsilon}$ (the Greek letter varepsilon), receiving values of plus and minus $\varepsilon > 0$ with equal probabilities, $\pi_1 = \pi_2 = \frac{1}{2}$. (For a brief introduction to random variables, see Mathematical Appendix, Section A.3; where necessary we distinguish random from non-random variables by the ~ symbol, but deviate from the practice where the distinction is clear enough.) Hence, $\tilde{\varepsilon}$ has a mean of zero and a variance:

$$E(\tilde{\varepsilon}) = 0,$$
$$Var(\tilde{\varepsilon}) = \sigma_{\varepsilon}^2 = \varepsilon^2,$$

where σ, the Greek letter sigma, squared, is commonly used to denote the variance of a random variable.

Now the question is whether the prospect of a 'good outcome', $+\varepsilon$, fully compensates the player for the possibility of a 'bad outcome', $-\varepsilon$, with the same (absolute value) magnitude and the same probability, so that in expectations, the risk add sup to zero. For an experimental answer, find the highest insurance premium, S, that the player is willing to pay for a policy that fully removes the exposure to the $\tilde{\varepsilon}$ risk (i.e. the insurance scheme, which, on top of the S charge, pays ε in case $\tilde{\varepsilon} = -\varepsilon$ and charges ε in case $\tilde{\varepsilon} = +\varepsilon$), so that the combined effect of the risk and the insurance is to leave the player with the riskless income, $\bar{c}$, less the premium S.

Definition 1.2. A player's subjective attitude to risk is measured through her coefficient of risk aversion, θ (the Greek letter *theta*), defined as

$$\theta = \frac{S}{\sigma_{\varepsilon}^2/2}.$$

A player with $\theta = 0$ is called *risk neutral.* Such player is not willing to spend any money on buying insurance against mean-zero risk. A $\theta > 0$ indicates an aversion to risk, where the player is averse to the effect of fluctuations in consumption over different eventualities even though, 'on average', the fluctuations add up to zero. The reader may notice a similar aversion to fluctuation of consumption over time has driven our analysis of the DUSV assumption in Section 1.7, above.[6] A player with a negative θ is called risk loving, a case that we shall ignore in this book.

Notice that both the risk, σ^2, and the premium, S, can be objectively measured, unlike the sentiment that is not observable and cannot be directly quantified. Notwithstanding, the strength of the risk-aversion sentiment can be inferred from the ratio between the risk and the premium. Hence, if two players face the same objective risk (and have the same basic income, $\bar{c}$) but one is willing to pay a higher premium in order to insure herself against that risk, then we shall deem the latter more risk-averse than the former and assign to her a higher coefficient of risk aversion. The reader may wonder why we divide σ_ε^2 by 2; the answer to this question is that it seems to be slightly more convenient; see Chapter 5.

It is worth relating this definition to the discussion of Allais' Paradox above. In fact, Definition 1.2 assumes that the subjective valuations of each event's outcome are independent of valuations of other events' outcomes. To see the point more clearly, notice that at the point where the player is indifferent about taking the insurance,

$$S = \frac{\theta}{2}\pi_1 \varepsilon^2 + \frac{\theta}{2}\pi_2 (-\varepsilon)^2,$$

from which follows:

$$\pi_1 \left[\bar{c} - \frac{\theta}{2}\varepsilon^2\right] + \pi_2 \left[\bar{c} - \frac{\theta}{2}(-\varepsilon)^2\right] = \bar{c} - S.$$

That is, the player's well-being can be found by calculating, separately, his event-by-event well-being then adding up these measures. (To find the within-event well-being, subtract from $\bar{c}$ the squared deviation in consumption multiplied by $\frac{\theta}{2}$, then multiply the result by the probability of the event.) The calculation therefore abstracts from the possibility that one event's valuation may be affected by another, as suggested by the Allais Paradox. Without taking a strong position on this matter, we comment that this level of abstraction serves well the sort of analysis conducted in this book. Other assumptions may be needed for the analysis of different phenomena.

1.9.3 Behavioural Finance

Behavioural finance is a new branch of financial economics that attempts to refine the modelling of decision-making under conditions of uncertainty, to account for

[6] Indeed, a more advanced analysis can establish a formal connection between the two sentiments through the principle of decreasing marginal utility of consumption.

more involved sentiments, in addition to the basic impatient and risk aversion parameters β and θ, as defined above. Even more ambitiously, behavioural finance attempts to explain players' propensity to making mistakes. Daniel Kahneman, (2002) Nobel prize laureate in Economics (himself a cognitive psychologist), has documented many of these mistakes; see his Nobel Lecture (2002). However, the label, behavioural, is somewhat misleading: all economics is behavioural, in the sense that it accounts for the role of sentiment in human behaviour. Behavioural finance is about a more elaborate modelling of such sentiments.

As for mistakes, in Chapters 7 and 8 we explore the possibility that players act to their own disadvantage, but only because they lack some information that is relevant to their decision-making. But then, given their limited information at the time, they still make a rational decision, taking a course of action that is best—given their knowledge and understanding of their situation. To be clear, only information that is not available at the time, and might not even be available with hindsight, may deem the original decision disadvantageous.

It is extremely difficult, however, to model miscalculations in the simple sense of 'making a foolish mistake' on the basis of existing information, especially if these mistakes re-occur on a regular basis and according to recognizable patterns. For if there is some regularity in the manner that a player makes mistakes, then that pattern can be used, by the player herself, to warn her against making the same mistake, repeatedly.

1.10 Positive Economics

Once an economist models players' motivations and sentiments into behavioural parameters, she can construct a model that predicts how they would act under different circumstances. For example, using behavioural (and technological) parameters, an economist can build a model of a certain market and estimate the effect of a tax (taking the interactions between the players into consideration). Once the tax is levied, the economist can test her predictions against the observed outcome. If the outcome falls too distant from the prediction, the model should be *rejected*; see Section 1.5.1 of the Mathematical Appendix for some additional detail about the statistical methods involved with hypothesis testing. To use Karl Popper's terminology, the model is falsified. This simple idea, much elaborated upon by Milton Friedman (1953), winner of the 1976 Nobel Prize in Economics, provides the foundations for empirical economics; a discipline tested by observation rather than just pure speculation.

Friedman also claims that the falsifiability test is the only criterion that economists should use in evaluating the validity of their theories. In particular, economists should be satisfied with a certain level of a model's abstraction provided that it yields predictions that are not falsified. It has to be noted, however, that a level of abstraction, deemed 'proper' by the Friedman criterion, is specific to a model that tackles a specific phenomenon. For example, a two-period model may be sufficient in order to predict the behaviour of a rational drug addict as in Proposition 1.3 but may not be sufficient in order to analyse the addict's behaviour following a treatment. Another example: the modelling of risk aversion as in Definition 1.2 may be sufficient in explaining, say, a household's demand for fire insurance, but may fail in predicting experimental results related to Allais' Paradox.

1.11 Correlation and Causality

A crucial implication of the above discussion is that a theory is not 'proved true' by passing the falsifiability test. Take, for example, the theory that a more developed financial industry is able to fund more investment, allocate capital to its most productive use, and thus promote economic growth. King and Levine (1993) put the theory to a statistical test by estimating the cross-country regressions,

$$GPY_i = \alpha + \beta \times Depth_i + \gamma \times X_i + \varepsilon_i, \tag{1.5}$$

where financial *Depth* is measured by ratios such as liquid liabilities to GDP in 1960, *GPY* is the growth rate of per-capita income in the years 1960–1989 (see Table 2 in the published paper). X stands for a set of other controls and ε is an error term. i is an index that runs across the 63 countries that are included in the study; R^2 is 0.55 and β is statistically significant at the 1% level; see Mathematical Appendix, Section A.5, for some additional information about regression analysis. Hence, King and Levine do not reject the hypotheses that developed financial markets contribute to economic growth.

So why can't we say that King and Levine 'have proved' the hypothesis right? For two reasons (at least). First, the positive correlation between financial depth and economic growth is also consistent with a causal relationship that operates in the opposite direction. That is, financial markets were developed in order to serve a growing economy. Second, both economic growth and financial depth might be caused by a third factor, that causes both but without any direct causal relationship between the two. For example, a better-educated population might increase productivity and generate economic growth. At the same time, a better-educated population might also have a higher demand for financial products. To ameliorate this problem, King and Levine also control for education by including in Equation (1.5)'s X variable the rate of secondary school enrolment in 1960. That may "strengthen" their claim but will not resolve the problem conclusively as education enrolment may have been a response to anticipated economic opportunities.

The deeper point here is that, ultimately, causal relationships originate in sentiments and other entities that are not directly observable. Once assumed, they can be parametrized and measured out of observed behaviour. Yet, such measurement cannot rule out the possibility that the behaviour originates in some other sentiment (that can be quantified via another behavioural parameter). If a theory fails to predict certain outcomes, we can conclude, with relative confidence, that the theory has no power against the facts and should be rejected. But if it is not rejected, we cannot rule out the possibility that another theory would turn up with superior predictive power, or, that the theory will be rejected when tested more rigorously.

Is there a way out of this problem? Only to some extent. One can formulate some other plausible alternative theories and reject them against the facts. Alternatively, one may refine the test. For example, King and Levine augment their regression results with 'event studies,' whereby they follow 27 countries that participated in 'intensive adjustment lending' programmes that included elements of structural market reforms, and measure their economic performance during the next 15 years. Figure 1.7 (Figure 2 in the published King and Levine (1993) paper) shows that countries with a high level of financial depth to begin with had GDP/capita growth rate, almost 3% (per annum) higher, relative to countries with a low level of financial depth. Again, such additional correlations, though useful in showing

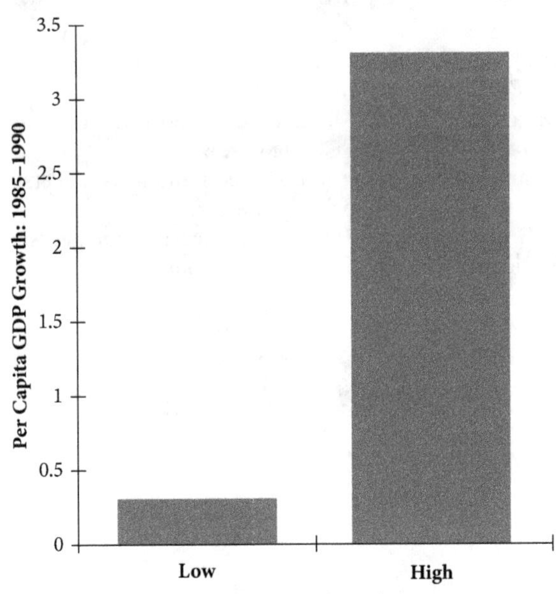

Figure 1.7 Finance and growth

that the theory has passed another hurdle, cannot prove that it will not fail the next one.

1.12 Conclusion

The main driver of this introductory chapter is the argument that the rationality assumption could be an acceptable, if not as an accurate description of real-world humans, at least as a starting point in economic modelling, abstracting from some properties of actual humans in order to focus on other, more important ones. Critical to this argument is the observation that the rationality assumption can accommodate a surprisingly broad spectrum of actual human attributes. Some of these attributes are so benign that they are taken for granted in many informal discussions.

Notwithstanding, the main business of economics is the modelling of human interaction rather than the modelling of decisions made in isolation of others. To that end, the current chapter provided some important building blocks. In the modelling of financial markets, two behavioural parameters are particularly important: the subjective discount factor and the coefficient of risk aversion. They play a central role in the analysis of subsequent chapters.

References

[1] Stigler George J. and Gary S. Becker (1977). 'De Gustibus Non Est Disputandum', *The American Economic Review*, Vol. 67, No. 2, pp. 76–90.
[2] Friedman, Milton (1953). 'The Methodology of Positive Economics', in *Essays in Positive Economics*, University of Chicago Press.
[3] Kahneman, Daniel (2002). 'Maps of Bounded Rationality: A Perspective on Intuitive Judgement and Choice'. Nobel Prize Lecture.
[4] King, Robert G. and Ross Levine (1993). 'Finance, Entrepreneurship and Growth: Theory and Evidence', *Journal of Monetary Economics*, 32, pp. 513–542.

2

Cutting Deals (the Coase Theorem)

2.1 Introduction

Frankie and Johnny decide to end an unhappy marriage.[1] There is no love or sympathy left between them; their only purpose is to walk away from a bad relationship and get along with their lives. The couple owns, jointly, some assets. Hence, the 'deal' that they are trying to execute is Frankie's acceptance of an asset split in return for Johnny's acceptance of the same split. Naturally, they prioritize an amicable separation, if only to avoid legal expenses. However, if they fail to reach an agreement, the fall-back option is legal proceedings. In the jurisdiction of their domicile, the rule is an equal split of the assets, after the deduction of legal expenses, which are massive: 50% of the estate. The purpose of this chapter is to develop a positive theory that predicts the outcome of such situations, as well as a normative evaluation of the outcome in terms of economic efficiency.

Simple as it is, the example captures the essence of many social interactions. First, it describes players in a state of conflict. Second, the conflict is about the *allocation* of *scarce resources*; each would like to increase her share of the 'pie' at the expense of the other player. Third, the players also have a common interest, to reach a consensual agreement so as to avoid the legal expenses. Hence, the first fundamental (positive) question is whether the intensity of the conflict is bound to undermine the players' ability to pursue common interests. Fourth, social interaction scarcely takes place in a void. Rather, the setting in which the conflict is resolved, in this case domestic divorce law, affects the outcome. Hence, the second fundamental (normative) question is whether by changing the setting a better outcome can be achieved.

The Frankie-and-Johnny 'story' can be considered as a *bargaining* situation. Some useful terminology is provided with the aid of Figure 2.1. The payoffs for players 1 and 2 are plotted against the horizontal and vertical axes, respectively. Clearly, players cannot receive, jointly, more then 100% of the estate, which means that all points within the straight-isosceles, shaded, unit-sided triangle make the *feasible set* of allocations. Since the players' common interest is to exploit their resources to the full, the hypotenuse of that triangle deserves special attention; we call it the *Pareto-efficient set*. Since, in case of disagreement, the courts implement

[1] The example of divorce is chosen for its similarity to the chapter's main application: corporate bankruptcy. Both deal with a similar problem, which is the winding up of an association that no longer generates value to its members.

The Economics of Financial Markets and Institutions. Oren Sussman, Oxford University Press. © Oren Sussman (2023).
DOI: 10.1093/oso/9780192869739.003.0003

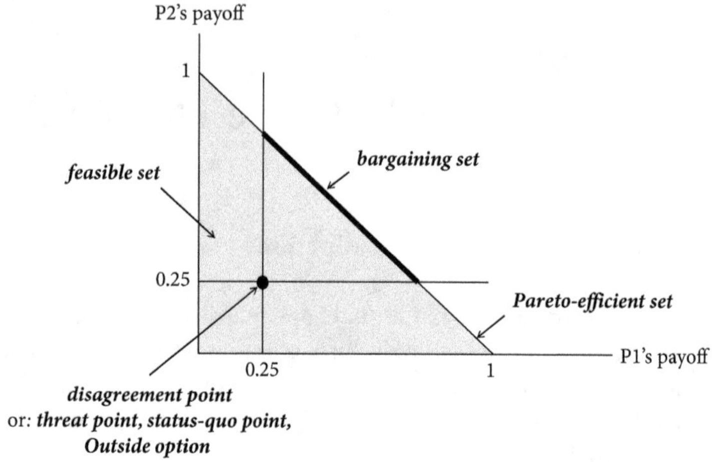

Figure 2.1 The bargaining problem

an equal split of the asset remaining after legal expenses, the (0.25, 0.25) is called the *disagreement point*, also the *status-quo point*, *outside option*, or *threat point*. Since players would reject any deal that offers them less than what they would get under that point, we call the intersection of the Pareto-efficient set and the positive quadrant spanned by the status-quo point the *bargaining set*.

2.2 Economic Efficiency

Can an economist make normative statements on the basis of technical analysis alone, without involving her own value judgement about right or wrong, good or bad, fair or foul? The answer is yes, to a large extent. When a certain choice makes everyone worse off (by their own subjectively defined motives and sentiments) we can say that the outcome is economically inefficient. Presumably, such an outcome can be deemed undesirable under any system of moral values. The definitions below operationalize this simple idea into the notion of *Pareto efficiency*, the most commonly used criterion of efficiency in economics.

Definition 2.1. An outcome is said to be *Pareto dominated* if there exist another feasible outcome such that at least one player is better off and all the others are not worse off.

and

Definition 2.2. An outcome is said to be Pareto efficient if there is no other feasible outcome that Pareto dominates it.

In Figure 2.1, all points in the Pareto-efficient set satisfy the definition of economic efficiency to the same extent. Some readers may feel that points towards the centre of that graph are 'fair' while points towards the corners are not. Economic theory accepts that issues of fairness are important but, at the same time, have little to say about substance of fairness; as it happens, political and social thinkers are bitterly divided about the meaning of fairness and, even more so, about the role of public policy in achieving it. The contribution that economists attempt to make to such policy debates is in drawing a clear distinction between efficiency and fairness, hoping that even ideologically opposed parties could accept that Pareto-dominated outcomes can be ruled out. Moreover, the economist who conducted the analysis on the basis of efficiency consideration can rightly argue that her personal convictions did not interfere with the analysis.

This position relies on the ability to make a clear conceptual distinction between matters of efficiency and matters of fairness. To illustrate the point, suppose that a politician suggests to move from a Pareto efficient but (in her view) unfair allocation (on the graph of the Pareto-efficient set but towards the corner) to a Pareto-dominated but fair allocation (inside the feasible set but towards the centre). An efficiency analysis should point out that there exists some other allocation that could benefit some (perhaps all) players and, at the same time, satisfies the politician's notion of fairness, regardless of the content and the detail of the fairness argument. It follows that there is little substance in the popular view that there is a fundamental conflict between efficiency and fairness: the more of the former, the less of the latter. Rather, efficiency considerations are independent of fairness considerations.

Another misperception is that efficiency considerations should be used in order to maximize the 'size of the pie,' while fairness considerations should be used in order to determine its allocation. Consider the case where 'fair' outcomes (towards the centre) generate an aggregate payoff that is smaller than the aggregate payoff of the unfair outcomes (towards the corners); see Figure 2.2.[2] In this case, Pareto efficiency does not require that overall output is maximized.[3] Rather, it deems outcomes like point *A* to be economically inefficient. Loosely speaking, there are points that generate the 'same level of fairness' with higher payoffs for both players. While 'more fairness' implies a lower average standard of living, it does not imply sacrificing economic efficiency.

[2] One (of many) possible 'stories' that can justify the type of a feasible set that is plotted in Figure 2.2 is that there is a single productive resource, a plot of land for example, which would be more productive if cultivated by a single player rather than split among the two of them (and excluding the possibility of giving it to one player and taxing him so as to support the other).

[3] For a diagrammatic representation of the aggregate (overall) payoff, draw a straight lines with −45° slope via the relevant allocation and read the quantity on the intersection of that line and the horizontal (or the vertical) axis.

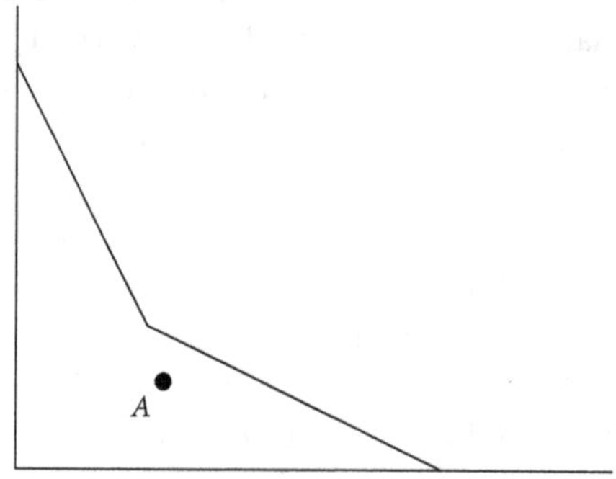

Figure 2.2 Efficiency and fairness

2.3 Rubinstein's Alternating Offers Bargaining Game

In order to analyse interactions among several players, the setting in which they operate needs to be described in greater detail. That includes the players, their motives, the possible choices that they can make, and the payoffs associated with any combination of choices. Such a setting may be captured by what is called a *game*. We use the Rubinstein (1982) alternating-offers bargaining model in order to analyse the Frankie-and-Johnny problem. Figure 2.3, which is called the *extensive form* of the game, provides more detail. In spite of the graphic similarity to Figure 1.1's decision tree, the two differ in that, here, a different player makes a move at each node. More accurately:

- There are two players, $P1$ and $P2$, who bargain over the allocation of a 'pie'.
- The players are selfish (they don't care about the well-being of their opponents), materialistic, rational, and impatient, so that they subjectively value next-round deliveries using β^{P1} and β^{P2} discount factors (both positive and smaller than 1, as discussed in Chapter 1). No other objective, say, building a reputation for 'toughness' or 'decency' affect their behaviour.
- The bargaining has T rounds, indexed by $t = 1, 2..., T$. Notice that T is the length of the game, while t is an index that runs throughout the bargaining rounds, from 1 to T.
- In the first round, $t = 1$, $P1$, gives an offer[4] $(x_1, 1 - x_1)$, $0 \leq x_1 \leq 1$ being his own share of the pie, the rest being allocated to $P2$. For simplicity, assume that the players' share of the pie is, also, their subjective valuation of that share. If $P2$ accepts the offer it is implemented right away. If $P2$ rejects the offer, she will get the right to make the next-round offer $(x_2, 1 - x_2)$, x_2 being $P1$'s share,

[4] As a general rule, we use subscripts to denote the time index and superscripts to denote the players' index.

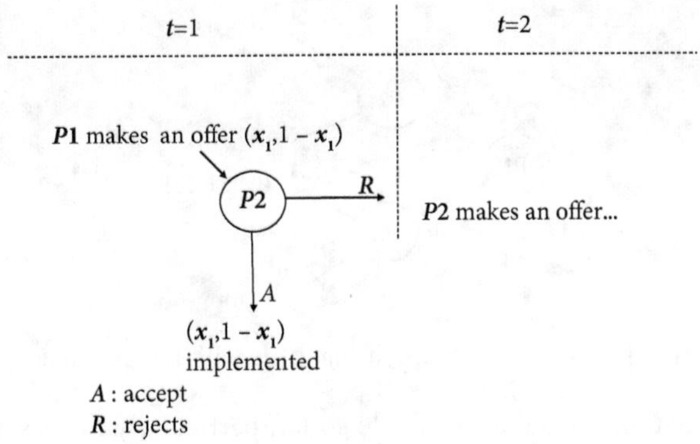

Figure 2.3 The alternating offers bargaining game

as offered to him at $t = 2$ by *P2*. If the offer is accepted it is implemented; if it is rejected, it would be *P1*'s turn to make an offer at the next round; and so on. Offers are exchanged until agreement is reached, at which point the agreed-upon distribution is implemented and the game terminates.

- If the players fail to reach an agreement in the last, $t = T$, round, the status-quo point is implemented. For simplicity of the exposition, we analyse the game with a $(0, 0)$ status-quo point, but comment on outcomes in games where there is a non-zero status-quo point.
- Each player knows and understands all the 'rules of the game': their feasible moves, payoffs, own subjective valuations, as well as moves, payoffs, and subjective valuations of their opponent. Moreover, each player knows that his opponent knows that he knows and understand the rules of the game. For example, *P1* knows that *P2* is rational, but also that *P2* understands that he, *P1*, is rational as well.

Some of the assumptions are unrealistic: for example that the players care only about their material payoff, free of other sentiments such as envy, fear, or grudge. The reader is not asked to believe in the realism of the assumptions, only to defer judgement of the proper level of abstraction that we apply until the conclusions of the analysis become clear. If necessary, we can refine the assumptions—at a cost of some extra analytical complexity.

2.3.1 Building Up Intuition: A Simpler Game

Consider the slightly simpler game with only one round, $T = 1$, and only two feasible offers: a 'fair' one $(0.5, 0.5)$, and an 'insulting' one $(0.95, 0.05)$, see Figure 2.4. Since *P2* cannot respond with a counter-offer, this is sometimes called a *take-it-leave-it* or an *ultimatum* game.

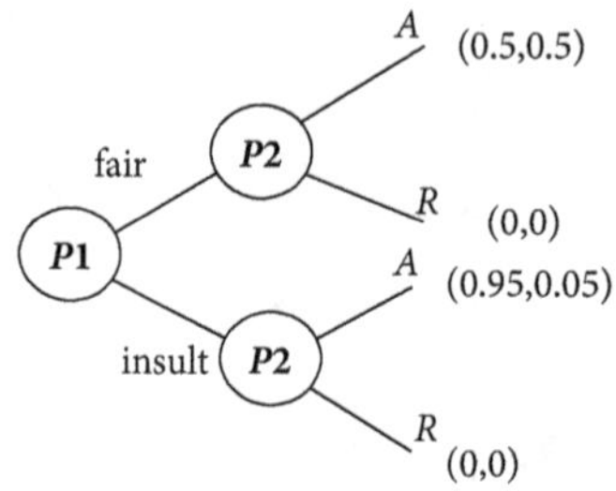

Figure 2.4 A one-round bargaining game with two feasible offers

Given the assumptions that we made so far, particularly the assumption that each player is rational and aware of the rationality of his opponent, it is hard to avoid the conclusion that this game's only plausible outcome is *P*1 making an insulting offer and *P*2 accepting it. The argument runs as follows: *P*1 is rational and thus forward looking. He should therefore ask himself: what will be *P*2's reaction to each one of my own offers? Knowing that *P*2 is also rational and cares only about her own payoff, he can predict her reaction: accept both the insulting and the fair offers. It follows that *P*1's own payoff of the two offers are 0.95 and 0.5, respectively. The former dominates. We can thus conclude that the plausible *equilibrium path* (namely, the sequence of moves that the players are predicted to take) in this game is an insulting offer by *P*1, which is accepted by *P*2.

Notice that in spite of the material difference between a game tree and a decision tree, the mechanics of 'solving the problem', by backward induction is similar—superficially. The technical name for such an equilibrium concept is *sub-game perfect.*

2.3.2 Non-credible threats

In this equilibrium, *P*1 takes advantage of *P*2's rationality, as well as her position in the game, namely being on the receiving end in a single-round game. Could *P*2 avoid this grim outcome by telling *P*1, up front: I will accept only the fair offer; if you give me an insulting offer I will 'teach you a lesson' and reject it, to my own, as well as your determent. If *P*1 believes that *P*2 would act in that manner, he would deliver the fair offer that pays him 0.5 rather than the insulting offer that would be rejected and thus pay him zero. If that happens, *P*2 will not have to exercise the threat of rejecting the insulting offer and can benefit from a payoff of 0.5. Clearly, *P*2's should do her best to convince *P*1 that she would reject the insulting offer.

But can *P*1 be convinced? Not if he knows (with full confidence) that *P*2 values only material payoffs and makes decisions rationally. For by the time *P*2 gets the insulting offer she already knows that the threat failed to achieve its desired effect. At that point, there is no cost in reneging on her threat, and there is a small gain to be made from doing so. *P*1 can thus discard *P*2's *non-credible threat* and deliver the insulting offer. It might seem unrealistic to suppose that *P2* does not care about making a fool of herself and about losing the reputation for 'toughness' that she tried to build up. Indeed, real-world individuals care about such things, perhaps because they are worried about future consequences of being revealed as a wimps. But such considerations were ruled out by assuming that this is a one-round game and that the 'world ends' thereafter. Hence, a valid conclusion to this discussion might be that the above assumptions fail to capture important aspects of real-world situations. It should not undermine the conclusion that for the game, as specified above, realistic or not, the analysis of Section 2.3.1 does make sense.

A more general and more fundamental conclusion from the discussion above is that the equilibrium path, in this case (insult, accept) and the (0.95.0.05) payoffs, is a very partial description of the players' considerations. For the actions that the players take in equilibrium are supported by a broader set of considerations about their opponents' reactions to other actions *off the equilibrium path.* In our case, that *P2* would not play 'reject' when she is given the insulting offer. To capture these considerations we define the notion of a *strategy*, one of the basic concepts of Game Theory:

Definition 2.3. A strategy is a complete action plan that describes how a player would respond to each and every move of the other player(s).

In our case, *P2* has to choose between four possible strategies: accept both the fair and the insulting offers; reject both; accept the former but reject the latter; reject the former and accept the latter. See further discussion in Section 2.7, below.

2.4 Equilibrium in the Alternating-Offers Game

We find the equilibrium by analysing, first, a one-period game, $T = 1$, then extending the length of the game to $T = 2$, and ultimately to $T \to \infty$.

2.4.1 Equilibrium for the $T = 1$ Game

This game differs only slightly from the one in Section 2.3.2. Although, now, there is an infinite number of feasible offers, the decision for *P1* is as simple. For $x_1 = 0.95$ dominates $x_1 = 0.5$, $x_1 = 0.96$ dominates $x_1 = 0.95$, $x_1 = 0.97$ dominates $x_1 = 0.96$, and so on, all the way up to $x_1 = 1$. Notice that when $x_1 = 1$, *P2* is indifferent between accepting the offer and rejecting it. So we can refine the argument and say that the offer should be just below $x_1 = 1$, so that *P2* gains a clear (though tiny) benefit from accepting the offer. Hence, from this point onwards, we adopt the practice of taking $x_1 = 1$ to mean 'just below one by a very small amount'.

'Unfair' as the outcome is, it is Pareto efficient, as it is impossible to make *P2* better off without making *P1* worse off. To see, more clearly, why this is an interesting statement, consider the case of a non-zero status-quo point, say (0.25, 0.25). Following the same steps as above, it is easy to see that the equilibrium path would be for *P1* to make the offer $x_1 = 0.75$, which is accepted by *P2*. Hence, *P1* is ruthless in pursuing his own interests, but also careful not to be too aggressive so as to push *P2* towards rejecting his offer. For example, suppose *P1* delivers the offer $x_1 = 0.8$. By rejecting the offer, *P2* can increase her share from 0.2 to 0.25, decreasing *P1*'s allocation from 0.75 to 0.25, in a sense, making him bear the entire burden of legal expenses. An important lesson here is that it is possible for a player to aggressively pursue self interest and, at the same time, accommodate his opponent so as not to undermine common interests. Such consideration does not rely on any sense of sympathy or altruism, nor does it require the intervention of any mediator or conciliator.

2.4.2 Equilibrium for the $T = 2$ Game

Adding one extra period would be to *P2*'s advantage, as she can now reject *P1*'s first-period offer and move to the second round, where she has the advantage of making a take-it-or-leave-it offer. But then, *P1* should try to make his $t = 1$ offer more attractive (relative to the $T = 1$ game), so that *P2* does not exercise her second-round option. At the same time, *P1* could exploit *P2*'s impatience and offer her a bit less than the entire pie, which she would get if she moves to the second round.

To be more precise, the equilibrium path in the $T = 2$ game is for *P1* to give a $t = 1$ offer of $(1 - x_1) = \beta^{P2}$, an offer that *P2* accepts as she is indifferent between getting β^{P2} at $t = 1$ and 1 at $t = 2$, thereby terminating the game without going to a second round. The precise argument is, again, by backward induction, assisted by Figure 2.5. (Notice that the receiving-offer player, namely *P2* in $t = 1$ and *P1* in $t = 2$, is placed on a straight segment between 0 and 1, to express the fact that an offer can be any number between 0 and 1.) If there is a second round, *P2* would fully exploit the situation, giving *P1* an offer of $x_2 = 0$. By giving *P2* a $t = 1$ offer just above the discounted value of the $t = 2$ delivery, β^{P2}, *P1* can avoid a second round, increasing his payoff to $x_1 = 1 - \beta^{P2} > 0$.

Two points are worth making. First, the two-period problem adds another dimension to the discussion of the efficiency. For now, economic inefficiency may arise either because the parties fail to reach an agreement (and, hence, fall back on the status-quo point) or because they fail to reach an early agreement. Due to impatience, a delay in reaching an agreement would 'eat up' into the present value of the pie. Technically, any second-period allocation with a discounted subjective value of $\left[\beta^{P1}x_1, \beta^{P2}(1 - x_1)\right]$ is Pareto dominated by the first-period allocation $(x_1, 1 - x_1)$.

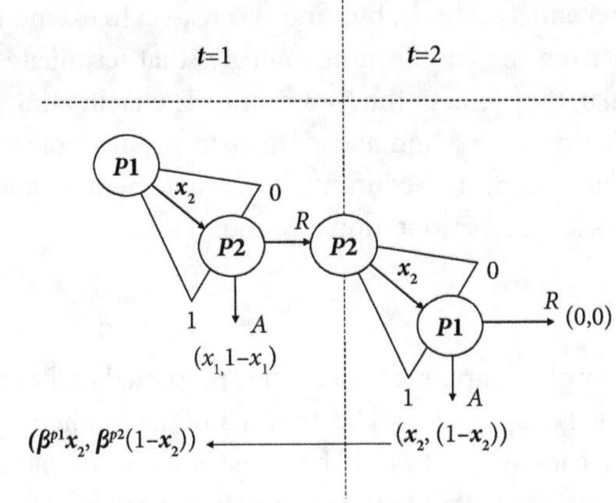

Figure 2.5 Alternating-offers bargaining with $T = 2$

Second, impatience is a disadvantage in bargaining: *P*1's share of the estate is smaller the larger is β^{P2}. That is, the more patient *P*2 is, the smaller is the 'concession' that *P*1 can extract from her by delivering an offer that terminates the bargaining earlier on.

2.4.3 Equilibrium for the $T \to \infty$ Game

By backward induction, a bargaining game of any length, *T*, would be settled up front. For the penultimate player should deliver an acceptable offer at $T - 1$, which would make the penultimate round, effectively, the last one. And so on.

Adding a second round to the $T = 1$ problem has taken away some of *P*1's first-mover advantage, but did not fully transfer it to *P*2. It is plausible that adding a third period, which will give *P*1 the 'last word' would restore some of the advantage that he had in the $T = 1$ game, but not completely. Intuitively, the longer the game, the more even the bargaining outcome is. Since, in reality, parties may respond to offers within a very short while, the number of rounds per a realistic bargaining situation, say a couple of days or a week, can be very large indeed, so that 'large *T*s' may be an object of practical, not just analytical, interest. But how should we select the 'right *T*', and how should we deal with the technical complexity of finding an equilibrium in such games? Surprisingly, the answer to both questions is to take *T* to infinity.

The difficulty, of course, is that such an *infinite-horizon* game has no final period from which to start the backward-induction process. We, therefore, use the following 'trick': suppose that there exists an equilibrium where *P*2 accepts the $t = 1$ offer. If so, it must be the case that, in making (accepting) this offer, *P*1 (*P*2) looks ahead to future (potential) rounds, but finds no reason to extend the bargaining; namely to deviate from the equilibrium strategies that terminate the bargaining at $t = 1$. In particular, they look to the $t = 3$ round. The facilitating property of the $T \to \infty$ game is that from $t = 3$ and ahead, the game looks exactly the same as it looks from $t = 1$ and ahead; in the infinite-horizon game, moving forwards does not take the players any closer to terminal round. If so,

$$x_1 = x_3. \tag{2.1}$$

Notice the similarity of this argument to the one presented in the calculation of an infinite, converging, geometric series Section A.1 of the Mathematical Appendix.

Moving one step backwards, it would be in the best interest of $P2$ to exploit $P1$'s impatience by delivering an offer that he can accept, namely:

$$x_2 = \beta^{P1} x_3. \tag{2.2}$$

Moving yet another step backwards to $t = 1$, it is now in the best interest of $P1$ to exploit $P2$'s impatience by delivering an offer that she can accepts, namely:

$$1 - x_1 = \beta^{P2} (1 - x_2). \tag{2.3}$$

(2.1) to (2.3) are three equations in three unknowns, that are easy to solve. Hence:

Proposition 2.1. *With $T \to \infty$, the alternating offers bargaining game would end after one round with P1's offer,*

$$x_1 = \frac{1 - \beta^{P2}}{1 - \beta^{P1}\beta^{P2}}, \tag{2.4}$$

being accepted by P2.

Now, consider the case where the two players have the same bargaining power: $\beta^{P1} = \beta^{P2} = \beta$, which substituted into Equation (2.4) yields:

$$x_1 = \frac{1 - \beta^{P2}}{1 - \beta^{P1}\beta^{P2}} = \frac{1 - \beta}{(1 - \beta)(1 + \beta)} = \frac{1}{1 + \beta}.$$

Now remember that the βs measure the subjective discount factor per period, a unit of time. Clearly, a player values a next-month delivery higher than a next-year delivery, not because her attitude towards deferred satisfactions is different but because the period of deferral is much shorter. At the limit, as the period of deferral approaches zero, the player's subjective discount factor approaches 1. In the context of bargaining where, virtually, players can respond to offers in an instant, the $\beta = 1$ benchmark is an interesting one. Hence,

Proposition 2.2. *With the same subjective time preferences and a very short time to wait for the next round of bargaining, Proposition 2.1's equilibrium offer reduces to:*

$$x_1 = x_2 = \frac{1}{2}.$$

However complicated, somewhat contrived, and perhaps unrealistic the model is, the bottom-line result is surprisingly simple and intuitive; possibly, our game is specified at the 'right level' of abstraction—after all.

2.5 Taking a Shortcut: Nash Bargaining

There are many economic problems where bargaining is important, albeit it is not the main focus of the analysis. In such problems, describing, again, the entire setting of the Rubinstein model, let alone repeating the entire argument behind Proposition 2.1, would make the analysis needlessly cumbersome, as well as distracting attention away from its main focus. In such cases it is common to take a shortcut and use a 'black box' formula that captures the main insights of the Rubinstein analysis: that, effectively, the players bargain just on that part of the pie which is beyond their status-quo points, giving each player a slice, $\lambda^i \geq 0$ (λ is the Greek letter lambda), $\lambda^{P1} + \lambda^{P2} = 1$; the more bargaining power a player has, the higher her respective λ^i. It is understood, informally, that λ^i is affected by a player's patience relative to his opponent's, by the number of bargaining rounds as well as the player's position in the game. The name of this shortcut is the Nash Bargaining Solution.

Consider a status-quo point, $(b^{P1}, b^{P2}) < 1$, so that, effectively, the parties bargain over $1 - b^{P1} - b^{P2}$. The Nash Bargaining solution allocates each player:

$$x^i = b^i + \lambda^i\left(1 - b^{P1} - b^{P2}\right).$$

Another way of thinking about this formula is that if $P1$ could give a take-it-or-leave it offer, his share would be $x^{P1} = \left(1 - b^{P2}\right)$. If $P2$ could give a take-it-or-leave-it offer, $P1$'s slice would only be b^{P1}. For the interim case of less than full bargaining power to any single player, take a weighted average between these two extreme cases, with the λs being the weights. Namely:

$$x^{P1} = \lambda^{P1}\left(1 - b^{P2}\right) + \lambda^{P2} b^{P1}$$

(and symmetrically for $P2$).

2.6 The Coase Theorem

Consider, again, the Frankie-and-Johnny 'story'. The legal setting guarantees the players certain legal rights: to bring their disagreement to a court of law, which would implement a 50 : 50 allocation of the estate, net of legal expenses. But since these expenses are significant, and since litigation offers no material benefit, the litigious course-of-action is economically inefficient. So could the parties avoid it? According to our analysis so far, the answer is yes. Moreover, even if the court favours one player over the other (on ground of, say, that the other was faulty of breaking the relationship), thereby deviating from the 50 : 50 rule, the answer would be the same: the parties would avoid litigation and bargain an out-of-court settlement to allocate the estate, which reflects the legal position of penalizing the faulty player. But how general is this conclusion? Should we expect it to hold under any conceivable legal setting? Ronald Coase, winner of the 1991 Nobel Prize in Economics, articulated in his famous 'theorem' an answer to this question:[5]

Proposition 2.3. *[The Coase Theorem] Provided that the players' dealings are free of any frictions, and provided that their rights over the disputed assets are well defined, the players would negotiate a Pareto efficient bargain.*

In his famous (1960) paper, Coase used the term *transaction costs* rather than *frictions*. We explain, below, the reason for deviating from Coase's terminology. It is worth noting that many have interpreted the Coase Theorems in the spirit of spontaneous order: since transaction costs are typically small, real world parties would always implement an economically efficient outcome, without help from any third party, and regardless of the setting, or the *environment* in which the players interact. As the following discussion shows, this interpretation is not adopted in this book.

2.6.1 Frictions: A Simple Example

Consider a slightly different setting to the one above. The parties can settle out of court (play S) and split the estate each getting one half. They can also litigate (play L), which will cost a fixed amount equal to 25% of the estate. However, the first player to file gains a *first-mover advantage*,[6] which we model in an extreme manner: the first mover gets the entire estate, net of legal expenses. The players

[5] See Coase (1960).

[6] In fact, an important aspect in some divorce cases, for the first mover chooses the jurisdiction. Jurisdictions differ in material respects, such as whether they recognize prenuptial agreements, or in the way they account for the contribution of the parties to the estate during the marriage. Searching for an advantageous jurisdiction is called *forum shopping*.

Table 2.1 The litigation game

		P2	
		L	S
P1	L	(0.375,0.375)	(0.75,0)
	S	(0,0.75)	(0.5,0.5)

make their decisions simultaneously. Clearly, if one plays *L* and the other plays *S*, the former is bound to be the first (and the only one) in court, implying a payoff of 0.75. If both play *L*, they have an equal probability of being first, which will deliver, in expectations, 0.375 each. (For the sake of the argument, assume that both players are risk neutral.) Table 2.1 shows the payoffs for each of the four combinations of the *L* and *S* strategies, retaining the notation that the first (second) number in parenthesis is *P1′s* (*P2′s*) payoff. Such matrix presentation of a *simultaneous-move* game is called the *normal form* of the game.

To find an equilibrium in such a game we look for a combination of strategies, one for *P1* and the other for *P2*, such that each player's strategy is a *best response* to the strategy of her opponent. Hence, *L* is *P1*'s best response to *P2* playing the *L* strategy, which delivers an expected payoff of 0.375—greater than the zero payoff for the *S* strategy. At the same time, *L* is also the best response in case *P2* plays the *S* strategy. Hence, in this case, *L* is *dominating strategy* and (*L*, *L*) is the unique *Nash Equilibrium* in this game, formulated by John Nash, winner of the 1994 Nobel Prize in Economics.

2.6.2 Frictions: Preliminary Discussion

Obviously, the above is a Pareto-dominated equilibrium; a *failure* to reach a *Coasian Bargain*. Like most failures in economics, this one results from a certain impediment to the exchange commodities or rights. In this case it is the right to be free of litigation, which is acquired in exchange for granting a similar right to the other player.

Behind the failure there seems to rest a more complicated 'story'. Perhaps, the parties met, discussed the mutual benefits of avoiding litigating, agreed to do so, then sealed their agreement 'with a handshake'. However, so the story goes, there is a time gap between making the agreement and 'delivering the goods', namely finalizing the process of dissolving the marriage and splitting the estate. Within that gap, each party may start doubting the other's commitment to the agreement. Notice that upon being informed that his opponent has filed a court case, a player would learn that the agreement was breached. In contrast, getting no information of such litigation does not guarantee that the bargain is being adhered to. If so, perhaps the best course of action is to litigate, preemptively. Notice, also, that once a court case is filed, the damage is already done and it is too late to cancel the bargain. For all these reasons, a player cannot trust her opponent handshake and would, therefore, prefer to avoid the bargain in the first place.

To rectify economic efficiency, the players need to institute some mechanism that would allow them to commit themselves to the deal, namely avoid litigation; for example, by signing a legally binding contract to that effect. It is not clear that the courts would enforce such a contract, as they might consider the right to justice fundamental, which the parties cannot wave off even by mutual consent.

Suppose, for the sake of the argument, that a no-litigation contract is viable. When should it be negotiated? Clearly not after the couple has already agreed to separate. For any communication, from one party to the other, suggesting such a contract, would reveal that the sender of message is contemplating litigation, to which the receiver might respond by litigating preemptively. Instead, the best time to agree the term of separation is when the marriage relationship is created, which raises additional questions. Would such negotiations undermine the parties (subjective) joy of creating the bond? Can the couple, at that point in their relationship, understand the issues involving separation? Even ignoring these 'emotional' aspects, we have assumed, so far, that the separation is consensual. In many cases it is not. For reasons of fairness, or in order to strengthen the bond, should the parties make the status-quo point *contingent* on the circumstances of the separation, penalizing the party responsible for breaching it? It follows that separation clauses in a prenuptial contract may be quite complicated to negotiate and articulate.

The 'stories' above make clear that frictions in human interaction are way more complicated than the impression conveyed by Coase's usage of 'transaction cost'. In many cases the relationship has a time dimension so that, first, the parties need to negotiate a contract that would regulate their dealings and, second to implement it, which might imply a renegotiation of the original contract (unlike in a *spot transaction* where the parties can agree the term of a deal and execute it—instantaneously). Since the contract is likely to rely on court enforcement (or, at least, the threat of it), it should be clearly articulated and documented, so that the court can interpret it later on. Moreover, the court's interpretation should be resilient to the possibility that at the point of litigating the parties are likely to come up with conflicting claims regarding the original intention of the contract.

Perhaps the most important implication of this discussion is that 'frictions', unlike 'transaction costs', are not something that the analysis should take for granted but, rather, something that should be an integral part of the analysis. That should be done by modelling the frictions and the mechanism, say a contract, devised to relax their effect into a single analytical framework. Of particular interest is the question whether the players can devise the contract on their own

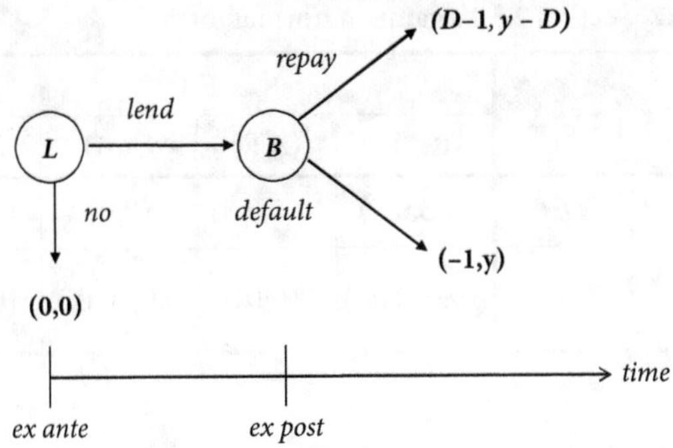

Figure 2.6 Financial distress

(spontaneously), without any support from a third party such as a priest, a clerk, a judge, or a legislator. This question, to a large extent, sets up the agenda for subsequent chapters

2.6.3 Ex-Post versus Ex-Ante Economic Efficiency

The dynamic element in the stories above requires a more careful distinction between ex-ante efficiency and ex-post efficiency. Consider the following example, illustrated in Figure 2.6. A lender, L, can lend £1 to a borrower, B, to fund a project that would yield an amount $y > 1$ (assume, for simplicity, that the interest rate is zero). It is agreed that upon maturity, B would pay back an amount D, $1 < D < y$. B may perform on the agreement by delivering the amount D, or she may default and pay nothing; there is no penalty, legal or otherwise, for default. Clearly, both options are *ex-post* efficient as they imply different partitions of the 'pie', y, none of which Pareto dominates the other. It is also clear that the only equilibrium in this game is one where L does not lend, anticipating a default if he lends. Clearly that equilibrium is ex-ante inefficient, for $(0, 0)$ is Pareto dominated by $(D - 1, y - D)$.

For most of the cases analysed in this book, the more interesting criterion is ex-ante efficency.

2.7 A Note on Equilibria in Games

The reader might get the impression that the sub-game-perfect equilibrium defined above is of a completely different nature to the Nash Equilibrium used here, which is not the case. To see the point more clearly, Table 2.2 describes Section 2.3.1's game in normal form. $P1$, who moves first, has two strategies available for him, either the fair or the insulting offer, F and I respectively. As already

Table 2.2 Section 2.3.1's game in normal form

		P2			
		(*A*,*A*)	(*A*,*R*)	(*R*,*A*)	(*R*,*R*)
P1	*F*	(0.5,0.5)	(0.5,0.5)	(0,0)	(0,0)
	I	(0.95,0.05)	(0,0)	(0.95,0.05)	(0,0)

explained in Section 2.3.2 above, since *P2* moves second, her strategy has to specify how she reacts to all of *P1*'s possible moves. For example, (*A*, *R*) is the strategy: accept the fair offer but reject the insulting one. It is easy to see that *P1* playing *I* and *P2* playing (*A*, *A*) is a Nash Equilibrium. However, *P1* playing *F* and *P2* playing (*A*, *R*) is also a Nash Equilibrium. In particular, *F* is *P1*'s best response to *P2* playing (*A*, *R*). Reinhardt Selten, winner of the 1994 Nobel Prize in Economics, pointed out that a normal-form analysis of dynamic games does not exclude equilibria that are supported by non-credible threats; see discussion in Section 2.3.2. He therefore suggested the sub-game-perfect equilibrium concept as a *refinement* that weeds out such equilibria from the more general set of Nash Equilibria.

2.8 Application: Insolvency Law

Moving from couples to companies, can the stakeholders in a failing business sort out their conflicts via a Coasian Bargain, or should we suspect that certain frictions would prevent them from doing so, requiring an active involvement of the courts, the regulators, or the government?

Risking oversimplification, it is sometimes helpful to sort actual insolvency[7] laws between two extreme ends. The first is *freedom of contracting* where the law limits the role of the courts to the strict enforcement of the contractual rights of all the parties involved. Ex ante, when the contracts are negotiated, the allocation of rights is determined by mutual consent. Particularly, the contracting parties may adopt an 'egalitarian' approach where all stakeholders have similar rights, or they may choose to allocate more rights to certain stakeholders, particularly the secured creditors. (We defer analysis of the rationale for securing certain debt by collateral to Chapter 3.) Ex post, the court would avoid any question regarding the allocation of rights, whether efficient or fair. Rather, it would assume that the contracting parties have taken all such factors into consideration, ex ante, and were well placed to devise the best-possible contract on their own (spontaneously). The

[7] In English law, the word 'insolvency' applies, exclusively, to companies, while the word bankruptcy is reserved for natural persons. In the US, the word bankruptcy applies to both.

second approach to insolvency may be described as *judicial activism*, where the creditors' rights are placed under judicial review (ex post). Particularly, the courts are empowered to block the liquidation rights of the secured creditors in cases where these are deemed not to be conducive to the common good. Nineteenth-century England was close to the first model, while 1980s US was close to the second, with judges sometimes acting as if any company, regardless of how poorly performing, was worthy of 'protection' from creditors who are trying to enforce their liquidation rights.[8] The public-policy question is which point between these two extremes better serves the economy.

2.8.1 Financial and Economic Distress

Definition 2.4. A company is said to be in economic distress if the discounted value of its future cash flow falls short of its liquidation value. A debtor is said to be financially distressed if the discounted value of its future cash flow falls short of the value of its debt.

That is, in the case of economic distress, liquidation is the NPV-positive line of action. In the case of financial distress, continuation is the NPV-positive line of action, though the company is unable to pay its debt. For example, consider a company with no debt and an asset that yields £5 per annum, in perpetuity. The risk-free interest rate is 10% and the liquidation value is 100. Since the company has no debt, by definition it cannot be financially distressed. Its owner is safe of any forced liquidation simply because no one has the right to impose it on him. Yet the company is economically distressed, since its going-concern value is $5/0.1 = 50$ while its liquidation value is 100. It is in the owner's best interest to liquidate the asset, 'put the money in the bank' and generate annual income of 10, over and above the company's cash flow—if continued.

Consider, next, a company with secured, senior debt of 70. There are two periods, $t = 1, 2$. For simplicity, assume that the interest rate is zero. Since the debt is in default, the secured creditor, C, has the right to repossess the company's asset and sell it. The $t = 1$ market price of the assets is 20, which depreciates to zero at $t = 2$, so that C's liquidation option effectively expires if not used at $t = 1$. If C does not exercise her liquidation right, and if the company's owner, F, can fund a $t = 2$ investment, of 10, in working capital, it can generate *verifiable* cash flow of 50; see Figure 2.7.[9] Verifiability implies that cash income is observable to third parties, particularly to a court of law, which can enforce any claim against this income; see Chapter 3 for a more exhaustive discussion of the concept. It is assumed that

[8] For an extreme example, see Weiss and Wruck (1998) for the case of Eastern Airlines.

[9] The figure is an abbreviated extensive form, as it does not fully describe the way the funding part of the game works.

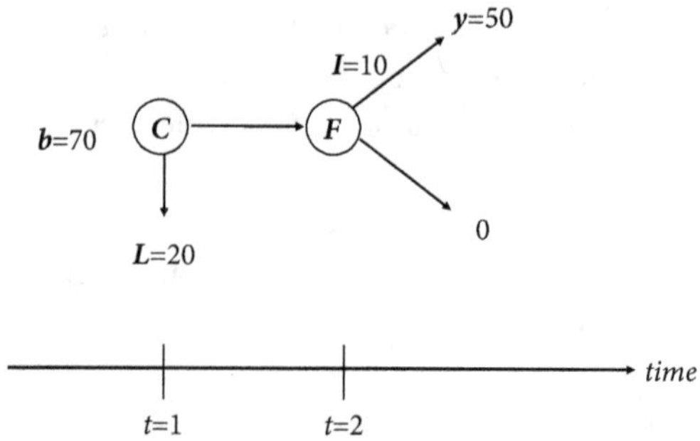

Figure 2.7 The lending problem

F has some exclusive know-how in managing the asset, which explains why the value of the assets, once separated from *F*, is just 20. Lastly, suppose that *C* has no will or, perhaps, is unable to fund the working capital himself. Clearly, the company is not economically distressed, for its net discounted cash flow, 50 – 10, exceeds its liquidation value, 20. Yet, it is financially distressed as it cannot pay back it debt—fully.

2.8.2 Debt Overhang

Could an economically viable company be liquidated prematurely due to financial distress? According to the *debt-overhang* scenario, the answer is yes; see Myers (1977). Consider a potential creditor who is approached by *F* for working-capital funding. Should he lend, he would be junior to *C*. Hence, when the income, 50, is generated, he would be second in line, to be paid only after *C* is satisfied. Since *C* has a claim to any income up to 70, nothing is left to the junior creditor. He should refuse lending. *C* should foresee this line of events and liquidate the assets up-front, and save 20 out of his unfortunate investment.

2.8.3 Debt Forgiveness

Is debt overhang a violation of the Coase Theorem? Not according to the description of the facts so far. For it is in the best interest of *C* and *F* to agree a debt forgiveness of between 30 and 50, that would decrease the value of the debt from 70 to between 40 and 20, allowing working capital to flow in, to the mutual benefit of both *C* and *F*. Notice that such a deal does not even require any communication between *C* and *F*, for the former can simply cancel 30 units of debt, unilaterally. Clearly, there is no need for any external intervention to convince *C* to 'show sympathy and help out' *F*, for that 'leniency' is entirely in his own self-interest.

The case for leniency is somewhat more dramatic if we interpret the story a bit differently. Suppose that *I*, instead of being an investment in working capital, is the opportunity cost of *F*: she can simply walk away from her failed business and find a job that pays her 10. It is still in the best interest of *C* to forgive the debt down, so as to leave *F* with a payoff of 10, which might explain the common incidence of managers of failed businesses still keeping a generous compensation package, to the fury of the public and other stakeholders.

2.8.3.1 Debt-for-Equity Swaps

A different but economically equivalent way of forgiving debt is for *C* to write off all his debt in return for the company's equity,[10] previously held by *F*. Such a 'swap' would place *C* at the end of the line, and would turn the provider of working capital to a senior creditor, allowing him to collect his debt of 10. Under the alternative interpretation whereby *F* has an outside option of 10, *C* could swap all his debt for up to 80% ownership stake in the company, leaving *F* with 0.2×50, just enough to compensate him for not exercising his walk-away option.

2.9 The Limits of Freedom of Contracting

In this section we examine several factors, including suspected frictions that could undermine the efficiency of a freedom-of-contracting regime.

2.9.1 Third Parties

It is sometimes argued that a company may be liquidated because the debtor and the creditor fail to take into consideration the loss of value to third parties, for example, the company's workers. Consider a modification of the example above where out of the company's cash flow of 50, 30 is already committed, by way of a contract with unionized labour, to paying wages. Moreover, the domestic legal system is pro labour and treats wage arrears as senior to any other liability. It follows that if the company is continued under the existing contract, $t = 2$ cash flow is divided 20 to *C* and 30 to labour. Since we carry on with the interpretation of *I* as *F*'s outside option, it is in the latter's best interest to leave the company, and in *C*'s best interest to liquidate the company up-front.

Clearly, a rescue deal can still be worked out once labour is brought into the Coasian Bargain. For example, once *C* writes down the debt to 20, and the workers take a pay-cut of 10 (leaving them with wages of 20), *F* is left with 10, the exact

[10] Namely, titles against the company's profits; a more detailed explanation is provided in Chapter 3, Section 3.5.1.

amount that would make him stay put. Other deals, more advantageous to C and F may be negotiated if the workers are at a weak bargaining position, that forces them towards greater concessions. Notice, that labour's $t = 2$ outside option is zero.

Hence, by themselves, third parties make no material difference to the analysis of the Coase Theorem. However, in order to achieve economic efficiency, any stakeholder should be brought into the restructuring negotiations. The word 'stakeholder' applies widely: any party who has a claim against the company or might be affected by its operations. If a stakeholder cannot be reached, or a class of stakeholders are so numerous and spread-out that they are unable to coordinate the appointment of a delegate that would represent them, a restructuring may fail and a viable company may be liquidated.

2.9.2 Private Benefits and Liquidity

A more complicated situation arises where some of the value that the company generates is non-cash benefits. Common, though somewhat contrived, examples are the subjective valuation of a sense of pride, security, or social status that F derives from owning her business. More realistically, even cash flows that are hard to trace and account for and, therefore, to monetize can be considered non-cash benefits. For example, the more activist American approach to bankruptcy originates in the late nineteenth century's railroads insolvencies, when a regular rail service was essential to the normal operation of many businesses: to bring in raw materials and take product to market; see Franks and Sussman (2005). In such a case, a cessation of rail service due to insolvency would result in material loss of cash to those businesses, but that loss is hard to account for, let alone to be brought into the Coasian Bargain. *Non-pecuniary* or *private benefits* are some of the technical terms used in the literature to describe such benefits.

Suppose that of the value of 50 generated by Figure 2.7's company, 30 is private benefits. It follows that the amount of cash generated by the company is just 20, short of the minimum 30 that is needed to keep C and F stay put. In theory, a Coasian Bargain can still be organized so as to keep the company afloat. It requires that the private beneficiaries inject in cash in lieu of the missing 10 units. The deal may be structured as follows: C swaps its senior debt for F's equity, and sells it to the private beneficiaries for 20. The private beneficiaries then grant F 50% of the equity, as an incentive package, and keep the rest to themselves. That would split the cash flow of the firm, 10 to F, to keep her on board, and 10 to the private beneficiaries, which would leave them at $30 - 20 + 10 = 20$, better than losing their entire private benefits.

There are two important implications of the current example. First, the expression 'claims against the company' has to be interpreted more broadly: any value generate by the company, whether it is backed by a formal claim (a contract) or just 'picked up' by a certain party, has to participate in the restructuring. Second, in this case, the private beneficiaries have to inject current cash in exchange for future benefits. Hence, a possible source of failure in debt restructuring is the lack of liquidity[11] by certain parties. Even if the private benefits materialize, in cash, at some future point, that does not imply that they can raise, at a short notice, enough cash to execute a Coasian bargain.

2.9.3 Activist Courts and the Availability of Credit

An activist bankruptcy court, recognizing the practical difficulties in organizing a Coasian Bargain, may decide to force *C* to write down the debt to 10 ('take a haircut'—in market lingo). Three points are worth making here.

First, such a forced write down is not to the benefit of all the parties involved, as *C* is worse off by 10—relative to what he could have, had he been allowed to exercise his legal right and liquidate the company's assets. In other words, this is not a facilitation of a Coasian Bargain. The activist court may still argue that it has rescued more value, 30, distributed across the many, rather than impose a loss of 10 on a single stakeholder. While that may be a valid (indeed a common) argument by some social calculus, it stands on weaker footing than the Pareto criterion. Second, the court should consider the precedent that it creates and, therefore, the effect on *C*, or other creditors, in future applications for credit. In other words, even though the court could improve the ex-post outcome of the distressed borrower currently in court, it might worsen ex-ante lending conditions for subsequent borrowers (some of whom will never be in distress). Third, a broader policy consideration should compare the effectiveness of legal intervention against other policy measures. In particular, the government may 'bail out' the company. Treasury bailouts have several advantages relative to court action. They do not create a legal precedent and, therefore, do not affect ex-ante lending decisions. It is worth noticing that judicial activism in the United States started with railroads but spread, over time, to industries where there is less of a public interest in preserving distressed companies. Treasuries may be better equipped than courts in assessing the social benefit of intervention. In addition, while the activist court burdens the cost of rescue on *C* alone, the treasury would roll it over to the tax payer, which is likely to overlap with the private beneficiaries. In that respect, the ultimate outcome of a bailout may be closer to a Coasian Bargain.

2.9.4 Uncoordinated Creditors: Creditors Run

The most dramatic instance of creditors unable to coordinate their moves, thereby putting at risk an economically viable company, is a *creditors run*. To capture this

[11] The word liquidity means value that can be converted to cash with minimal loss; various formulations appear in subsequent chapters.

situation, consider a company, *F*, that has an outstanding debt of 100. If carried on, the company would generate a cash flow of 100, plus a significant amount of private benefits to its insiders—workers and management. Hence, the coordination problem apart, the company is neither economically nor financially distressed. The company's debt, 100, is held by two risk-neutral creditors, 50 each. The debt is secured on the company's assets, that have a liquidation value of 40. However, the debt is not prioritized so that, in liquidation, the creditors are paid on a first-come first-served basis. The creditors make the decision whether to claim for repayment simultaneously. It follows that if both decide to *run* on the company's assets (play *R*), each has a 50% chance to be first and be paid the entire liquidation value of the company—40. In expectation, their payoffs are (20, 20); see Table 2.3. If both allow the company to carry on (play *S*, for 'stay'), the company would yield its full economic potential, with payoffs (50, 50). If one player runs and the other stays, the former would be paid 40 and the latter would be paid zero.

Clearly, there are two Nash Equilibria, (*S*, *S*) and (*R*, *R*), as the best response to *S* is *S* and the best response *R* is *R*. It follows that a company may be liquidated just because the creditors lost faith in its financial stability. The root cause of the inefficiency is the first mover advantage, already discussed in Section 2.6.1. The literature sometimes likens such an outcome to a *common pool* where, absent regulation, fishermen tend to engage in over-fishing, perhaps to the point of exploiting the pool's natural resource to depletion.

Whether the problem calls for court (or any other regulatory) intervention is not at all clear. For the problem of creditors' run has a simple and widely used contractual solution: to prioritize the creditors, ex ante, by way of a contract, so as to remove the first-mover advantage and, hence, to avoid the run, ex-post. So far, no friction is identified that could explain why the parties could not deploy this simple mechanism. By itself, a company that suffers the consequences of a badly structured debt does not falsify the Coase Theorem. More so when most real-world debt is prioritized. Nor does it give grounds for intervention. For (probably) it is not the job of the courts to correct flawed managerial decisions.

To highlight the effectiveness of prioritized debt, Figure 2.8 describes two alternative situations: on the left (right) hand sides, the senior (junior) creditors,

Table 2.3 Creditors run

		creditor 2	
		R	*S*
creditor 1	*R*	(20,20)	(40,0)
	S	(0,40)	(50,50)

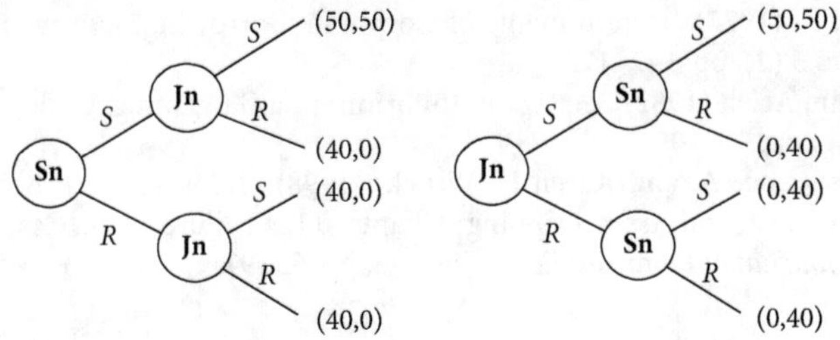

Figure 2.8 Prioritized debt

Sn (Jn), is in the position of being first, considering whether it is in their best interest to demand repayment, i.e. play *R*, or abstain from doing so, i.e. play *S*. However, regardless of who moves first, if the firm is liquidated, payments to the senior creditor are prioritized over the junior creditor. Evidently, in both cases the, only sub-game perfect equilibrium is for the first mover, whether she is the junior or the senior creditor, to play *S* and for the second player to follow. Since neither the senior creditor nor the junior creditor can increase their share of the liquidation value, the first-mover advantage is eliminated, and with it the hazard that the conflict of interest between the creditors would cause a viable company to fail.

2.10 Conclusion

In this chapter we take the first step in analysing social interaction. As an example, we look at the case of players conflicted about the splitting of a given resource, a so-called pie. Under the Rubinstein alternating-offer modelling of the bargaining process, the outcome is Pareto efficient. The Coase Theorem claimed such a result to be of broader applicability and generality. Yet, Coase offers no explicit modelling and the no-friction condition seems to be somewhat vague, lacking any precise definition of 'frictions'.

Our analysis of the financial restructuring of a distressed company suggests two potential sources of frictions: a difficulty in writing binding contracts, and a difficulty of reaching all the parties that could benefit from a potential Coasian Bargain. Subsequent chapters offer more elaboration of these and other sources of frictions. In particular, we shall elaborate on the inherent difficulty to trade (rights in) certain commodities, the paradigmatic example being information.

References

[1] Coase, R. H., (1960). 'The Problem of Social Cost'. *Journal of Law and Economics*, Vol. 3 (October), pp. 1–44.

[2] Franks, Julian and Oren Sussman. (2005). 'Financial Innovations and Corporate Bankruptcy'. *Journal of Financial Intermediation*, 14, pp. 283–317.

[3] Myers, S. C. (1977). 'Determinants of Corporate Borrowing'. *Journal of Financial Economics* 5 (2), pp. 147–175.
[4] Rubinstein, Ariel, (1982). 'Perfect Equilibrium in a Bargaining Model'. *Econometrica*, 50 (1) pp. 97–109.
[5] Weiss, Lawrence A. and Karen H. Wruck, (1998). 'Information Problems, Conflicts of Interest, and Asset Stripping: Chapter 11' s Failure in the Case of Eastern Airlines', *Journal of Financial Economics*, 48, pp. 55–97.

3
Property Rights

3.1 Introduction

Of all the institutions that were developed in order to support the market economy, private property is probably the most important. But what exactly is the right to property? What frictions is it supposed to alleviate and, if so, how does it operate towards this end? Surprisingly, economists have found these questions hard to answer; to some extent, the available answers (below) are, still, not entirely satisfactory.

Legally speaking, the owner of an object obtains full discretion to *control*, deploy, or benefit from the object in any way that pleases her. However, only scarcely is that right exclusive, for other stakeholders may have rights in the same object. For example, the tax authorities may have a claim against some of the income generated by the object. More interestingly, parties who provided funds towards the purchase of the object are typically rewarded with certain rights, such as voting rights or security interests, in the owner's business. Clearly, these potentially conflicting rights need to be reconciled one against the other by prescribing who gets what under each conceivable eventuality.

Here comes an important observation: that the owner's rights are typically defined by what is left over after other stakeholders have carved out some rights for themselves: ownership is a *residual claim*. This observation raises a few 'big questions':

- *BQ1*: why should the owner's right be defined as a residual where other stakeholders have their rights explicitly defined? For example, a debtor's security interest is defined by the right to take possession of an asset *contingent* on the owner defaulting on payment. Otherwise, the owner stays in control and keeps the residual cash that is left after making the payment. Is that a reflection of some fundamental difficulty in the contracting, documenting, and implementing rights? Are financial contracts inherently *crude* and *incomplete*?
- *BQ2*: what is the efficient allocation of ownership rights? For example: it is a very common practice, in market economies, to allocate control and residual cash rights to the investors who provide the capital (and to the managers appointed by them). Typically, labour is granted the right to a fixed payment and hardly any control rights. In fact, some social reformers suggest

The Economics of Financial Markets and Institutions. Oren Sussman, Oxford University Press. © Oren Sussman (2023).
DOI: 10.1093/oso/9780192869739.003.0004

a switch, where labour hires capital, pays it a fixed amount and holds control and residual cash rights. While some may dismiss this idea as an 'impractical utopia', an economist would like to have a more analytical argument (for or against), grounded in the concept of economic efficiency.

- *BQ3*: could the efficient allocation be achieved, spontaneously, via voluntary exchange among the stakeholders? As already noted in Chapter 2, voluntary exchange implies not just spot trading in commodities but, also, free exchange of rights, that parties write into contracts, to be implemented as intended.

The questions above are clearly among the most fundamental in the analysis of any market. But as we shall see below, answering these abstract questions also sheds light on some business practices, such as mergers, acquisitions, outsourcing, and leveraged buy-outs (LBOs).

3.2 The Nature of the Firm

The economic theory of property rights is closely related to the theory of the firm. Modern investigation starts with Coase (1937), who asked a surprisingly simple question: what is the *nature of the firm*? His answer was: a set of transactions, removed from the marketplace because of high transaction costs, enclosed into a small internal market, where the cost of transacting is lower. As in the case of his famous theorem, Coase does not provide a precise definition of transaction costs, let alone suggest a method to identify and measure them in practice. In the absence of such identification, it is very difficult to operationalize the theory and test it empirically. Hence, we suggest an alternative definition, which is more operational and directly related to the notion of property:

Definition 3.1. The firm is a set of assets under joint ownership. Implied by ownership is an allocation of control and cash rights, perhaps contingent on certain eventualities.

It is common to order the assets that a firm could potentially own along a vertical line (from inputs to final goods) and along a horizontal line by the degree of substitutability or complementarity with the firm's core product. Hence, when a supermarket chain acquires a dairy farm, we say that it integrates vertically, while if it creates its own credit card we say that it integrates horizontally, to consumer finance—see Figure 3.1.

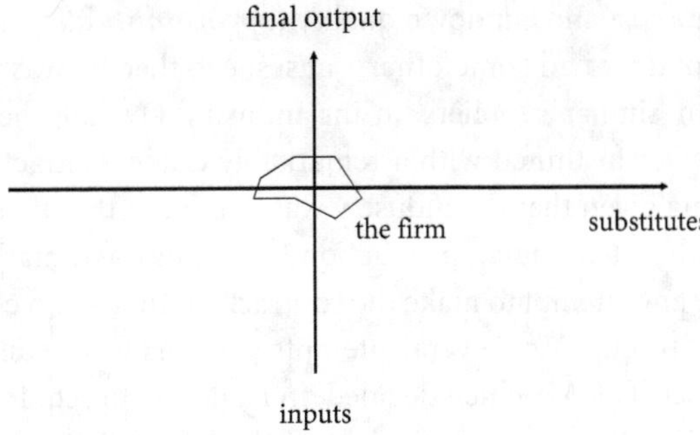

Figure 3.1 Vertical/horizontal integration

3.2.1 An Outline of a Theory

Relying heavily on a single historical event, the 1926 acquisition of Fisher Brothers (FB), a supplier of automobile bodies to General Motors (GM), Klein, Crowford, and Alchian (1978) suggests a theory of vertical integration and thus, by Definition 3.1, a theory of the firm. The event took place at a time when a new technology was introduced to the automobile industry: metal-closed bodies. (In the early days of the industry, automobile-bodies were built, like horse-drawn carriages, by covering a hand-made wooden frame with metal sheets.) GM, still a small operator in an industry not yet consolidated, hoped to use the new technology in order to become a market leader. However, it relied on FB to provide the metal-closed bodies (the word 'outsourcing' was invented, yet). These bodies were manufactured using heavy stamping machines that pressed sheets of metal against heavy forms so as to shape them into various body parts. The stamping forms are expensive and, also, specific to the automobile manufacturer: a bonnet made for a GM car could not be used in, say, a Ford automobile. As a result, the investment in a stamping forms is a *sunk cost*: once made, it cannot be recovered or redeployed.

Clearly, a stronger relationship between GM and FB was required. If not, once FB's cost was sunk, GM could bargain the price of the metal bodies down to their unit cost, leaving FB's sunk cost uncovered and the company at a loss. Hence, in 1919 a ten-year contract was signed, which gave FB an exclusive-supplier status with a guaranteed profit of 17.6% over the unit cost of producing a body.[1] Doing so, the contract placed FB in a monopolistic position with the deliberate aim of granting it with a *rent*,[2] so as to cover the sunk cost. As a result FB had a strong

[1] Such pricing formula is called *cost plus*.

[2] The word 'rent' implies profit derived from monopolistic, political or some other special position, rather than from the production of goods and services; see further discussion in Section 6.2.1 of Chapter 6. Since, here, the ex-post rent actually compensates for an ex-ante sunk cost, it is sometimes called 'quasi rent'.

incentive to inflate cost and cut down quality (*opportunistically*). To control such behaviour, the contract had some other clauses, e.g. that *FB* was not allowed to charge more than 'similar suppliers' in the industry. Overall, the impression is that relationship was instituted with a remarkably crude contract, which is particularly surprising given that the industry was young, in the 'disruptive' stage of development, with fast-changing production technology and market conditions. There was hardly any attempt to make the contract contingent on changes in market size or cost of production. Several attempts were made to refine the contract, but they did not satisfy GM, which decided, in response, to acquired FB in 1926.

It is worth articulating the main insight of the 'story'. i) While GM acquired FB's asset out of a profit motive, by itself, the change of ownership does not affect the asset's physical characteristics and, hence, its productivity. The question how a change in ownership structure is to enhance profitability therefore deserve some serious analysis and rigorous modelling. ii) It follows that the burden that separate ownership imposed on the relationship was not an automatic result of asset specificity and sunk cost. Rather, these physical characteristics gave rise to a friction that undermined the parties, ability to manage their assets effectively. iii) The friction had to do with the need to ex-ante articulate, document, contract, and (potentially) ex-post enforce the delivery of a certain product, made to a certain specification, at the right quality and for the right price. A failure to implement any one of these characteristics left either side with a strong incentive to exploit any gap in the contract, to its own advantage, thereby inflicting an extra cost on the other side. iv) The advantage of ownership is that it gave GM the right to control the asset 'the way it felt like' provided that it did not breach a well-specified right that was handed out to a third party, e.g. a secured lender or a bank. Whatever GM did not give away was, simply, its own business.

Notice, however, that in order to control the asset post acquisition, GM's management still had to communicate, to the production-line operators, the specification that they wanted, as well as incentivizing them to deliver the required specification at the right quality, for a wage rate that left GM with a profit. Somehow, for a reason that is not entirely clear, in-house communication seems to be easier than cross-party contraction. As we argue, below, this lack of clarity is more than just an aesthetic defect of this chapter's analysis.

3.2.2 Relationships: Weak and Strong

It is useful to think of the two ownership structures, joint or separate, in the MG–FB story as special cases of a wider spectrum of relationship structures, differentiated by their strength. On one end, we have an *arm's-length relationship* where parties trade one with the other, perhaps regularly, but without any firm commitment that binds them together. Stronger relationships are formalized by way of

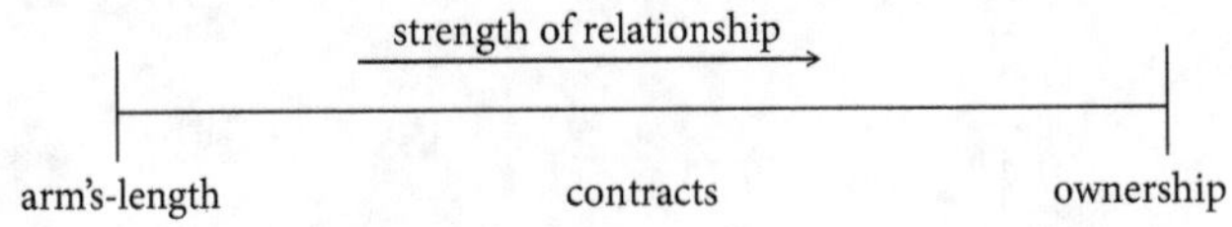

Figure 3.2 Relationships, strong and weak

contracts. These contracts can also vary in strength, depending on how binding the commitments the contract imposes, including its length. At the far end of the spectrum is ownership, where a party takes full control of the assets of another party, for an unspecified duration (see Figure 3.2).

3.3 Technological Complementarities and Synergies

Not every relationship is affected by frictions. Some production relationships are frictionless, in which case production decisions, as well as the distribution of surplus across the players who are party to the relationship, are independent of ownership structure. To demonstrate the point, we lay down:

Definition 3.2. Assets are said to technologically complement one another if they can generate higher value by operating jointly (say, one providing an input to the other) relative to their combined stand-alone value.

Definition 3.3. A *synergy* is the extra value generated by placing assets under joint ownership relative to their combined, stand-alone value.

Clearly, the two notions above are logically distinct. Yet, it is a common mistake to assume that synergies are automatically implied by technological complementarities, a mistake that cost many billions of dollars in failed acquisitions. We thus start our formal analysis with the following:

Proposition 3.1. *Synergies are not a necessary consequence of technological complementarities. That is, the joint value of two technologically complement assets, as well as the distribution of that value across the stakeholders, may not be affected by ownership structure, either arm's length or joint ownership.*

We demonstrate Proposition 3.1 by constructing a simple numerical example where an acquisition of a supplier would affect neither the joint value of the assets nor the distribution of that value. In other words, the example demonstrates a case of positive technological complementarities but zero synergies. An asset, $A1$, generates an input for another asset, $A2$, producing output valued at 100 (net of

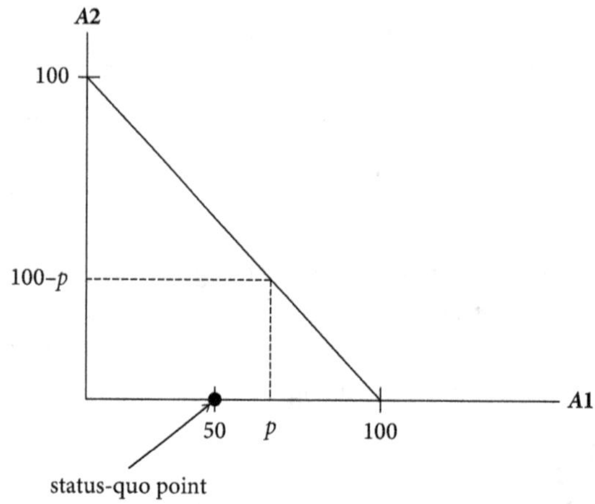

Figure 3.3 Technological complementarities with no synergies

costs of production born by *A2*).[3] *A1* can be deployed to another use (i.e. it has an outside option) valued at 50; there is no alternative use for *A2*. Unless otherwise stated, we assume that the owners of these assets have an equal bargaining power, $\lambda = 0.5$, where λ is used as in the Nash Bargaining sense of Chapter 2. Hence, the straight line from (0, 100) to (100, 0) is the Pareto-efficient set, (50, 0) is the status quo point, and 50 is the gain from trade (see Figure 3.3).

The analysis of the arm's-length relationship is straightforward. Since the owners have equal bargaining power, the value generated by the trade, 50, would be equally split among them. Hence, the final payoff for each owner is his outside option plus 25, namely (75, 25). It follows that the negotiated *transfer price* of the input, p, paid by *A2* to *A1*, is 75.[4]

Next, we analyse the acquisition game; see Figure 3.4. Suppose the owner of *A1* offers to sell the asset to the owner of *A2* for a price q. If the owner of *A2* accepts the offer, she will take possession and use it in order to generate the input for *A2*. Since she no longer needs to pay for the input, her final payoff would be $100 - q$. If she rejects the offer, then in the next stage, the owners of *A1* and *A2* would revert back to an arm's-length relationship. One might think that the owner of *A1* would benefit from a first-mover advantage, but this is not the case. For the owner of *A2* would not accept any offer higher than 75, for that would leave her with a payoff less than 25, lower than her arm's-length payoff. Obviously, the owner of *A1* would not offer to sell the asset for any less than 75. It follows that $q = 75$, regardless of the exact structure of the acquisition game.

[3] We can also think of the 100 number as discounted cash flow.

[4] Transfer prices, unlike 'market prices' (see Chapter 4), are negotiated in a non-competitive environment.

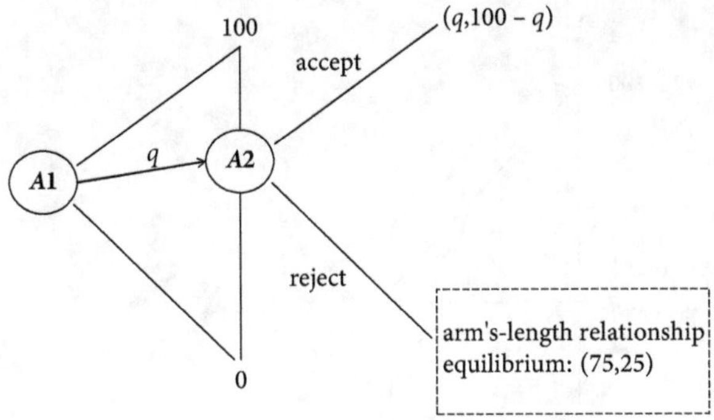

Figure 3.4 The acquisition game

It is worth noting that the result above is valid for any distribution of bargaining power. That is, for any λ, $p = q$.

3.4 Joint Ownership and Synergies

This section present a much simplified version of Grossman and Hart (1986).[5] Oliver Hart was winner of the 2016 Nobel Prize in Economics.

Proposition 3.2. *Synergies may arise when technologically complementing assets, otherwise owned separately by players whose exchange of rights is undermined by frictions, are brought under joint ownership.*

To demonstrate the proposition, consider an example of two assets, $A1$ and $A2$, owned (initially) by two players, $P1$ and $P2$, respectively. Suppose that both assets are nearby oil-fields with similar geological structure. Exploiting the fields requires a geological survey (test-drill) that can be performed only by $P1$, on $A1$, at a cost of 100. The test has no value outside of the $P1$–$P2$ relationship. Using the survey results, both fields can be exploited, generating 60 units of income each. Once the survey is done, the cost of its executing is no longer recoverable. The example thus captures the main characteristics of the GM–FB story: a time-spanned relationship, an ex-ante sunk-cost investment in a relationship specific asset, with cross-assets interrelated cash flows. As emphasized above, it is important to distinguish the physical characteristics and the frictions that arise from them.

Clearly, the oil-fields are worthy of exploitation, for their joint value, 60 + 60 = 120, exceeds the cost of the survey, 100; that is, the test is NPV positive. At the

[5] See also Hart (1995).

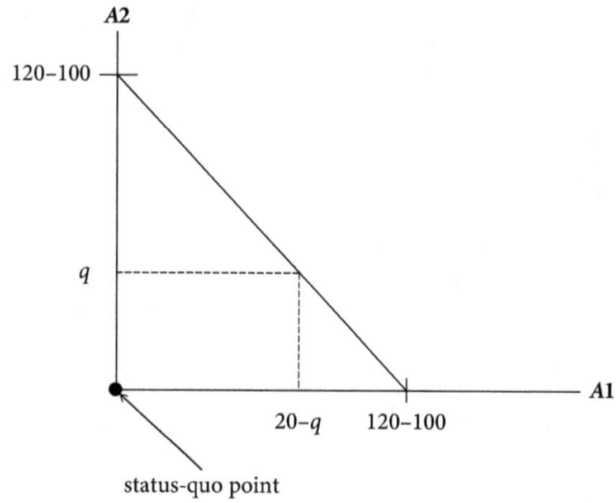

Figure 3.5 Ex-ante bargaining on the acquisition price

same time, *P*1 has no incentive to execute the survey on his own because the cost exceeds his own benefit, 60. Absent a survey, *A*2 cannot utilize her asset either.

Joint ownership of both *A*1 and *A*2 restores *P*1's incentive to execute the test: the value generated by both fields is 120, so the survey is worth executing, at a cost of 100. The more interesting question is whether the value can be unlocked through ex-ante voluntary (spontaneous) trading in assets. Figure 3.5 analyses the ex-ante bargaining over the acquisition of *A*2 by *P*1. The status-quo point is (0, 0), so the gains from trade are the entire joint-value of the fields, net of the cost of the survey, namely 20. With $\lambda = 0.5$, that value is equally split, implying an acquisition price, $q = 10$. Notice that an acquisition of *A*1 by *P*2 cannot unlock the value, as, by assumption, only *P*1 can execute the survey (on *A*1. Economic efficiency requires that assets are owned by player best placed to increase their value.

Next we check whether other types of relationships can unlock the value of the assets. The first arrangement to be examined is an arm's-length trade in information. Namely, *P*1 executes the survey and then bargains a transfer price at which he would sell the results to *P*2. Here comes an important observation of very general applicability: that information is not a commodity that can be traded like any other. The reason is simple: one cannot 'test drive' information. When a player is offered information that is claimed to benefit her, she cannot (subjectively) value the information without examining it. But once she examines the information, she already acquires it, with no need to pay for it. The setting described above is a good example. *P*2 cannot verify that it got all the survey results until she sees them. Or, to put it differently, *P*1 cannot guarantee the delivery of all the results (at an agreed price), that is to commit, credibly, not to censor parts of the report on grounds that these parts are irrelevant and, therefore, not included in the deal. (When *P*2 discovers the censoring, *P*1 may offer to sell it for an additional fee.)

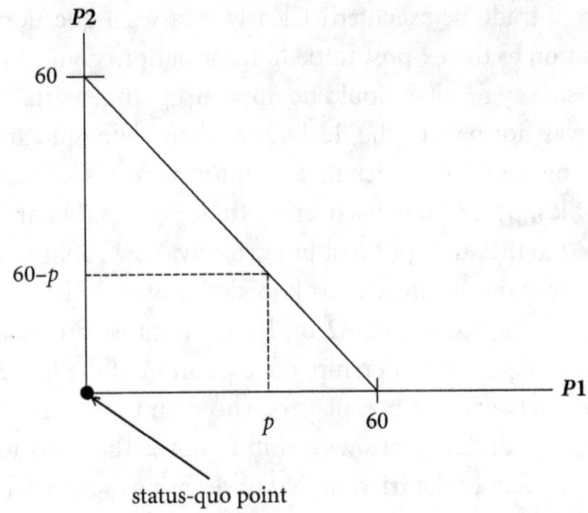

Figure 3.6 Ex-post bargaining on survey results

Clearly, *P2* should take this possibility into consideration when buying the results. We have thus identified a powerful source of friction that can undermine the Coase Theorem (in addition to those described in Chapter 2): some object simply resists the process of exchange; see Chapter 6 for a more elaborate analysis.

Suppose, just for the sake of argument, that such trade in test results is possible. Figure 3.6 analyses the ex-post trade, which would allow the unlocking of *A2*'s value, 60. The ex-post status-quo point is (0, 0). With $\lambda = 0.5$, information is traded for 30. Clearly, such transfer price is not sufficient to incentivize *P1* to execute the survey, which costs *P1* a 100 and generates benefits of 60 from the exploitation of *A1* plus 30 from selling *P2* access to the results; a loss. Hence, the survey would not be executed in the first place and both players end with a zero payoff. The reason is obvious: to deliver ex-ante investment, all values associated with the investment (along its life) need to be properly accounted and specified. Here, one important aspect of the transaction, the information's transfer price, is left out, to be determined ex-post through bargaining. At that point, the cost of the investment is already sunk, so there is nothing to anchor the price to the ex-ante expense.

3.4.1 Contract and Property

Consider, next, a test-sharing contract: *P2* contributes 50 to the execution of the survey and, in return, shares the survey results. If such a contract can be implemented, the survey is executed, economic efficiency is restored, and the value of the investment is equally split, 60 + 50 – 100 = 10 to *P1* and 60 – 50 = 10 to *P2*, same as in the acquisition scenario.

But could such a trade be executed? Clearly it raises a question similar to the one raised in relation to the ex-post trade in information: could *P*1 credibly commit to deliver all survey results? Could he not censor some parts of the report on grounds that 'it was not part of the deal' (and, then, demand extra payment for sharing them)? How could *P*2 check that no information is hidden away without searching all *P*1 files, potentially discovering trade secrets that are genuinely private and unrelated to the survey? Most importantly, how could a court deliberate on such a dispute without having expert knowledge of the oil business?

It follows that an acquisition of *A*2 by *P*1 is the most promising solution to the problem. Under separate ownership, the execution of the test depends on the exchange of rights between the two players who own the assets. Placing the two ends of this exchange under joint ownership removes the need for trading and, by implication, the effect of the friction that undermines such trade. By the residual nature of ownership, the rights of the owner need no elaborate contracting or implementation. The owner simply collects the residual left by other stakeholders whose rights were, presumably, easier to specify. The very 'crudeness' of ownership is also the source of its advantage, as it avoids the need to negotiate, articulate, document, and implement more refined contractual relationship. To summarize:

Proposition 3.3. *To answer the three question posed in the introduction:*

BQ1: ownership (of property) is the residual right to control an asset and collect the cash that it generates. Structuring relationships in terms of property rights might be advantageous compared with a more refined contracting of contingencies that are hard to articulate, document, and enforce.

BQ2: an allocation of ownership rights can be a result of spontaneous interaction between the parties to the relationship.

BQ3: economic efficiency requires that the party whose action can increase the value of the asset (P1 in the example above) should become the owner of the asset.

The reader must realize that in order to derive a notion of property, we had to make a somewhat unsatisfactory assumption about the difficulties of articulating certain contractual schemes. The problem is not so much that we have to make 'lots of assumptions'; hopefully, at this stage, the reader is already comfortable with the idea that 'making assumptions' is the staple of economic analysis. It is that the main object of the analysis, to demonstrate how frictions can be relaxed by instituting certain exchange mechanisms, is 'pushed through' (at the very last step of the argument) by assuming away the test-sharing contract, on grounds of non-viability. Although a 'story' regarding non-viability is offered, that story falls way short of a comprehensive theory, let alone precise modelling, of the limits of contracting. How far can contracts go? Which mechanisms are too complicated to document in contract form? Such questions become even more acute in cases where, unlike in the above example, a refined contract can deliver a higher value relative to a crude, ownership-based mechanism; see Section 3.5 for an example and a further discussion.

3.4.2 Buy Outs

In the analysis so far, we have demonstrated how, exactly because of its crude nature, mechanism based on the notion of ownership can generate value that a contract affected by frictions cannot. Crucially, there are cases in which that very crudeness generates economically inefficient outcomes. To put it more technically, The synergies can be either positive or negative. While the former case justifies a policy of integration, the latter case justifies a policy of ownership separation, a spin-off or a buy-out in business lingo. Although the argument is virtually the same, for its wide practical applicability, it is worth making it explicit:

Proposition 3.4. *There are cases where economic efficiency requires that certain assets are placed under separate ownership.*

To substantiate this interpretation, consider the case of two players, and only one asset; think of *P*2 as the (original) owner of the asset and *P*1 its manager. The asset is an oil-field that can generate income of 120 conditional on a survey that only *P*1 is capable of executing. The cost of the survey is 100 (better think of the cost as the subjective value of the effort that *P*1 would have to put in for the execution of the survey). Although *P*2 contributes nothing to unlocking the value of the asset, as the owner of the asset she needs to consent to any related action allowing her to extract rent from giving consent. Particularly, with $\lambda = 0.5$, following a (potential) survey, *P*2 will extract half of the ex-post payoff, 60. That would leave *P*1 with $120 - 60 - 100 < 0$; anticipating such outcome, he would avoid the survey altogether, leaving both parties with a zero payoff. On the other hand, ex-ante bargaining of a management buyout should end up with an acquisition of the asset by its manager with $q = 10$; see Figure 3.7.

In most cases, management doesn't have enough cash to execute the transaction. It is common to use debt, rather than equity, in the funding of the transaction, so as to provide the management with a strong incentive to 'work hard'. Hence the name: levered buy out (LBO).

3.4.3 A Reconsideration of the GM–FB Case

For completeness, we rehearse the 'story' of General Motors and Fisher Brothers that has motivated this chapter using a (fictional) numerical example. Ex ante, GM needs to make a decision whether to develop the market for metal-closed

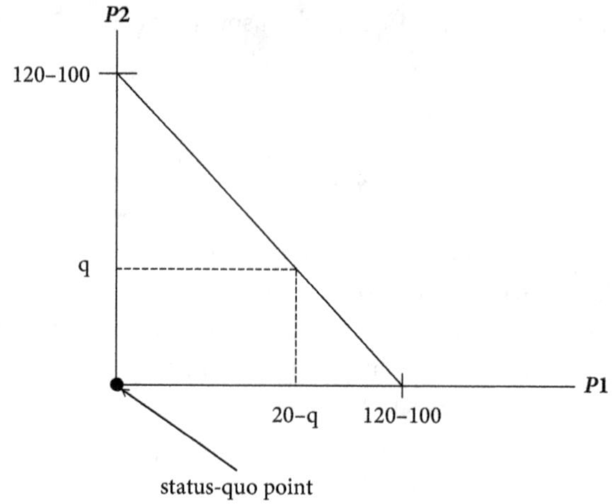

Figure 3.7 Management buy-out

bodies—or not. Developing the market would cost it 50, a sunk cost. The ex-post value of the developed market is 150 (gross of the sunk cost) while the value of the undeveloped market is 80, distributed (70, 10) between GM and FB, respectively. For simplicity, we ignore FB's sunk costs. For simplicity we also assume that once GM develops the market for metal-closed bodies, it can no longer exploit its old market (valued at 70), though FB still retains its outside option of 10. A more substantial assumption is that the skill of developing the market is embodied in GM and cannot be acquired by any other operator, in particular FB. In contrast, FB's technology can be transferred to another operator, in particular GM. We keep the assumptions of an equal bargaining power, $\lambda = 0.5$ and a zero interest rate.

Notice, first that the market is worth developing: its value, net of the cost of investment, is $150 - 50 = 100$, while the combined GM–FB value of the existing market is only 80. The surplus created by the new market is, thus, 20.

Next, aided by Figure 3.8, we demonstrate that the market cannot be developed on the basis of an arm's-length relationship between the two companies. Ex post, the parties would bargain a transfer price, *p*, that MG pays FB for the metal bodies: $10 + (150 - 10)/2 = 80$. In line with previous analysis, GM's sunk cost is not priced into the transfer price. Ex ante, net of the sunk cost, MG payoff from developing the market is $150 - 80 - 50 = 20$; FB stays with the ex-post transfer price of 80. Clearly it does not pay GM to develop the market as its outside option, 70, is way above its profit within the arm's-length relationship. The root cause of the failure is that the excessively high transfer price that GM has to pay does not compensate it for the investment that it made in developing the market.

Crucially, the value of the market can be unlocked if GM acquires FB, at a price of *q*. With equal bargaining power, that acquisition price splits the surplus created

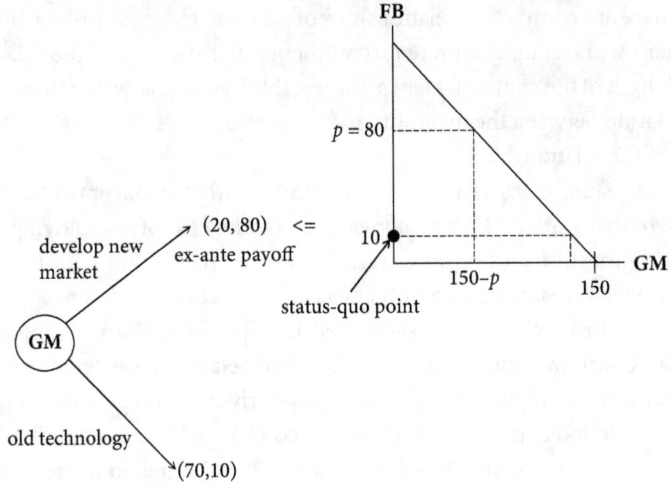

Figure 3.8 Arm's-length relationship in the GM–FB example

by the new market, 20, equally between the two companies. Given that the status quo point is (70, 10), an acquisition should deliver a profit of (80, 20). Hence, net of the acquisition cost, MG profit should be $150 - 50 - q = 80$, implying $q = 20$.

Lastly, it is worth pointing out, again, the important role played by FB specific technology. Had the marker for metal-closed bodies been competitive, competition would drive the transfer price down to 10, in which case GM's profit in an arm's-length relationship would have been $150 - 50 - 10 = 90$, in fact allocating all the surplus created by the new market to GM.

3.4.4 An Empirical Test of the Theory

Our theory is obviously abstract, perhaps even contrived. It is already noted in Chapter 1, above, that the ultimate test of a theory is not its level of abstraction but, rather, its ability to produce a testable hypothesis that is consistent with the data. The real ingenuity in empirical work is, often, in the ability to identify a correlation that captures an essential attribute of a theory and, then, find the data that allows testing—often a scarce resource. Such is the case in Paul Joskow's (1987) study of the vertical relationship between coal-mining companies and owners of coal-fired power stations.

Taken literally, the theory predicts a switch, from contracts to ownership beyond a certain level of a friction, in our case a friction that is directly related to the asset's specificity and the investment's sunk cost. The Joskow's study assumes, without a precise formal theory, that relationships vary in a more continuous manner, between arm's-length relationship and ownership; see Figure 3.2. In the middle, there are contractual relationships of various strengths. Joskow then associates, again without an elaborate formal theory, the strength of the relationship with the length of the contract. Hence, the testable hypothesis is that there is a positive correlation between the magnitude of the frictions (specific sunk cost) and the strength of the relationships.

Measuring sunk costs is not a trivial matter either. Conceptually, one may hypothesize that sunk costs can be measured by the cost of redeploying an asset out of a relationship. Notice, however, that in our theory, sunk costs affect the equilibrium via the status quo point; assets are not actually redeployed.

Here comes Joskow's crucial insight: coal-fired power stations are not only substantial sunk-cost investments, they are also designed to use a specific type of coal. A coal market with a highly varied quality may derive a power generator and a coal mine into a relationship that is burdened by contractual frictions similar to those in the GM–FB case. A competitive coal market would ameliorate the problem as it sets a market price for the coal of each quality; weak competition enhances the friction. On the East Coast of the United States, the quality of coal is uniform, production is more dispersed (smaller coal mines) and the transportation system is better, which creates a more competitive market relative to the West Coast, with the Mid West in between. That allows East Coast producers to buy 18% of their coal from suppliers with whom they have only an arm's-length relationships. That figure drops to 2% on the West Coast, with 8% in the Mid West; see Table 3.1. An extreme case of asset specificity is when a power-generating plant locates right at the mouth of a coal mine, limiting coal supply to that coal mine alone. In these cases, the cost of redeploying the assets is supposed to be exceptionally high and so is the need for long-duration contracts.

Statistical testing is done using linear regressions with contract duration as the independent variable:

$$duration_i = \alpha + \beta_1 \times X_i + \beta_2 \times mouth_i + \beta_3 \times midwest_i + beta_4 \times westcoast_i + \varepsilon_i.$$

(The study looks at a period starting in the late 1970s and ends in the early 1980s.) i is an index that runs across the sample of contracts used in the study. *midwest*

Table 3.1 Coal mines and power stations, cross-regional differences

	Regions within the US		
	East	**Mid-west**	**West**
coal quality	uniform	more variable	highly variable
mine size	small (underground)	medium	large (surface)
transport system	good	medium	poor
spot market/delivery	18%	8%	2%

Table 3.2 Regression results, Joskow's (1987)

Independent variable: contract duration		
variable	**coefficient (years)**	**standard error**
mine-mouth	16	2
Mid-west	3–4	1
West Coast	5–6	1
R^2 is between 0.6 and 0.7 and N is either 169 or 277		

(*westcoast*) is a dummy variable that receives a value of 1 if observation i belongs to a power-generating plant located in the Mid West (West Coast) and 0 otherwise. For a brief explanation of dummy variables, see Section A.5.2 of the Mathematical Appendix. As explained there, a third dummy variable for the East Coast should not be included in the regression. Rather, for an observation, k, such that $midwest_k = westcoast_k = 0$, the regression's intercept captures contract duration for an East-Coast power-generating plant. X is a string of variables that capture 'other factors' that may affect duration without being explicitly covered by the theory. *mouth* is another dummy variable that receives a value of 1 if the contract is between a producer and a supplier such that the former is located right at the mouth of coal mine and 0 otherwise. ε is an error term. The results of the estimation are presented in Table 3.2[6]. West Coast (Mid West) tends to be 5 to 6 years longer (3 to 4 years longer) than on the East Coast. Being a mine-mouth producer tends to increase the duration of the contract by an extra 16 years. Estimated coefficients are more than two standard errors away from zero, making them statistically significant different than zero by a common rule of thumb; see Section A.5.2 of the Mathematical Appendix. R^2 is 'respectably high'. N is standard notation for the number of observations.

3.5 Property Rights and Secured Debt

An obvious link between property rights and traditional financial analysis is the wide-spread phenomenon of companies creating, by way of a contract, security interests in assets that they own, by pledging them as collateral against credit. Hart and Moore (1998) suggest a theory of secured debt. To better appreciate the role that security interests play in the funding of companies, we provide, first, a more general description of the financial instruments that are used in the funding of companies.

[6] Taken from Table 3 in Joskow's (1987).

3.5.1 Contracts and Capital Structure

The capital structure of a company is defined by the contracts that are used in its funding. In general, contracts are functions, a mapping from eventualities to deliveries. For example, debt and equity are functions from the company's income, x, which varies across eventualities, and the amount paid to the company's debt and equity holders, d and e, respectively. x is defined as revenue from selling the company's product, net of the cost of production; interest payments, that is d, should not be treated as an expense though they are treated that way by the accounting profession. Debt is characterized by a flat repayment segment, R, which is independent of x, and another segment where $d = x < R$. That is, whenever x falls short of R, the company's entire income is allocated to debt holders; see Figure 3.9 for the *piece-wise linear* relationship between x and d. Equity takes the residual, $x - d$. Claims against the company's debt and equity are sold out ex-ante, raising amounts of funding D and E respectively. The total value of all claims issued by the company adds up to its value: $V = D + E$. The composition of V in terms of debt and equity is referred to as the company's *capital structure*. The share of debt in the company's value, D/V, is called *leverage*. The more the company relies on debt funding, the more levered it is. Understanding the determinants of capital structure is one of finance's oldest questions.

While, traditionally, the analysis of debt and equity focused on cash rights, it is quite clear that other aspects of capital structure are of fundamental importance. Most importantly, the equity-holders jointly control the firm when $e > 0$, but lose control to the debt-holders when $d = x$ (i.e. when $e = 0$), that is when the company is insolvent. Arguably, it is the transfer of control from the owner to the debtor which is the most remarkable characteristic of insolvency and bankruptcy. A related point, already highlighted by the analysis in Chapter 2, is that the parties

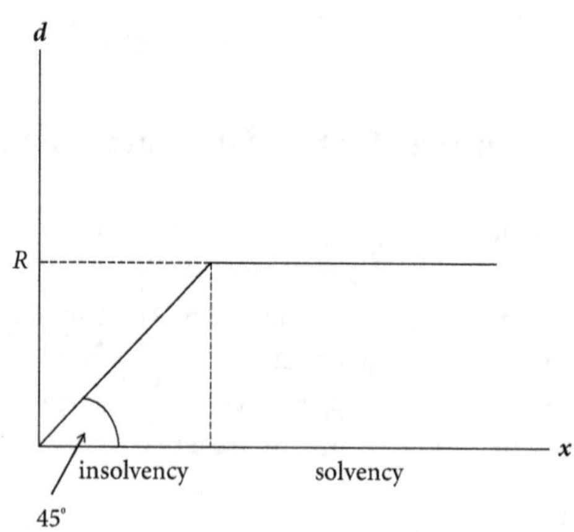

Figure 3.9 The debt contract

may renegotiate payments ex post. Hence, while *d* and *e* are the amounts formally written into the contract, actual repayment may be different.

Notice that the transfer of control from company's owners to its creditors originates in the debt contract, which can use the company's assets as security. That is, as part of the debt contract, the debtor transfers ownership of the company to the creditor—contingent on a default to pay the full amount *R*. In fact, the debt contract can be viewed as a combination of two transactions: the debtor sells the assets to the creditor, in return for funding, and a (call) option to buy back the assets at a price of *R*.

Before we turn to a simple exposition of the Hart–Moore theory, it is worth making one additional comment on capital structure. Some companies, particularly larger ones, list their equity for trading on public markets. Typically, small equity holders have no interest in taking part in the management of the company. To use a famous expression coined by Berle and Means (1933), in such large companies, there is a 'separation of ownership and control'. Namely, small and large shareholders may hold identically worded documents that, in legal theory convey the same amount of control (voting) rights—per share. Notwithstanding, only the large shareholders are practically capable of exercising their control rights. In such situations, we make a distinction between the company's *internals*, i.e. the large shareholders whose effective control of the company far exceeds their equity position, and the *external investors*. Obviously, the distinction is of no significance in the models presented in Chapters 2 and 3, where the company is assumed to be controlled by a single owner-manager; in fact, even General Motors was modelled as an owner manager, no doubt a dramatic abstraction.

3.5.2 A Theory of Security Interests

We present the basic idea of the Hart–Moore model by taking the numerical example of Chapter 2's debt restructuring and extending it backwards to an earlier period, $t = 0$, when the debt was created. (In fact, the reader should have asked himself, while reading Chapter 2, what economic purpose a debt of 70 has served in the first place.) More accurately, since the theory attempts to explain secured debt, we should think about initial funding more generally, as some external funding contract that, in equilibrium, looks like secured debt. We keep the basic structure: there are two risk-neutral players, the company's owner-manger, *F*, and the creditor *C*. At $t = 0$ the latter provides the former some funding, needed in order to operate a project. *F* has a unique ability to operate the project. In return, *C* must be assured that he would be compensated for the contribution that he made. The asset's liquidation value is 20, firm's cash flow, if continued, is 50 and *F*'s outside option is 10. The players have equal bargaining power. For simplicity, suppose the risk-free interest rate is zero.

The most important modification to Chapter 2's assumptions is that we now assume that F's cash flows are *not verifiable*. Remember that in Chapter 2 we assume that since cash flows are verifiable, they can be written into a contract and be enforced by a court of law, as intended. As a result, we concluded that debt restructuring would take place as follows: C would write down the debt, unilaterally, to 40 so as to provide C with an incentive to stay put. The liquidation option is not exercised and the company is allowed to carry on. At $t = 2$, F would repay his debt of 40. If he fails to do so, C would take her to court and enforce the payment. Given the certain outcome of court proceedings, F would save herself the cost and the trouble of litigation and pay her debt.

The non-verifiability of cash flows changes this situation considerably. Even if C knows, with absolute certainty, that F can generate a cash flow of 50, if continued, he also knows that he will not be able to provide the court with the evidence necessary to enforce payments. In absence of such evidence, F's best $t = 2$ line of action (if ever the game progresses to that point) is to claim that the project has failed to generate any cash and keep the amount, 50, to herself. Foreseeing that outcome, at $t = 1$, C concludes that he has no hope of extracting any cash from F past the point of liquidation and act accordingly. Notice that had F been in possession of any cash in excess of 20 at $t = 1$ this outcome could have been avoided, but that possibility was already assumed away. Hence the basic intuition of the model: since cash is non verifiable, the only way C can extract cash payments from F is under the threat of liquidation.

But how did the debt of 70 came about? Ex ante, at $t = 0$, C and F must have had some other, more optimistic scenarios in mind. For simplicity, suppose there were only two possible outcomes, H and L. The L outcome is described above, yielding equilibrium payoffs of $(20, 0)$. The H outcome, assumes that F collect a cash flow of 200 at $t = 1$ and an equal amount at $t = 2$; both amounts are not verifiable. H and L have equal probabilities; see Figure 3.10.

Building upon the intuition derived from the analysis of event L, it should be clear that C can enforce no payment on F at $t = 2$. At $t = 1$, F has two options: to

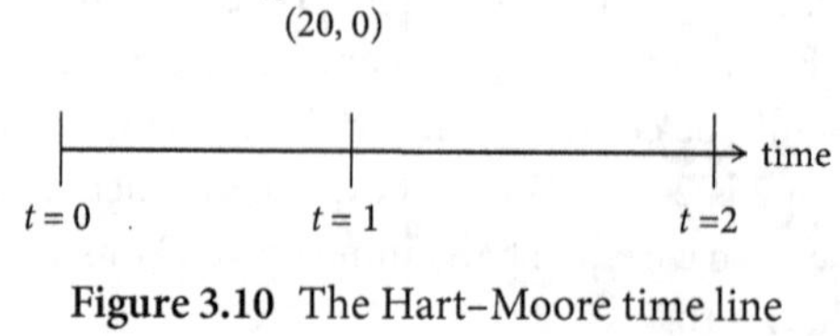

Figure 3.10 The Hart–Moore time line

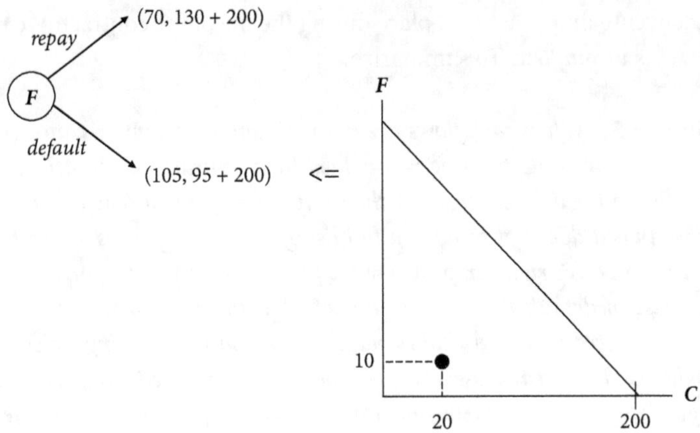

Figure 3.11 The $t = 1$ game in the H event

pay back the debt or to default. Paying the debt would yield the following payoffs: (70, 130 + 200) (see Figure 3.11). The other option is to default, perhaps hoping to negotiate better terms. In case of such *strategic default,* the players would fall back on their status quo point, (20, 10), losing the cash flow of 200 that is due at $t = 2$. Hence, under the equal bargaining power assumption, these negotiations would end with F paying C and amount $20 + [200 - (10 + 20)]/2 = 105$. Obviously, strategic default is a dominated strategy. It is in F's best interest to pay his debt as agreed in the debt contract, 70. Notice that although the asset is not liquidated on this path of the game, the asset liquidation value plays a role in deterring strategic default. The higher the liquidation value, the less attractive is strategic default. We conclude by noting that the amount of funding that C is willing to supply, ex ante, under this scheme, is

$$E(d) = \frac{70 + 20}{2} = 45.$$

Hence the main insight of the Hart–Moore analysis. In order to obtain funding, the parties need to design a contract that generates enough cash payments so that, in expectations, C's payoffs are (at least) 45. Since cash flows are not verifiable, the contract must include some mechanism that enforces repayments without relying on the court's ability to verify cash flows. That is obtained by giving C the right to repossess F's assets in case of default. (Notice that, unlike cash flow, default is an event that the court can verify.) Hence the transfer of asset ownership, from F to C in case of default is a sanction that is used in lieu of court cash verification. Notice that actual repayments differ from the amount that is formally written into the contract, R. In that respect, the contract is crude, missing a description of some important eventualities that take place during the life of the contract. We say that the contract is *incomplete*. To summarize:

Proposition 3.5. *When cash flows are not verifiable, incomplete-contract theory predicts that corporate funding is provided by a contract that has the following similarities to the debt contract: i) the company's payment schedule is crude in the sense that it does not provide a full list of the contingencies facing the company; ii) company's rights in property are pledged as security against funding, so that in case of default the external investor has the right to repossess the security; iii) repossession actually takes place in low cash-flow contingencies; iv) even when the asset is not repossessed, the amount of repayments that is resilient to strategic default is partly determined by the asset liquidation value; the higher the liquidation value the less attractive strategic default is.*

The funding scheme above involves a certain 'waste' as an economically viable (though financially distressed) company is liquidated in the L event, leaving F with her outside option, 10, instead of the 50 that she could collect if allowed to continue. To see the point more clearly, compute F's expected equity payoff:

$$E(e) = \frac{330 + 10}{2} = 170$$

Alternatively, consider the hypothetical case where cash flows are verifiable. In which case, an alternative funding contract, with payoff contingent on cash flows, (R_L, R_H) could be designed. To avoid liquidation in the L event the contract would have to set $R_L = 0$.[7] Assuming that the same amount of external funding has to be raised, 45, payments in the H event must be set up higher, at $R_H = 90$, so that, in expectations, C breaks even. However, F's expected equity payoffs would increase to:

$$E\left(e|_{\text{full information}}\right) = \frac{310 + 50}{2} = 180. \tag{3.1}$$

Hence, unlike in the analysis of synergies, above, the use of an incomplete contract involves a certain loss of value. It is therefore, more difficult to avoid the question whether the loss of value is, indeed, an unavoidable consequence of the informational friction. More so as, by assumption, both F and C are fully informed about realized cash flows; otherwise, they would not be able to renegotiate payoffs where necessary. If so, perhaps there is a way to utilize that information, implement a more sophisticated contract, and rescue the full value of the relationship as in Equation (3.1). The Hart–Moore model leaves the question somewhat

[7] Although, with verifiable cash flows, $t = 2$ payments are possible, to facilitate the comparison to the non-verifiable case, we limit attention to contracts where payments are limited to $t = 1$ only.

unanswered. To put it more technically, the contract above is constrained Pareto efficient in the following sense:

Definition 3.4. We say that an outcome is *constrained Pareto efficient* if no Pareto improvement exists given the distribution of information in the model's environment.

In Chapter 7 we present an alternative modelling approach that does address this question head on.

It is interesting to note that the concept of incompleteness is first introduced in Simon (1951), winner of the 1978 Nobel Prize in Economics. Simon observed that labour contracts do not contain a complete list of contingencies and tasks to be performed by the employee in each and every one of them. Instead, the typical employment contract has a simpler, more crude structure, whereby the employee grants the employer the *authority* to select the task, ex post. (Notice the similarity between authority over employees and property rights over assets.) It is implied that the mental cost imposed, by a complete contract, on both employer and employee is too great to bear. At the same time, rather than providing a complete theory of mental costs, Simon suggested that players' *bounded rationality* makes the writing and execution of complete contracts too costly, if not impossible. Many years later, economists still lack a comprehensive theory of authority. Academic views are split between those who are attracted to the realism of concepts such as authority or property, and 'purists' who prefer to carry on with the full-rationality approach, albeit keep on searching for the frictions (mental or informational) that would generate contracts with more realistic properties—one day.

3.6 Trade in a Lawless Environment: Reputation

The entire analysis so far, in both Chapters 2 and 3, is conducted under the assumption that the *rule of law* prevails. That is, players can acquire property and sign contracts with confidence that their rights would be enforced. In fact, that the very threat to seek justice in court is sufficient in order to prevent a breach of the contract and guarantee delivery—out of court.

Unfortunately, the rule of law does not prevail always and everywhere. However, it is well documented that certain trades survive even the most lawless of environments, including trade that requires a certain level of commitment, that is for one player to sink in a certain cost for a future benefit that requires the participation of another player.

Avner Greif (1989) provides an excellent example of medieval commerce, across the Mediterranean, operated by Jewish traders. Even within a city or a region, let alone 'internationally', law-enforcement was extremely weak. Moreover, maritime traffic being unsafe, modern communication lines non existent and prices being volatile due to exposure to natural hazards (such as drought or plagues) it took a great deal of trust for a trader to send off merchandise to an agent across the sea and expect payment weeks or months later. Nevertheless, trade survived, supported by trust and personal reputation or, what the traders themselves describe in their correspondence as 'honour'. The following identifies conditions for such trade.

A Merchant, M, can deliver a good that costs him $c < 1$ to an overseas agent, A, who would sell it for a price $p > 1$, so that the joint gains from trade are $p - c$. For simplicity, we fix the transfer price that A pays M to 1. A can make the repayment or default. The trade may be repeated, $t = 1, 2, \ldots, T$ times. Players' subjective discount factors are β.

The $T = 1$ game is described in Figure 3.12. Clearly, the backward induction, sub-game perfect, equilibrium path in this game is no trade, an inefficient outcome: if M delivers, A needs to choose between repayment and default with payoffs $p - 1$ and p, respectively; default dominates. Hence, M's payoff for sending the goods is $-c$ while the payoff for no trade is 0; no trade dominates. The result has an intuitive interpretation: short-term relationships are strongly affected by lack of trust. In absence of an external mechanism of commitment (such as law enforcement) valuable trading opportunities will be lost.

So can trade be sustained through repeated interactions, which allow players to build up a reputation of honesty by delivering in the early rounds of trading? Somewhat surprisingly, though straightforwardly on backward-induction considerations, the no trade result prevails for any (finite) T. Figure 3.13 presents the $T = 2$ game. Notice that the figure already eliminates the option of supplying the goods at $t = 2$ following default at $t = 1$, thereby implementing a *penalty* that M imposes on A for not performing. For ease of exposition, the payoffs on the right-hand side of the figure include only the payoffs of the second round, so that the ex-ante (discounted) payoff for two rounds of trade (if executed) would be $(1 + \beta) \times (1 - c, p - 1)$. That is, the predicted gain from trade is $(1 - c, p - 1)$ and it accumulates from one round of trade to the next. Clearly, maintaining trade is in the (ex ante) best interest of both players.

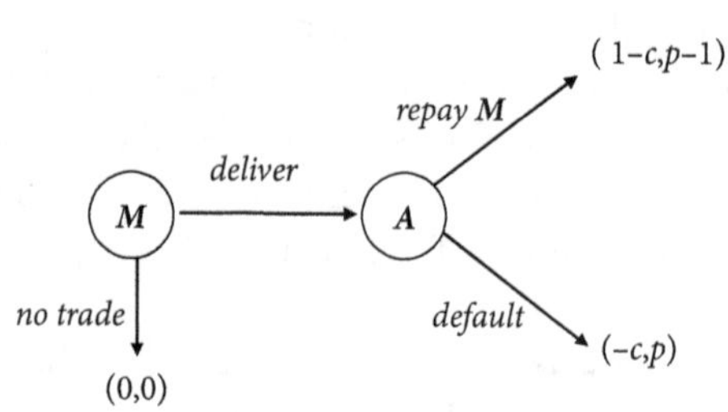

Figure 3.12 A $T = 1$ agent problem

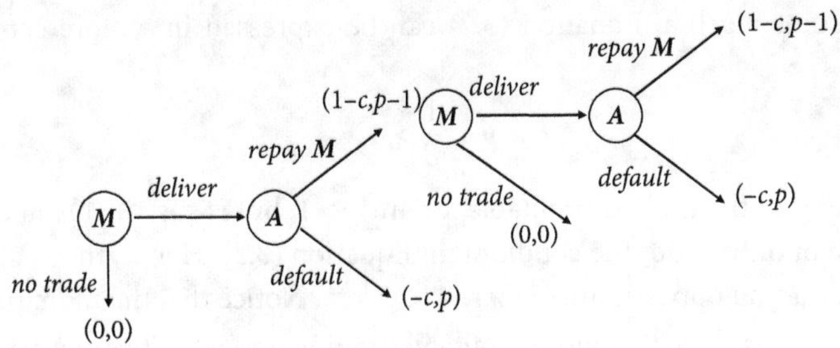

Figure 3.13 A $T = 2$ agent problem

The reason why trade is not a sub-game perfect equilibrium for the $T = 2$ game is that looking forward at the beginning of the second round, the game looks exactly the same as the $T = 1$ game, in which the equilibrium was: no trade. Notice that both players keep the first-period gain, $(1 - c, p - 1)$, which, at this point, is already sunk, with no effect on $t = 2$ decisions. Given that there will be no trade at $t = 2$, looking forward at $t = 1$ the game looks exactly the same as a $T = 1$ game, save for the insignificant addition of $(0, 0)$ to the first-period gains (on the 'repay *M*' arm of the game). Hence, there is no trade in the first round either.

The same argument applies for any (finite) higher *T*. Intuitively, the agent is always tempted to breach confidence at $t = T$. Foreseeing such conduct, *M* responds by terminating the game after $T - 1$ rounds of trade. Now the argument can be repeated on the $T - 1$ game, taking away one extra period, and so on to $T = 1$.

To get a more positive result we extend the game to infinity (namely $T \to \infty$), so as to avoid the 'last round effect'. As noted in Chapter 2, such games cannot be solved by backwards induction. A different sort of equilibrium can be derived if we allow strategies to be defined as follows: *M* sends merchandise at $t = 1$, and carries on doing so if *A* repays; once *A* defaults, *M* shifts to a penalty mode and stops the trade – for ever.

Consider round *t*, and assume that *M* has delivered the goods in all previous rounds. *A* can default, for which the payoff is *p*; or she can adopt a repayment strategy. She knows *M*'s response would be to maintain the trade for all subsequent rounds, generating her a payoff of $p - 1$, in all subsequent rounds. It follows that *A*'s repayment strategy is a best response to *M*'s strategy if:

$$\frac{p-1}{1-\beta} > p \tag{3.2}$$

(using, again, the formula for a converging geometric series; see Section A.1 of the Mathematical Appendix).

Using some algebra, Equation (3.2) can be expressed in a more economical manner:

$$p > \frac{1}{\beta} > 1. \tag{3.3}$$

Remember that the trade is profitable for any $p > 1$, but is sustainable in a lawless environment only under the condition in Equation (3.3). Hence, there is a loss of profitable trading opportunities where $1 < p < \frac{1}{\beta}$. Notice that the more impatient A is, the higher is, $\frac{1}{\beta}$, so that more profitable-trading opportunities are lost. Hence:

Proposition 3.6. *Some reputation-based trade can survive in a lawless environment, but certain trading opportunities may be lost. The more patient the players are, the less trading opportunities are lost.*

3.7 Conclusion

The statement that well-defined property rights are essential to prosperity and welfare has become almost a cliché of political-economy discussion. Regardless, property right are not easy to fit into the conceptual framework of economic analysis. In this chapter we present some common wisdom on the subject. Property rights give owners control rights over asset and residual right in the cash generated by these assets. They should be allocated to the party that is best placed in take the action that would increase the value of the asset. Some alternative contractual arrangements are excluded using 'stories' that are not fully modelled. At the same time, these stories point at imperfect information as a major source of friction in financial markets, and a potential explanation of the institutional structures that we observe in the market.

References

[1] Berle, Adolf A. Jr., and Gardiner C. Means (1993). *The Modern Corporation and Private Property*, The Macmillan Company.

[2] Coase, Ronald H. (1937). 'The Nature of the Firm', *Economica*, New Series, Vol. 4, No. 16, pp. 386–405.

[3] Greif, Avner (1989). 'Reputation and Coalitions in Medieval Trade: Evidence on the Maghribi Traders', *The Journal of Economic History*, 49(4), pp. 857–882.

[4] Grossman, Sanford J. and Oliver D. Hart (1986). 'The Costs and Benefits of Ownership: A Theory of Vertical and Lateral Integration', *Journal of Political Economy*, Vol. 94, No. 4, pp. 691–719.

[5] Hart, Oliver (1995). *Firms, Contracts and Financial Structure*, Oxford University Press.

[6] Hart, Olive and John More (1998). 'Default and Reegotiation: A Dynamic Model of Debt', *Quarterly Journal of Economics*, Vol. 113, No. 1, pp. 1–41.

[7] Joskow, Paul L. (1987). 'Contract Duration and Relationship-Specific Investments: Empirical Evidence from Coal Markets', *American Economic Review*, Vol. 77, No. 1, pp. 168–185.
[8] Klein, Benjamine, Robert G. Crawford, and Armen A. Alchian (1978). 'Vertical Integration, Appropriable Rents, and the Competitive Contracting Process', *Journal of Law and Economics*, Vol. 21, No. 2 (Oct.), pp. 297–326.
[9] Simon, Herbert A. (1951). 'A Formal Theory of the Employment Relationship', *Econometrica*, Vol. 19, No. 3, pp. 293–305.

4
Competitive Markets

4.1 Introduction

So far, we have modelled economic interactions between players as if they were taking place 'one on one'. We had in mind a small number of players, typically two, responding *strategically* to their opponents, taking into consideration how their opponents would respond to their own moves. Each player was acutely aware of her opponent's identity, personality, motivation, and circumstances.

However, in reality, many transactions are hard to fit into such a theoretical construct. Often, transactions take place in a *competitive market*, an environment where a multitude of buyers and sellers trade *anonymously*. In such an environment there is no room, nor is there any need, to consider counter parties' identity or motivations. Rather, 'the market' sets up a price, so that any vendor (buyer) who tries to charge (bid for) a price above (below) the market price will not be able to complete her transaction as planned. The purpose of this chapter is to provide a brief exposition of the competitive model and some of its applications.

An important advantage of the competitive model is that it allows for a comprehensive analysis of the entire market (or even the entire economy): all the participants, the terms on which they trade, and, as a result, their respective gains, including the response of these variables to changes in the environment. There is a price to be paid for these analytical advantages: our micro-modelling of the actual buyer–seller interaction is about to become even more abstract. In fact, we shall abandon a line of investigation that we have pursued in Chapters 2 and 3: the economic consequences of frictions. In this chapter (and in the next one) players have all the information that they need in order to make their decisions. They can also participate in any trade that would be beneficial for them. Starting in Chapter 6 and onwards, frictions will, again, play a central role in the analysis.

4.2 Perfect Competition

A perfectly competitive environment is characterized by the *law of one price* and by the *atomistic* nature of each and every player trading in each market.[1] By the law of one price we mean that each commodity has its own market, but all transactions

[1] It is customary among economist to call traders in a competitive market 'agents' rather than 'players', a practice that we avoid here.

The Economics of Financial Markets and Institutions. Oren Sussman, Oxford University Press. © Oren Sussman (2023). DOI: 10.1093/oso/9780192869739.003.0005

within a market are executed at the same price; remember that it takes more than physical properties to define a commodity. We have already noted, in Chapter 1, that if two physically identical objects are differentiated by the time of their delivery, the price of a late delivery is likely to be lower than the price of an early delivery. A chemist, a physicist, or an engineer may regard the two objects as identical, but an economist would regard them as different *commodities*. Obviously, transportation costs imply that two physically identical objects delivered in two different locations have different prices. Though the price difference can be easily explained by the cost of transportation, strictly speaking these are two different commodities traded in two different markets. In Chapter 5, below, we shall see that two identical objects delivered under different circumstances should also be viewed as different commodities. In fact, the entire economic analysis of risk rests on this observation.

By 'atomistic' we mean that even 'heavy traders' cannot affect the market price. Though some players may be much wealthier than others, thereby trading much higher volumes, relative to the size of the market all players are of insignificant size and, therefore, have no effect on the market price. To use standard economic terminology, all players are *price takers*. Clearly, market prices change according to circumstances; such circumstances are incorporated into market prices through the trades of the players who are active in the market. Notwithstanding, no trader on his own can affect the market price. Hopefully, these seemingly contradicting statements will become clearer as we progress our analysis of competitive markets.

4.2.1 A Note on Profit Maximization

The main focus of Chapters 2 and 3 is potential conflicts of interest among the company's stakeholders. In particular, the possibility that, in the presence of certain frictions, conflicts of interests among the stakeholders may cause an economically viable company to fail. In the frictionless environment of this chapter, much as in an idealized Coasian environment, these conflicts of interests play no role. It may still be the case that each stakeholder wants to increase her 'share of the pie' at the expense of others, but such disagreements have no effect on the company's operational decisions, for *profit maximization* is in their common interest, independently of other issues that they face. In addition, the competitive environment limits, considerably, the amount of rent on which the stakeholders might be conflicted.

A 'firm' in the competitive model reduces to a production facility, defined purely by *technological* considerations. Accordingly, profit maximization is not an empirical statement about the reality of the corporate world but, rather, a statement about a model that abstracts from trading frictions. The abstraction is useful to the extent that it helps us to understand how competitive markets operate. Likewise, Chapters 2 and 3 may be blamed for being too abstract, ignoring competition and technology. Neither this chapter nor the previous one claims to present an accurate and complete image of reality.

A point about terminology: we tend to use 'company' when discussing organizational aspects and 'firms' when we discuss technological aspects, but we do not apply the distinction in a consistent manner.

4.3 Supply and Demand Curves

If players are price takers, then the functional relationship between the market price and the quantity that a player buys (sells) constitutes his demand (supply) curve. In fact, Chapter 1's decreasing unit subjective valuations (DUSV) is just an instance of a demand curve.

There is, however, an alternative way to derive demand and supply curves, relying solely on players' heterogeneity (henceforth the HP derivation), which is more useful for certain analytical purposes. Consider the demand for labour by an industry where each firm is operated by a single owner-manager, who makes a decision whether to operate or not. If it operates, the firm employs a single worker and produces a fixed amount of γ (the Greek letter Gamma) units of output, where γ differs across firms, between 0 and Γ (capital γ). Notice that γ, i.e. output per worker, is just the firm's *productivity*. Workers are homogeneous in their qualities so, due to the law of one price, all firms pay workers the same wage rate, w, and sell their product at the same price, p. Differences of productivity are due to firms, not workers. Employing a worker, the firm would make a profit of $\gamma p - w$, the value of its sales net of the wage that it pays. Obviously, the firm would prefer not to *participate* in the market when $\gamma p - w$ is negative. Demand for labour is, thus, a function that maps market prices to the number of workers the firm employs:

$$l = \begin{cases} 1 & \text{if} \quad \gamma p - w \geq 0 \\ 0 & \text{if} \quad \gamma p - w < 0 \end{cases}. \tag{4.1}$$

The graph of that function, the demand curve for labour, is the step-like solid line that 'jumps' from 0 to 1 when the wage rate drops below γp; see Figure 4.1. (The reader may recognize that the analysis in this section is just an elaboration on the simple principle already described in Proposition 1.1 of Chapter 1.)

Consider a market wage rate of w. The profit of a firm that *participates* in the market, $(\gamma p - w) \times 1$, is described by the shadowed rectangle in Figure 4.1. It is the area enclosed below the demand curve, above a horizontal line at the level of w. More generally, it is the *gain* or the *surplus* that the participating firm derives from

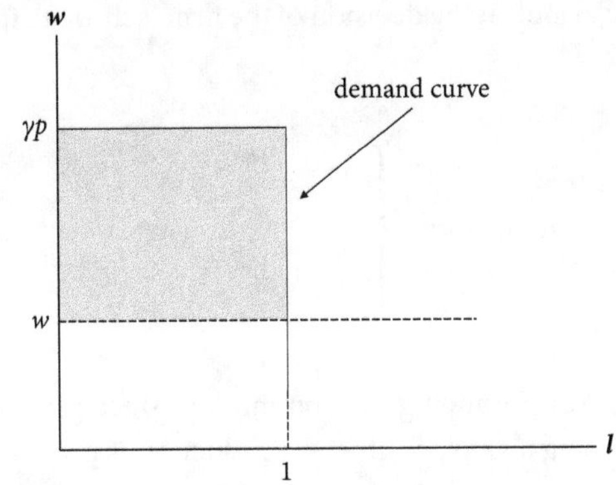

Figure 4.1 An individual firm's demand for labour

trading on the markets, in this case the *producer's surplus*. It plays an important part in the analysis below. Notice that the trader's surplus is denominated in the same units as w and p, in this case, money.

Alternatively, the labour demand function can be written as

$$l = \begin{cases} 1 & \text{if} \quad \gamma \geq \dfrac{w}{p} \\ 0 & \text{if} \quad \gamma < \dfrac{w}{p} \end{cases}$$

where $\frac{w}{p}$ is called the *real wage*, to be distinguished from the *nominal wage*, w, or from the output's *money price*, p, both of which are denominated in terms of money. $\frac{w}{p}$ is the cost of labour in terms of product: for example, if the firm manufactures shoes, and if the daily nominal wage rate is $w = £100$, and the money price of a pair of shoes is $p = £50$, then the daily cost of labour is 2 pair of shoes. Since money has no intrinsic value, it is sometimes useful to express the firm's decision in terms of real rather than nominal magnitudes. Likewise, the worker's decisions are likely to be based on her real wage rate, namely on the things that money wages can buy. As we shall see below, the real wage is just a special case of a *relative price*, the price of a commodity (in this case—labour) in terms of another commodity (in this case—shoes). In general, we assume that rational players are immune to the illusion that a high money denomination actually makes them better off:

Proposition 4.1. [No Money Illusion] *If both* w *and* p *change proportionately, neither the firm's nor the worker's decision would be affected; neither is prone to 'money illusion'.*

Another useful way to look at the decision of the firm is through its product *supply*, which is

$$production = \begin{cases} \gamma & if \quad p \geq \dfrac{w}{\gamma} \\ 0 & if \quad p < \dfrac{w}{\gamma} \end{cases},$$

$\frac{w}{\gamma}$ being the *unit cost* of producing the commodity: since producing γ units cost w, the cost of producing a single unit is $\frac{w}{\gamma}$. Production is profitable whenever the price of the commodity, p, exceeds its unit cost, $\frac{w}{\gamma}$. The supply function therefore indicates a jump from 0 to γ when the price of the final product exceeds unit cost, implying a step-like supply curve with higher production at higher product price.

The next step is to derive the demand for labour by the entire industry. Figure 4.2 plots the entire range of firms' productivity, from 0 to Γ, and a certain market real wage rate, $\frac{w}{p}$. As already discussed above, only firms with productivity greater (or equal) than $\frac{w}{p}$ would participate in the market. Hence, if the real wage falls, the cut-off point $\frac{w}{p}$ shifts to the left. As a result, some of the firms that did not participate in the market when real wages were high would participate at the lower real wage. Each of the new participants would employ one additional worker. The conclusion is that there is an inverse relationship between the market's wage rate and the demand for labour by the entire industry.

Figure 4.3 plots a graph of the industry's demand-for-labour function, mapping nominal wages to a certain amount of labour. (The linear shape of the demand curve is not a necessary implication of the assumptions above though it is a possible one.) The downwards slope of the demand curve is a consequence of the argument of the previous paragraph: with lower wages, some lower-productivity firms, not profitable beforehand, become profitable and employ more workers. Notice that every point on the demand curve maps to a certain firm. For example, point A in Figure 4.3 maps to a firm that becomes just profitable at a wage rate of w_A or, more accurately, to a firm with productivity of $\gamma_A = \frac{w_A}{p}$. Hence, points towards the upper left (bottom right) end of the curve map to relatively high (low) productive firms. Points on the demand curve but below the market wage w, map to firms that, had they operated, would not be profitable; hence, they do not participate. Next to the demand curve we note the market price that the industry faces, p. A different product price would imply a different demand curve (see below).

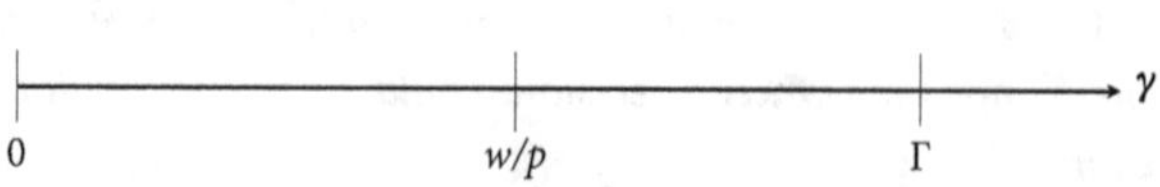

Figure 4.2 Heterogeneity of productivity across firms

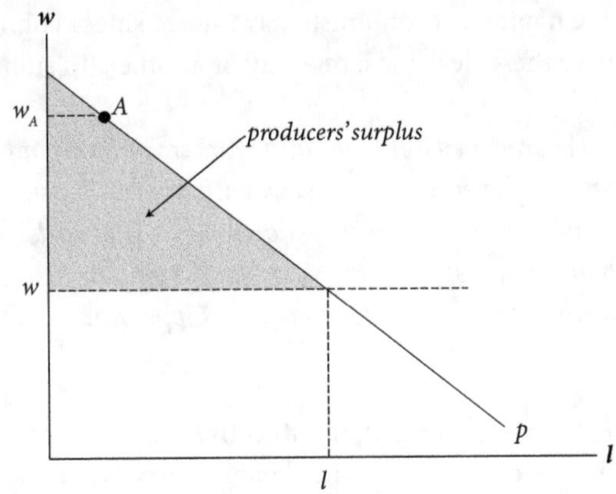

Figure 4.3 Industry demand for labour

The shaded area enclosed below the demand curve and above the market price is called the industry's surplus. Since each point on the demand curve maps to a firm, the vertical distance between the demand curve and the market wage rate measures that firm's surplus. For example, the surplus of the firm mapping to point A in Figure 4.3 is (using the above $\gamma_A = \frac{w_A}{p}$):

$$\pi_A = \gamma_A p - w = w_A - w.$$

Then, adding up the surplus of all the *participating* firms, the resulting shaded area equals the profits of the entire industry. Like the surplus of the individual firm, the industry's surplus is also denominated in money.

In much the same manner we can derive the supply of labour. Consider a population of potential workers, differentiated by their subjective valuation of free time, v, between zero and V. Each would make a decision whether the real wage offered on the market compensates for the loss of the pleasure of being idle, or, more technically, the opportunity cost of *leisure*. His decision could be summarized as follows:

$$l = \begin{cases} 1 & \text{if} \quad \frac{w}{p} \geq v \\ 0 & \text{if} \quad \frac{w}{p} < v \end{cases}.$$

Following the same steps as before, we derive an upwards sloping supply curve of labour and the workers' surplus. Notice that all those potential workers who decided not to seek a job have done so, voluntarily, on the assessment that staying idle brings them more joy than taking up a job (and of spending the earned wages).

As emphasized in Chapter 1, economists have no business commenting on the sentiments that drive these decisions, one way or another. To summarize:

Proposition 4.2. *Heterogeneity of firms and workers in terms of productivity and subjective valuation of leisure, respectively, with binary decisions about participation, is sufficient in order to derive a downwards (upwards) sloping demand (supply) for labour with respect to the wage rate. A similar heterogeneous-player (HP) approach can be used in order to derive supply and demand functions in other markets.*

As noted above, the Decreasing Unit Subjective Valuation curve of Chapter 1, DUSV, is an alternative derivation of the demand curve for a player whose consumption decision is not limited to either zero or one. (Chapter 6 elaborates on the production decisions of a firm that is not restricted to binary production decisions.) The notion of consumer surplus also applies. To see why, consider a DUSV curve for some arbitrary commodity as in Figure 4.4. (This is just an extension of the Chapter 1 argument.) Take a specific quantity, q_0. The subjective valuation of an extra unit at that level of consumption is v_0. Since the market price is $p_m < v_0$, the player can make herself better off by buying an extra unit of the commodity, generating a surplus of $v_0 - p_m > 0$. At a higher level of consumption, say, q_1, the subjective valuation of an extra unit is only $v_1 < v_0$. Since it is still the case that $v_1 > p_m$, it is in her best interest to increase consumption even further. And so on, until she reaches the quantity q_m, where the subjective valuation of an extra unit equals the market price p_m. Beyond q_m, the subjective valuation of an extra unit of consumption is lower than p_m, so consuming above q_m would actually undermine her well-being. It follows that q_m is the amount of consumption that best serves the player's interests, and the DUSV curve is, also, a demand curve. Adding up the

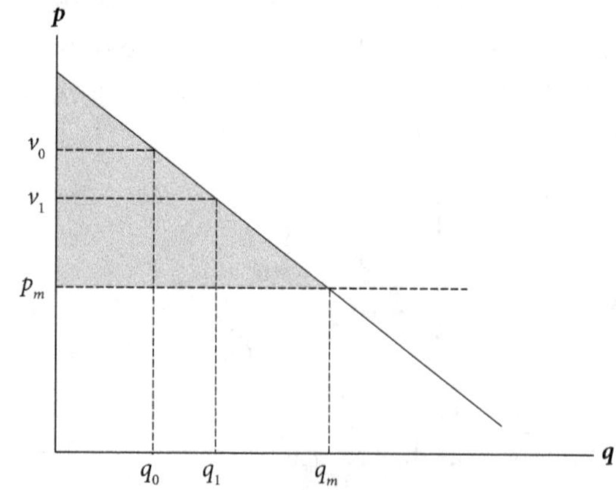

Figure 4.4 The DUSV representation of demand

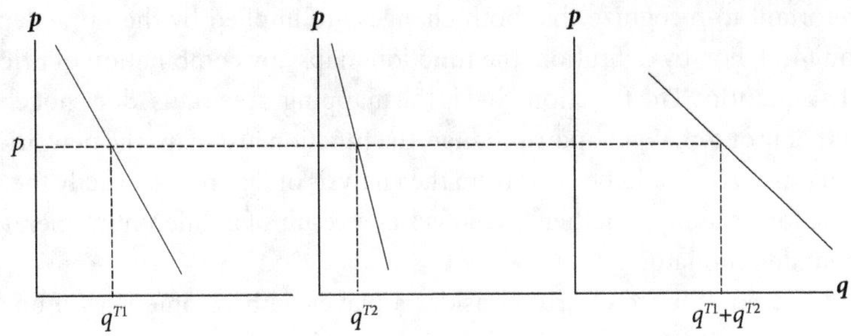

Figure 4.5 Horizontal summation of demand curves

surplus generated by each and every unit consumed up to q_m, geometrically represented by the shaded area below the demand curve and above the q_m horizontal line, measures the total surplus that the player has derived from buying q_m units of the commodity at a price of p_m. Notice that consumer surplus is denominated in the same unit as p_m, in this case—money.

The DUSV derivation can still accommodate heterogeneity, but requires an additional step called *horizontal summation* of curves. Consider a market with two types of players (consumers), *T1* and *T2*. Players within type are identical in their subjective valuations and, therefore, in their demand curves. At the same time, demand curves differ across types; see Figure 4.5. (For simplicity, think of each type as if it has one player only who, nevertheless, behaves in an atomistic manner, as a price taker.) To derive the industry's demand curve, consider a certain market price, *p*. Due to the law of one price, both types face the same market price, so deriving the quantities that each demands is easy: just draw their demand curves side by side and plot a horizontal line at *p*. Clearly, if the quantities demanded, at *p*, by *T1* and *T2* are q^{T1} and q^{T2}, respectively, then the market demand (at *p*) is $q^{T1} + q^{T2}$. Repeating this process for each and every conceivable price derives the industry's demand curve. (Notice that the horizontal summation is actually built into the HP derivation of demand.)

4.3.1 'Shifts' on and of Supply and Demand Curve

It is worth warning the reader against misleading terminology that is very common in economics (including in this book) regarding 'shifting curves'. Worse, economics tutors often urge their students to make a clear distinction between 'a move on the curve' (say, when *w* in Figure 4.3 drops) and a shift of the curve (say, when *p* in Figure 4.3 rises). Though the geometry of the analysis seems different, it is important to recognize that both changes are implied by the same demand function (4.1). For, by definition, the function maps any combination of prices, w and p, to a quantity. The function, that is the mapping 'apparatus', does not change when either w or p change; upon a change, the function just maps the new prices to a new quantity. As should be clear from the analysis of Figure 4.2, exactly the same economic forces apply, whether $\frac{w}{p}$ changes as a result of a different numerator or a different denominator.

To see the point more clearly, consider a player with income y, who operates under the following simple rule: she allocates 10% of her income to the consumption of a certain commodity, whatever the price of the commodity, p, is (and regardless of the price of other commodities). It follows that the quantity demanded of the commodity, q is:

$$q = \frac{0.1y}{p}. \tag{4.2}$$

Evidently, the consumption of the commodity is increasing in income and decreasing in the price of the commodity. A complete description of the demand function would be a three-dimensional manifold as in Figure 4.6. Any combination of p and y is a point on the 'floor' of the box; to find q, one should move vertically from that point until one hits the manifold, then move horizontally and read the quantity on the vertical scale. Since such a three-dimensional diagram is awkward to handle, a common practice is to fix the level of income at various levels of income, say, y_0, y_1 or y_2, with different p and q graphs. Each graph captures the variation of q with respect to the price p, given a certain level of income. Each can be visualized as a 'slice' of the manifold at a certain level of y; see Figure 4.6.

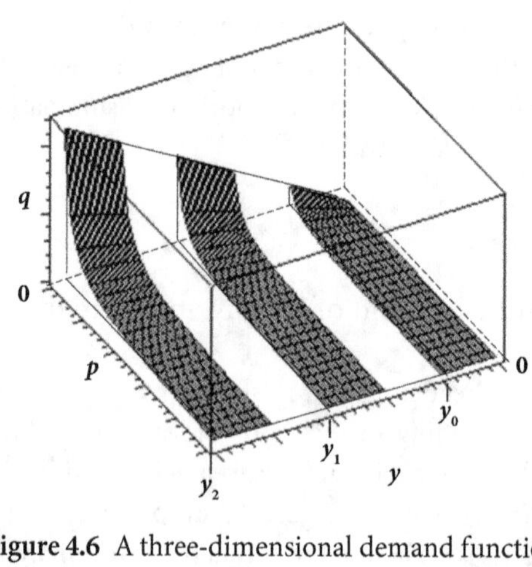

Figure 4.6 A three-dimensional demand function

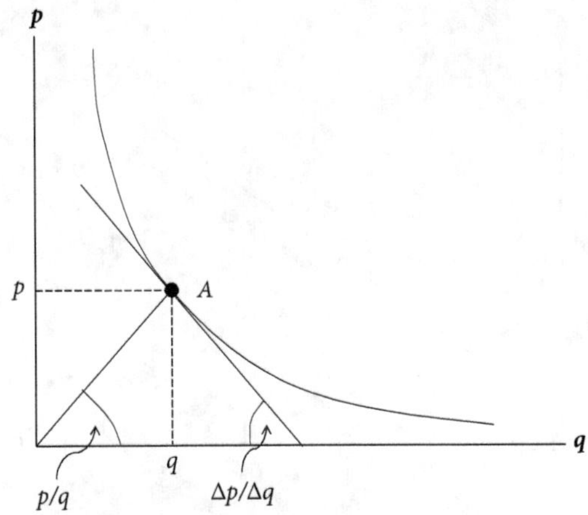

Figure 4.7 Elasticity of demand

4.3.2 Diversion: Elasticity of Demand

Another concept on which economics students spend too much time is that of the elasticity of the demand curve, defined as the ratio between a percentage change in the quantity and a certain percentage change in the price, at a certain point on the demand curve. Commonly denoted by η (the Greek letter eta):

$$\eta = \frac{\Delta q/q}{\Delta p/p} = \frac{p/q}{\Delta p/\Delta q}.$$

Figure 4.7 provides a geometric interpretation. We make no use of the concept in this book. For general reference, it is useful to note that when the demand curve is horizontal (vertical), $\eta \to \infty$ ($\eta \to 0$), the demand curve is said to be perfectly elastic (inelastic).

4.4 Market Equilibrium

We start with a formal definition:

Definition 4.1. A competitive equilibrium is a price, p^*, such that the market *clears*, so that the quantity demanded by all the buyers equals the quantity supplied by all the vendors in the market—at that price.

It follows that in equilibrium, each player can execute their production and consumption plans, as intended.

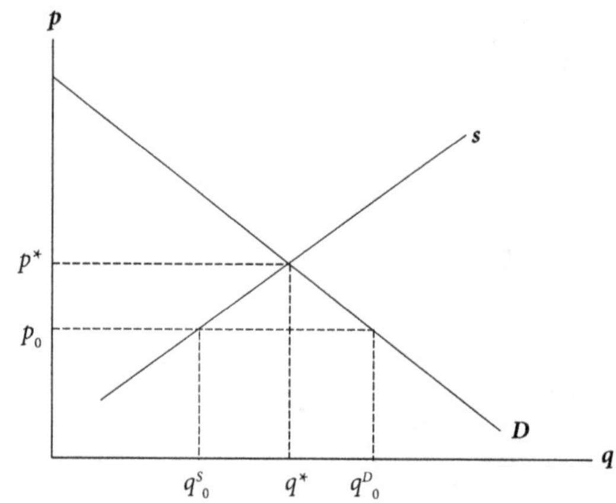

Figure 4.8 Competitive equilibrium

Figure 4.8 illustrates. A demand (supply) curve for a certain commodity is downwards (upwards) sloping: the higher the price the lower (higher) is the quantity demanded (supplied) by consumers (producers) who participate in that market. The equilibrium price, p^* is the intersection point of the two curves. At that price, the quantity demanded equals, exactly, the quantity supplied, q^*. In that sense, the market *clears*. With downwards (upwards) demand (supply) curve, p^* is the only price that clears the market; equilibrium is *unique*. To be sure, at any other price, say p_0, the quantity supplied, q_o^S differs from the quantity demanded, q_0^D, so that the market is in a state of *excess demand*, with some buyers frustrated by the inability to execute their plans. The market-clearing equilibrium price is the only one that avoids such frustration. That is, every vendor finds a buyer and every buyer finds a vendor.

4.4.1 Stability of Equilibrium

The market is the paradigmatic example of spontaneous order, a social system that is self-organizing, with no guidance from the outside, be it a government or a regulator. To put it differently, economic decisions are *decentralized* to the traders in the market, who need not worry about economic theory. All they need to do is to act in their best interests, given the market price.

The existence of an equilibrium would be of very little interest without it being *stable*, that is having the tendency to gravitate towards the equilibrium point, by forces that operate within the market itself. More precisely, any initial non-equilibrium price, say p_0 in Figure 4.8, would initiate a process whereby the price increases, until it converges to the equilibrium price, p^*.

To see why, remember that at a price like p_0 the market is in a state of excess demand: $q_0^D > q_0^S$, so there must be some frustrated buyers who cannot find a vendor, as all the vendors (who participate in the market) are already engaged with other buyers. (We are still using the HP derivation of supply and demand.) Crucially, these frustrated buyers value the commodity above p_0; remember that each buyer maps to points on the demand curve above p_0. If so, it is in their best interest to approach a participating vendor and offer him a price higher than p_0. In such a case, it would be in the best interest of the vendor to leave the buyer to whom she was just about to sell the commodity at a price of p_0 and trade, instead, with the higher-offer buyer. Doing so, the frustrated buyers bid up the market price. Since this argument is valid for any price lower than p^*, the upward trend in the price would stop only when the market price reaches p^*. Notice that along the process, vendors who did not participate at p_0 are drawn into the market, while some buyers leave the market.

A mirror image of this argument can be articulated for prices above p^*. In a state of excess supply, some vendors are frustrated, so it is in their best interest to try and sell their product below market price. It follows that at any price other than p^*, it is in the best interest of some traders to trade below (above) the market price, driving the price up (down) when $p < p^*$ ($p > p^*$). In contrast, at p^*, it is not of the best interest of any player, neither buyer nor vendor, to offer a price other than p^*, so that the *price discovery process* ends.

The reader may feel a certain tension between the argument above and the notion of price taking. Indeed, no player can change the market price. However, any buyer (vendor) may offer a price higher (lower) than the market price. The point is that it is no-one's best interest to do it in equilibrium, but it might be in the best interest of some to deviate from market price when the market is out of equilibrium, thereby driving the price towards equilibrium.

It is also worth noting that the stability argument, above, is a 'story' that is not fully integrated into our theory of supply and demand. For stability is a dynamic process, where our theory of supply and demand is a static one. As such, it does not incorporate the trades of the players along the convergence path, which must be associated with their expectations regarding the speed of the convergence, as well as the likelihood of being matched with a trading partner before prices fully adjust. We shall say more about the price-discovery process in Chapter 8.

4.4.2 Welfare Theorems

While decentralization is an attractive property, particularly to those who do not trust governments, it lacks any normative property. Surely, there is no reason to adopt a decentralized form of organization if all it produces is just poverty and misery. Fortunately, competitive equilibria have two properties that make them significantly more attractive. These properties are labelled, simply, "First" and "Second" Welfare Theorems.

Proposition 4.3 (First Welfare Theorem) *Provided that all commodities are traded in competitive markets, the equilibrium is Pareto efficient.*

The condition 'all commodities are traded in competitive markets' may seem benign—deceptively so. Its full consequences are to be better realized in Chapters 5 and 6.

The argument runs as follow: consider, for example, an intervention in the competitive equilibrium that forces an expansion of production, and consumption, by several units. For this to be a Pareto improvement, the non-participating firms who are induced to expand production need to be compensated for their extra production. Given their relatively low productivity (high unit cost), they should be granted a price *higher* than p^*. For similar reasons, the consumers who buy the extra product should be charged a price *lower* than p^*. Hence, the intervention creates a deficit, which must be funded by a third party, who would not benefit from the intervention.

Essentially, the equilibrium price, p^*, is above the unit cost of any participating firm and below the subjective valuation of any participating consumer. It separates the market to participating and non-participating, high productivity and low productivity firms, high-valuation and low-valuation consumers. It is worth writing down, explicitly, those properties of a competitive equilibrium that guarantee its Pareto efficiency:

Proposition 4.4. *The following separating conditions guarantee that a competitive equilibrium is Pareto efficient:*

i) Even the least productive participating firm is more productive than the most productive non-participating firm.
ii) Even the lowest-value participating consumer values the commodity higher than highest-value non-participating consumer.
iii) The unit cost of even the most productive non-participating firm is above the valuation of the highest value non-participating consumer.

When the three properties above are satisfied, it is hard to see how tweaking the allocation across participating and non-participating, high-valuation and low-valuation players can make some players better off without undermining others.

As already noted in Chapter 2, Pareto efficiency does not guarantee fairness. A competitive equilibrium might end up with vastly unequal levels of income and standard of living, which some may find morally unacceptable. We take no position on matters of fairness, but we do recognize the need to reconcile the calculus of economic efficiency with any notion of fairness that society might have. We have already developed the argument, in Chapter 2, that the implementation of such policies *need not* conflict with efficiency considerations. *Second Welfare Theorem* adapts that argument to the context of perfect competition (the concept of a lump sum transfer is explained below).

Proposition 4.5. (Second Welfare Theorem) *Any Pareto efficient allocation can be implemented by a competitive equilibrium accompanied by certain lump-sum transfers.*

To motivate the result, consider a market for some staple commodity, say rice or lentils. Following a *lump-sum transfer* (see below) of income from 'rich' to 'poor' players, decreasing (increasing) the income of the former (latter) 'type' by the same amount. (Suppose that there are no other 'types' and that each group is of the same size.) The rich are not heavy consumers of the commodity and, therefore, their post-transfer demand curve, D_1^R, is only slightly below their pre-transfer demand curve, D_0^R. In contrast, the poor spend much of their income on the commodity so that their post-transfer demand curve, D_1^P, is significantly above their pre-transfer demand curve, D_0^P. As a result, production and total consumption expands, but the consumption of the rich falls slightly; see Figure 4.9. The key observation is that both the pre-transfer and the post-transfer equilibria are Pareto efficient because both satisfy the separation conditions as formulated in Proposition 4.4 above.

It is clear that a transfer of this sort is not Pareto improving: it is intended to improve the well being of the poor, with the full awareness that the rich would have to burden the cost. Nevertheless, both pre-transfer and post-transfer allocations are Pareto efficient: an allocation is Pareto efficient when it impossible to Pareto-improve upon it. In fact, it is built into the definition of Pareto efficiency that any transition from one Pareto-efficient allocation to another involves loss of well-being for some players.

The Second Welfare Theorem is of tremendous political significance. It demonstrates that concerns about the fairness of certain market outcomes are not a sufficient reason to abolish the market economy. Rather, fairness-oriented policies can be implemented within a market economy, without giving up the efficiency gains that the system can deliver. It is sufficient to reallocate income across players but, then, let them trade as they wish, leaving the final outcome to be determined by the market.

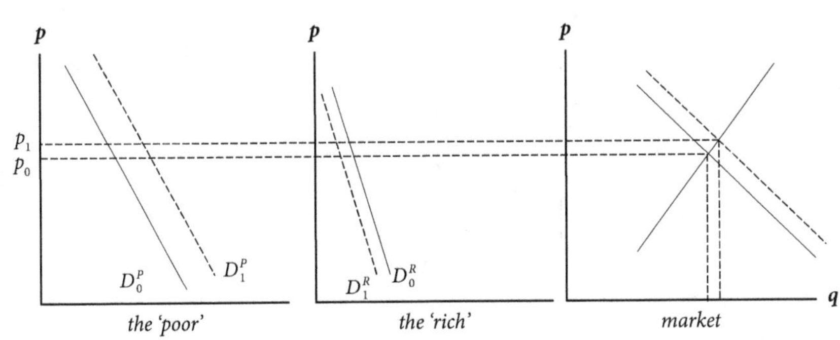

Figure 4.9 Lump sum transfer and a staple commodity market

4.4.3 Tax Distortions and Lump-sum Taxes

The somewhat casual treatment of lump-sum taxes, above, ignored some important issues. First, lump-sum taxes do not exist in reality. Second, any real-world tax is *distortionary* in a sense to be explained, below.

Consider a labour market, in equilibrium, where the wage rate is w^* (£s/month), say, and the employment level is l^*. To fund operations, the government levies an income tax, of t (£s/month) on any worker-firm transaction. (To facilitate the analysis, we express the tax rate in £s/month rather than as a percentage of income—as is the common practice of income tax.) As a result, a wedge is inserted between the wage rate that the firm pays, w^F, and the wage rate that the worker collects, w^L, so that $w^L = w^F - t$. Given after-tax wage rates, the amount of labour demanded equals the amount of labour supplied and the market clears at l_t, with firms (workers) paying (receiving) a higher (lower) effective wage rates relative to the pre-tax wage rate, w^*. The government's monthly tax revenue, $l_t \times t$, namely the *tax base*, l_t, multiplied by the tax rate t. The government's tax revenue is represented by the shaded areas $A + B$ in Figure 4.10.

Income tax is 'distorting' in the sense that a lump-sum tax would Pareto-improve on the income tax. A lump sum tax is a fixed levy, enforced on each and every player in the economy, independently of any action that the player takes. Lump sum taxes do not, and cannot, exist in reality, as players can always take some action to decrease their tax incidence: for example, leave the country or decrease their participation in the labour market so that there is no income from which tax can be deducted. Rather, lump sum taxes are a theoretical construct, invented by economists, so as to conceptualize the notion of tax distortion.

To see why a lump-sum tax Pareto dominates (still using the HP representation), let the non-affected players, whether firms or workers, be those who participate in the market even after the levy of the income tax. (These are firms with unit costs

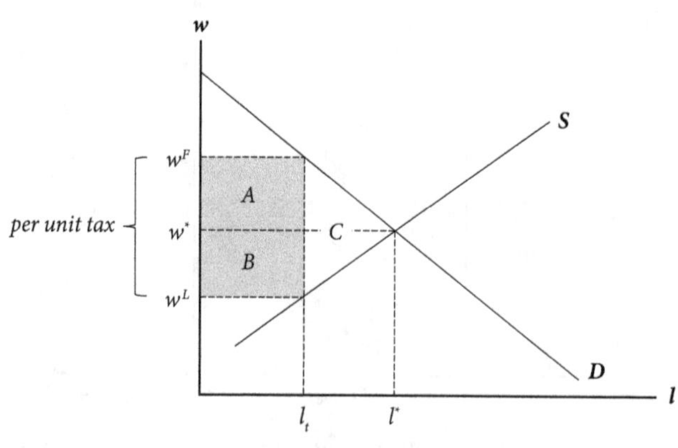

Figure 4.10 Income tax

higher than w^F.) In a similar manner, let the affected players be those who stop participating in the market after the levy of the income tax. (These are firms that value labour between w^* and w^F.) The lump sum tax works as follows: only the non-affected firms (workers) are taxed, by $w^F - w^*$ ($w^* - w^L$). Affected players, namely those who stop participating after the levy of the income tax, are not lump-sum taxed. Now confirm that w^* is the equilibrium wage under the lump-sum tax. After-tax income for non-affected players is the same under the lump-sum and income tax. Since they participate under the income tax they also participate under the lump-sum tax. Obviously, since the lump-sum tax does not apply to the affected players, they also participate. Hence w^* is the equilibrium wage with lump-sum tax. Conclusion: the non-affected players are indifferent between the two taxes, while the affected players are better off under the lump-sum tax. Intuitively, the income tax distorts as it drives beneficial trades by the affected players out the market. The lump-sum tax avoids that distortion.

Notice that the government raises the same amount of revenue under both lump-sum and income tax. Conclusion:

Proposition 4.6. *A lump sum tax Pareto dominates any same-revenue income tax.*

To quantify the difference between the two taxes, find the total loss of surplus under the income tax for affected firms. That is the trapezoid below the demand curve and between w^F and w^*. In a similar manner, find the total loss of surplus under the income tax for affected workers. Netting out the government's revenue, $A + B$, which is probably used to the benefit of the 'public', lightly shadowed triangle, C, in Figure 4.10, marks the total loss of surplus, due to the income tax, namely its tax distortion.

Intuitively, any tax on economic activity, that is any tax that is not a lump sum tax, distorts as it *crowds out* positive-surplus transactions from being executed. Needless to say, this is not an argument against taxation, provided that the government uses the tax revenue appropriately; see Chapter 6 below. It is, however, an argument in favour of using taxes that distort less, and it is an argument for netting out the surplus lost to taxation from the value generated by government operations, be it the production of 'public goods' or transfers to promote fairness and equity, along the lines of the Second Welfare Theorem.

4.4.4 Endogenous and Exogenous Variables

Exogenous variables are taken as given by the model so as to explain the *endogenous* variables. The former is an input to the model (so to speak) while the latter is an output. It should be emphasized that this classification is model specific. For example, all firms' γs in the HP derivation are taken as exogenous, but may be turned into endogenous variables in an extended model that includes an explanation of technological change. Likewise, market prices, are treated as exogenous in the firm's decision problem, but are *endogenized* once we move to a market analysis. Hence the common expression is that 'price takers treat the price as exogenous' (to their decision). Notice that exogenous variables need not be fixed, rather their change is determined by changes in the model's exogenous variables.

4.5 'Free Trade'

The two welfare theorems are commonly taken as a strong argument for free trade. An immediate question to be asked is why, in the real world, there is so much resistance to free trade. The answer is that the 'win–win' interpretation of free trade is, at best, an oversimplification and, at its worst, plainly wrong.

4.5.1 Trade Liberalization

Consider a market for a certain commodity in a small open economy. By 'small' we mean that the entire economy is atomistic with respect to the rest of the world, taking the world's price of the commodity as given, at p^*. Initially, local production is protected by an import prohibition, resulting in an initial equilibrium at point A, with a price of p_0 and a domestically manufactured quantity of q_0. Once a trade liberalization removes the import prohibition, previously participating domestic firms with a unit cost higher than p^* lose out to foreign competition and shut down, so domestic production falls from, q_0 to q^F. At the same time, previously non-participating consumers with subjective valuations above p^* find the post-liberalization price attractive. Domestic consumption expands from q_0 to q^C. The gap between domestic consumption and domestic production, $q^C - q^F$, is satisfied by imports; see Figure 4.11.

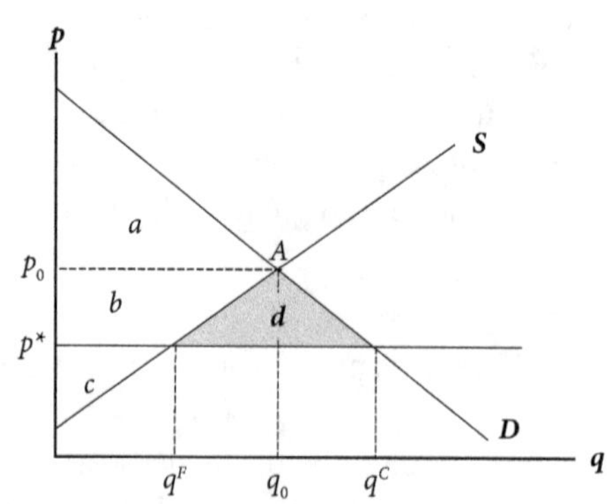

Figure 4.11 Trade liberalization

It is easy to see that domestic consumers gain from the lower price while domestic firms lose out. If some win and other lose, then on its own the liberalization is not Pareto improvement. A more refined argument would be that *if* the winners, after *fully* compensating the losers, can still retain some positive surplus, then the liberalization is a Pareto improvement. The precise argument goes as follows: consumer surplus grows from the a area before the liberalization to the $a + b + d$ area after the liberalization, a gain of $b + d$; see Figure 4.11. At the same time, producer surplus falls from the $b + c$ area before the liberalization to the c area after the liberalization, a loss of b. Since both gain and loss are denominated in the same units, money, losses can be netted of F gains to generate a net surplus of d. That is:

Proposition 4.7. *By itself, trade liberalization creates both winners and losers. However, after the winners fully compensate the losers, they there still retain some surplus. Only lump-sum transfers from winners to losers would guarantee that trade liberalization is a Pareto Improvement.*

4.5.2 A note on Coase, Pareto, Spontaneous Order and the State

It follows from Proposition 4.7 that a trade impediment, say an import prohibition, undermines economic efficiency. At the same time, there are winners and losers in its removal. That is consistent with our initial analysis of Pareto efficiency in Chapter 2: for any Pareto-dominated point a, there is a set of Pareto-efficient points, A, such that moving from a to any point in A makes every player better off. At the same time, since A is typically just a subset of the Pareto set, it is not the case that moving from a to an arbitrary Pareto-efficient point necessarily makes every player better off. It is, however, the case that for any point like a there exists a Coasian Bargain: a multi-party agreement that reallocates commodities and transfers, to everyone's benefit.

Now the 'folklore' of the Coase Theorem says: let the players get together and negotiate the terms of the bargain by themselves. That may be a credible idea for some of the cases discussed in Chapter 2, but quite inconceivable in the current context. When the entire population is affected by a certain policy, how can citizens 'get together' and commit themselves to action (including gifting funds to other citizens)? Moreover, the very idea of atomistic competition is alien to such civic gatherings.

It follows that the economy needs some arbiter to negotiate (and enforce) the Coasian Bargain. It is hard to see who, besides the state, can perform the task. But then, free-market reformers usually start by defining their purpose as removing state intervention from certain markets, towards a Spontaneous Order. But that transition may not be possible without the state playing a pivotal role.

Table 4.1 Labour productivity, steel, and computers, *ADV* and *BCK*

	ADV	*BCK*
S	200	100
C	10	2

The apparent tension in the above argument may identify the hard political problem that failed quite a few liberalizations.

4.5.3 David Ricardo's Comparative Advantage Theory

It is sometimes argued that less developed countries cannot participate in international trade because they have no technological advantage in any commodity. The great 'classical' economist David Ricardo (1772–1823) demonstrated the fallacy of this claim; some consider his argument to be the most elegant in economics.

We demonstrate the argument using a simple numerical example. Consider two countries: one is more technologically advanced than the other; call the former *ADV* and the latter *BCK*, respectively. There are two commodities, steel and computers, denoted by the letters *S* and *C*, respectively. Labour productivity, the γs of Equation (4.1) above, across countries and industries, are presented in Table 4.1 below. The crucial point is that *ADV* has an *absolute advantage* over *BCK* in both commodities, as it has higher labour productivity in both.

Ricardo's ingenious observation is that in spite of *ADV*'s absolute technological advantage, both countries can still benefit from bilateral trade because relatively, *ADV* has a technological advantage in computers: its labour is five times more productive than *BCK*s when deployed to computers but only twice as productive when deployed to steel. Likewise, *BCK* has a *comparative advantage* in steel. Hence, *ADV* and *BCK* should specialize in computing and steel, respectively, to their mutual benefit.

A more formal demonstration of the result goes as follows: there exist a combination of steel and computers prices, p^C and p^S respectively, and a combination of *ADV* and *BCK* wages, w^{ADV} and w^{BCK}, such that profit motives direct *ADV* (*BCK*) firms towards specialization in computers (steel):

$$\begin{aligned} 200p^S - w^{ADV} &< 10p^c - w^{ADV}. \\ 100p^S - w^{BCK} &> 2p^C - w^{BCK} \end{aligned} \tag{4.3}$$

Notice that the law of one price applies to steel and computers as they traded internationally; at the same time, since labour is not internationally mobile, there are differences in the wage rates across countries (but not across industries within each country). With some simple algebra we conclude that both inequalities in (4.3) are satisfied if, and only if:

$$20 < \frac{p^c}{p^S},$$

$$50 > \frac{p^c}{p^S}.$$

Since players are free from money illusion, only the relative prices matter; or, alternatively, we may set, conveniently, $p^S = 1$, and draw the conclusion that any computer price $20 < p^C < 50$ would achieve the desired specialization.

Does it follow that absolute advantage is economically irrelevant? Certainly not: it determines the standard of living in both countries. To see the point, consider *ADV*'s labour market, assuming that $p^C = 35$ so that the country is fully specialized in the manufacturing of computers. For simplicity, assume that workers in both countries are scarce relative to the number of firms that try to employ them, so that competition drives the wage rate up to the point that firms make zero profit; see Figure 4.6 for the case of *ADV*'s labour market. Solving out the wage rate from the zero-profit conditions,

$$35 \times 10 - w^{ADV} = 0,$$

$$1 \times 100 - w^{BCK} = 0,$$

we conclude that $w^{ADV} = 350$ while $w^{BCK} = 100$, a significant difference in the standard of living.

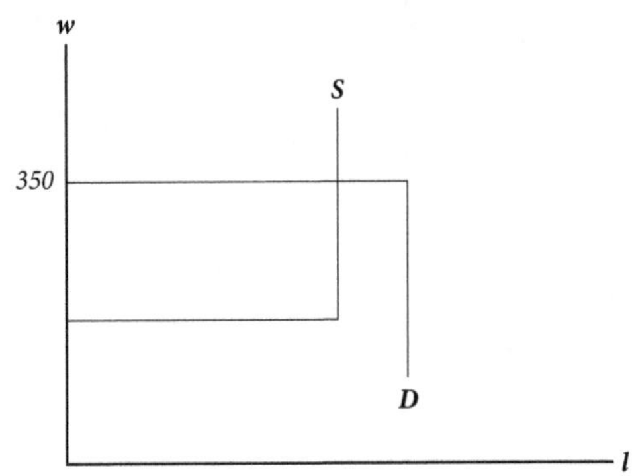

Figure 4.12 The *ADV* labour market, $p^c = 35$

4.6 Fitting Data: Estimating Supply and Demand Curves

Being functional relationships between prices and quantities, supply and demand functions are not observable; neither are their graphs. There is, of course, plenty of statistical data about prices and quantities, which can be presented as Figure 4.13-like plots, each point indicating the price–quantity combination that prevailed on the market at a certain point in time. Each point is *assumed* to be generated by an intersection between supply and demand curves. It follows that the 'cloud'-like shape of the data is generated by changes in the exogenous variables that move around the equilibrium point. We have already seen how to use regression analysis in order to estimate a single functional relationship; but how should we treat two functional relationship that interact one with another?

The idea is simple: on the basis of theory, we can predict which exogenous variables affect each curve. For example, the demand curve is affected by consumers' income, Y, and the supply curve is affected by the cost of raw materials, C. Now, suppose that we could identify a subset of observations (data points in Figure 4.13) where the cost of production is the same, but consumers' income changes, so that all the points within that subset can be treated as intersections of the same supply curve with different demand curves; see Figure 4.14. In which case, the supply curve is *identified* and can be estimated by linear regression on the subset. Likewise, data points with the same level of income but different cost of raw materials can identify the demand curve.

The problem with this method is that it might be difficult to find a significant number of data points where either Y or C are exactly the same. A more satisfactory solution starts with an explicit statement of the *structural equations*, namely the demand (4.4) and supply (4.5) functions,

$$q^D = d_0 - d_P \times p + d_Y \times Y + \varepsilon^D, \tag{4.4}$$

$$q^S = s_0 + s_P \times p - s_C \times C + \varepsilon^S. \tag{4.5}$$

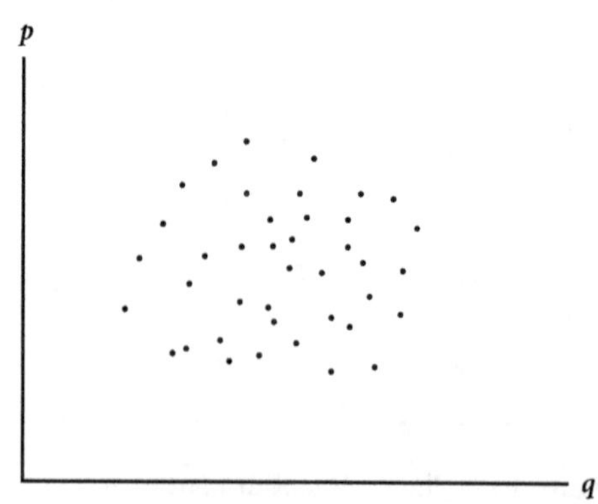

Figure 4.13 Market statistics

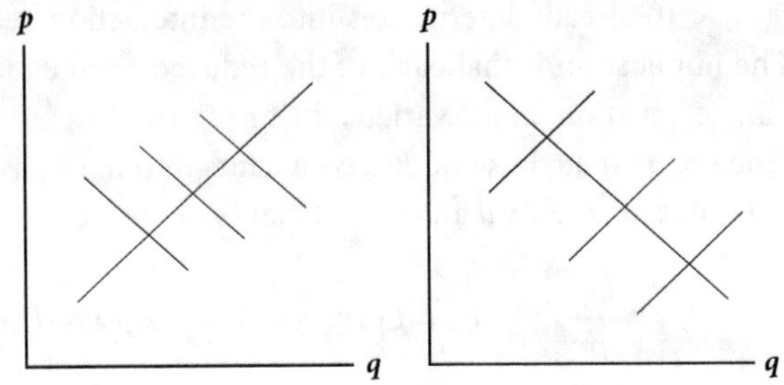

Figure 4.14 Identification of supply (left) and demand (right) curves

There are six (positive) structural parameters: d_0 and s_0 are the intercepts, d_P and s_P capture the price effect on supply and demand, while s_C and d_Y capture the effect of the exogenous variables, income and the cost of raw materials, on supply and demand. The εs are error terms, uncorrelated with Y and C; see Section A.5 of the Mathematical Appendix. The structure highlights the *simultaneity* problem in estimating, say, a demand curve, as the 'shift' from one point in the cloud to another relates to the simultaneous changes both supply-related cost factors and demand-related income factors—a direct implication of the concept of equilibrium.

Next, we equate supply and demand, $q^D = q^S \equiv q$, and find out the *reduced form*, two linear equations each relating the endogenous variables, p and q, to the model's exogenous variables, Y and C:

$$q = \alpha_0 + \alpha_Y \times Y + \alpha_C \times C + \upsilon^Q, \tag{4.6}$$

$$p = \beta_0 + \beta_Y \times Y + \beta_C \times C + \upsilon^P, \tag{4.7}$$

where

$$\alpha_0 = \frac{d_0 s_P + s_0 d_p}{s_P + d_P}, \qquad \alpha_Y = \frac{d_Y s_P}{s_P + d_P}, \qquad \alpha_C = -\frac{d_P s_C}{s_P + d_P}, \tag{4.8}$$

and

$$\beta_0 = \frac{d_0 - s_0}{s_P + d_P}, \qquad \beta_Y = \frac{d_Y}{s_P + d_P}, \qquad \beta_C = \frac{s_C}{s_P + d_P} \tag{4.9}$$

(for brevity, we omit the two expressions for the two error terms υ^P and υ^Q, where υ is the Greek letter upsilon). The reader is advised not to spend too much time on the derivation of the reduced form: it is sufficient to observe that since the two linear equations, (4.4) and (4.5), have only two unknowns, and since the price effects in the structure have opposite signs, a unique solution is guaranteed. The important point is that the reduced-form equations are free from the simultaneity problem: holding Y constant, C's positive price effect ($\beta_C > 0$) and negative quantity effect ($\alpha_C < 0$) already internalizes into the interaction between supply and demand. The implication is that each of the reduced form equations can be estimated by a single equation, multi-variate, linear regression.

Substituting the six estimated αs and βs coefficients into the six (4.8) and (4.9) equations, we solve out for the six d and s coefficients of the structure:

$$s_P = \frac{\alpha_Y}{\beta_Y}, \qquad d_P = -\frac{\alpha_C}{\beta_C}, \qquad d_Y = \beta_Y (s_P + d_P) \qquad s_C = \beta_C (s_P + d_P),$$

$$s_0 = \alpha_0 - s_P \beta_0, \qquad d_0 = \beta_0 (s_P + d_P) + s_0.$$

The estimation of the structural equations is of tremendous practical importance. Notice that for the sake of predicting prices and quantities for Ys and Cs the reduced form will do. But using structural equations we can go one step further. For example, we can use them in order to predict the revenue due to a suggested unit tax (where the supply price does not equal the demand price as in the income-tax example above) even if there is no data on past unit taxes, say, because they were never levied before. In fact, the structure can even be used in order to estimate the loss of consumer and producer surplus due to the new tax.

4.7 Applications

The conceptual framework of competitive markets, together with the statistical tools that were developed in order to 'take it to the data', is highly effective in the analysis of practical policy problems. Here are a few examples.

4.7.1 The Effect of Import Quotas on the US Economy

A quota is a policy that restricts the quantity of imports allowed into a country, so that the supply of the commodity becomes vertical at the point that the quota binds; see Figure 4.15. Clearly, a similar effect on the quantity of imports can be obtained by an import tariff. The difference is that a tariff would generate revenue, represented by the area $(a + b)$ in Figure 4.15, which the domestic government could use to the benefit of its own citizens. Under a quota, that tax revenue is lost to the foreign producers. Hence, a quota *increases* the loss of surplus to the domestic consumers to $a + c$, relative to just c in the case of a tariff. As for the foreign producers (suppose there are no domestic producers), the quota creates a rent, $a + b$ that mitigates some of the $b + d$ loss in the case of a tariff. The net change in producers' surplus is, thus,

$$-(b + d) + (a + b) = -d + a,$$

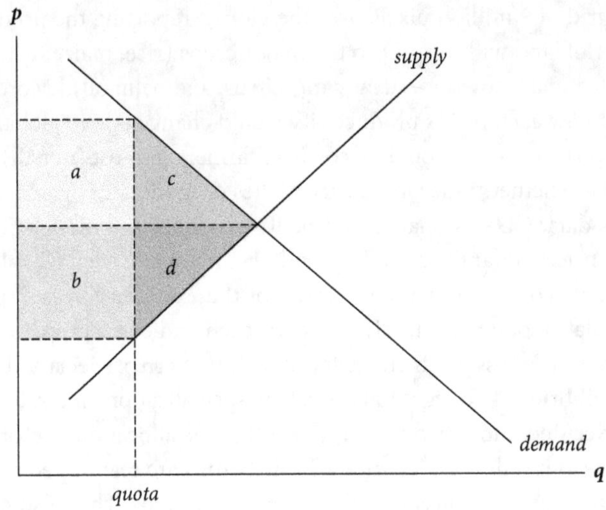

Figure 4.15 Import quota

which might even be positive: a quota may help the foreign producers to monopolize the domestic market (see Chapter 6).

In spite of their clear disadvantages, quotas are used in practice. For example, in 1981, the US government succumbed to lobbying by the domestic automobile industry that found it difficult to compete with small, reliable, and energy-efficient Japanese automobiles. (Try to re-plot Figure 4.15 accounting for both domestic and foreign production.) Hence, the US government negotiated with its Japanese counterpart a 'voluntary' restriction to the number automobile exported from Japan to the US. Feenstra (1992) summarizes the empirical estimates of the loss of surplus due to trade barriers in the automobile and other industries. It turns out that the annual loss of surplus (namely area c in Figure 4.15) from all trade barriers around the year 1985 was between \$8 and \$12 billion. The annual value of the rent transferred to the Japanese producers (namely the area $a + b$ in Figure 4.15) was between \$7 and \$17 billion. Clearly, the quota was a much less effective policy relative to a tariff. At the same time, the total cost to the US economy, given an annual GDP of \$4 trillion, was relatively small.

4.7.2 The Effect of Climate Change on Farmers Income

Costinot, Donaldson, and Smith (2016), henceforth CDS, estimate the effect of global warming on agricultural income. The exercise is based on data collected by the Food and Agriculture Organization (FAO), a United Nations agency that documents the productivity of agricultural land around the world. It does so by spanning a grid of 9 million pixels over the globe,[2] reporting the productivity of a typical plot of land with respect to ten major crops (rice, maize, wheat, cotton, tomato, white potato, soybean, sugar cane, citrus, and palm oil).[3] Moreover, FAO also predicts how each pixel's productivity would change due to global warming. While the global worming would be costly to farmers in most (not all) countries, the question is whether trade would exacerbates or moderates that cost.

Using this data, CDS estimate a competitive equilibrium model and *simulate* equilibrium prices, quantities, and agricultural income under global warming. Notice the huge computational complexity of the exercise: for each pixel, CDS need to calculate a potential supply curve for each and every crop, execute horizontal summation across pixels and determine the pattern of specialization in each pixel—in equilibrium.[4] To highlight the role of specialization and trade, the simulations are executed under two assumptions: that the allocation of crops to pixels stays the same as it is now or, alternatively, that crops are reallocated according to farmers' profit considerations and new climate conditions. They also make a distinction between national and international trade, autarky being the setting where trade takes place only within countries.

A sample of the results is presented in Table 4.2, taken from Table A in the appendix of the published paper. Evidently, Canada is a global warming winner (+45%) while Morocco is a massive loser (−27.4%); see first column to the left. The next two columns detect the source of the effect. For example, with international trade but with no change in the allocation of crops across pixels, Morocco's agricultural income falls 71%. With only internal trade but with

Table 4.2 Change in income due to climate change (% of agricultural expenditure)

	Trade + reallocation	**Autarky + reallocation**	**Trade + no reallocation**
Canada	45.4	47.1	15.0
Ethiopia	−11.5	−20.0	−64.3
India	−8.5	−9.8	−38.9
Morocco	−27.4	−28.0	−71.1
Russia	33.2	34.8	−3.0
USA	−0.8	−3.4	−55.4

Source: Costinot, Donaldson, and Smith (2016), Appendix, Table A.

[2] Since most of the globe is covered with water or ice, and since the CDS study is limited to 50 countries (that account for 91% of the value of agricultural output), 'only' 1.7 million pixels, or 'fields', are considered.

[3] These crops account for 72% of the value of the world's agricultural output.

[4] Indeed, the exercise is even more complicated because CDS also take into consideration the transportation cost (which we have ignored so far). The effect is to fragment each world crop market into regional crop markets.

reallocation of crops across pixels, agricultural income drops by 28%. Hence, international trade plays a relatively modest role in softening the blow of global warming, while internal trade supported by adaptive crop allocation make a significant contribution to that effect.

4.7.3 Environments with Both Strategic and Market Interactions: 'Fire Sales'

As already noted above, there seems to be a fundamental difference between the frictionless environment of this chapter and the one described in Chapter 3 where various frictions give rise to institutional arrangements such as secured debt. Notwithstanding, secured debt and competitive markets are interrelated in practice. For example, the Hart and Moore (1998) model predicts a positive relationship between the value of assets pledged as collateral and the amount of funding that can be obtained in return. Such a relationship raises the possibility that a drop in the values of productive assets may cause lenders to cut down exiting credit lines thereby forcing companies to sell assets into the second-hand market, to fund the early repayments.[5] So called *fire sales* are likely to go below the going market price. Worse, fire sales are likely to affect entire industries. As a multitude of companies fire-sale simultaneously, they drain liquidity out of the market, creating an adverse price reaction, that feed back into collateral values and, hence, further fire sales; see Shleifer and Vishny (1992). (Further discussions of the concept of liquidity are provided in Chapters 6 and 8.) As a result, a chain reaction may develop that would amplify an initially limited event many times over.

As we have already seen, empirical work may need to invent ad hoc solutions so as to fit in phenomena that are not quite covered by theory. For example, the story above conflicts with the law of one price so that distressed and non-distressed assets are traded at a different price. In addition, liquidated assets are not homogeneous. The work of Pulvino (1998) addresses these points through a technique known as the *hedonic-price* regressions, applied to the second-hand market of narrow-body commercial aircraft in the United States. The basic idea is that a relatively small number of characteristics. e.g. model, age, or quality of maintenance affect certain deviations from some benchmark price. At the same time, that benchmark price fluctuates over time according to market conditions: strength of demand, fuel prices, salaries, etc. All these can be summarized into a simple equation:

$$PRICE_i = \beta_0 + \beta_1 \times AGE_i + \Sigma_{m=1}^{M} \gamma_i \times MODEL_{m,i} + \Sigma_{t=1}^{T} \delta_t QURAT_{t,i} + \varepsilon_i, \quad (4.10)$$

[5] The last sentence applies to debt that is *callable*. Such debt is quite common. It serves the purpose of giving the secured creditor more power to 'discipline' the borrower. See Calomiris and Kahn (1991).

where $PRICE_i$ is the transaction-i price and AGE_i is the age of the aircraft at the time of the transaction. Then, there are M dummy variables with γ_i coefficients for the transaction's model and T dummy variables with δ_i coefficients for transaction's quarter.[6] ε_i is an error term. The equation is estimated using 1,079 market transactions during the period 1978–1991. R^2 is 0.762.

The time dummies capture the benchmark price, while the *AGE* and the *MODEL* variables span the price of a specific aircraft around that benchmark. For example, a $\beta_1 < 0$ implies that the older the aircraft the further below the benchmark it trades. A time series of the benchmark price is plotted in Figure 4.16.

To see whether fire-sale transactions are priced below the market price of a comparable aircraft at that quarter, Pulvino (1998) estimates the following regression:

$$\varepsilon_i = \alpha_o + \alpha_1 \times FIRE_i + \eta_i, \tag{4.11}$$

where ε is the error term from Equation (4.10) and *FIRE* is a dummy variable that receives a value of 1 if the transaction is a fire sale and zero otherwise. A transaction is defined as a fire sale if the vendor is considered to be in financial distress: above median leverage (debt over total assets) and below median current ratio (short-term assets over short-term liabilities). It turns out that fire sales are priced

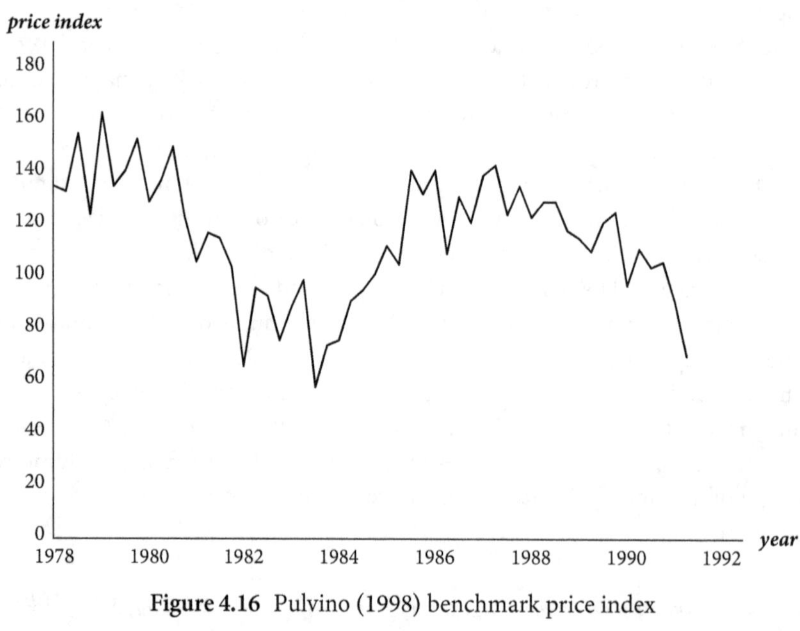

Figure 4.16 Pulvino (1998) benchmark price index

[6] In fact, Pulvino's formalization is slightly more sophisticated. It also includes dummy variables to account for the amount of noise that an aircraft releases, which might impose some restriction on its use within the United States.

about 14% below the benchmark. The effect is stronger during industry busts and vanishes in industry booms.

Although the feedback effect from the fire-sale price to secured debt is not modelled by Pulvino, a 'story' can be told. Suppose that for some exogenous reason, suspected maintenance issues at some low-cost operators, say, some enter economic distress and are forced to liquidate assets. By Equation (4.11), these sales are executed below the *PRICE* benchmark; indeed, they might drive the entire benchmark downwards. By point iv) of Proposition 4.5 of Chapter 3, that could affect the borrowing capacity of some healthy operators, as creditors suspect that such debtor would default strategically in order to renegotiate lower repayments. As a precaution, lenders may cut down the amount of lending, or call back existing loans, which might create some additional fire sales, with further effect on the benchmark. A contagion effect might arise.

4.8 Conclusion

The perfect-competition model is a cornerstone of economic analysis. It gives precise meaning to concepts such as competitive markets, decentralization, or comparative advantage. The two Welfare Theorems provide a clear benchmark against which to evaluate alternative models. The statistical methods that were developed in order to fit the model to the data define the standard of empirical work in economics. The model has very wide applicability, including international trade, taxation, and asset pricing—see Chapter 5.

The frictionless nature of the model is a source of doubts and criticism among many. Chapter 6 demonstrates how to use the model as a foundation upon which at least some frictions can be modelled, with substantial implications to the welfare analysis. Some results in Chapter 5 imply that even in an environment with frictions, some predictions of the competitive model apply, while others may not. In other words, while frictions is obviously an important topic for economic analysis, models without frictions could still be a useful analytical tool—sometimes.

References

[1] Calomiris, Charles W. and Charles M. Kahn (1991). 'The Role of Demandable Debt in Structuring Optimal Banking', *American Economic Review*, Vol. 81, No. 3, pp. 497–513.

[2] Costinot, Arnaud, Dave Donaldson, and Cory Smith (2016). 'Evolving Comparative Advantage and the Impact of Climate Change in Agricultural Markets: Evidence from 1.7 Million Fields around the World', *Journal of Political Economy*, Vol. 124, No. 1, pp. 205–248.

[3] Feenstra, Robert C. (1992). 'How Costly Is Protectionism?', *The Journal of Economic Perspectives*, Vol. 6, No. 3, pp. 159–178.

[4] Pulvino, Todd C. (1998). 'Do Asset Fire Sales Exist? An Empirical Investigation of Commercial Aircraft Transactions', *The Journal of Finance*, Vol. 53, No. 3, pp. 939–978.

[5] Shleifer, Andrei and Robert W. Vishny, (1992). 'Liquidation Values and Debt Capacity: A Market Equilibrium Approach', *Journal of Finance*, Vol. 47, No. 4, pp. 1343–1366.

5
The Market for Risk

5.1 Introduction

In Chapter 1 we already demonstrated the analytical benefit in treating physically identical objects, delivered at different points in time, as different commodities. In this chapter we apply the same idea to the economic analysis of risk by distinguishing deliveries of physically identical objects across different eventualities. Quite intuitively, a commitment to deliver £100 in the circumstances of personal duress has a higher subjective valuation than a commitment to deliver £100 in normal circumstances; hence the market for insurance. (The current chapter uses the DUSV derivation of demand.) As we shall see, the analysis of risk is just an application of the competitive model as presented in Chapter 4. As noted by Robert Lucas (1980), winner of the 1995 Nobel Prize in Economics, the theory of trade under uncertainty is developed not through 'an extension of general equilibrium theory [i.e. the theory of competitive markets] not in a mathematical sense, but rather [through] the observation that the range of applicability of this body of theory could be vastly broadened by some ingenuity in specifying what is meant by commodity'.

5.2 The Description of Uncertainty

It is time to define the notion of uncertainty in a more precise manner. Think about two points in times: 'before and after the event', *ex ante* and *ex post*; see Figure 5.1. Beforehand, one may conceive that the world can 'come out' in many possible shapes and forms. We use ω (the Greek letter omega) to index these conceivable outcomes, *states of nature* is the technical economic terminology,

$$\omega = 1, 2, 3, \dots, \Omega. \tag{5.1}$$

Since it is not known, ex ante, which state of nature will be *realized*, we can say that the world is uncertain. Yet, we accept that some outcomes are more likely than others. We measure the likelihood of each outcome by its probability, $\pi_\omega \geq 0$, the higher the probability the more likely the event. We assume that these Ω (capital ω)

The Economics of Financial Markets and Institutions. Oren Sussman, Oxford University Press. © Oren Sussman (2023).
DOI: 10.1093/oso/9780192869739.003.0006

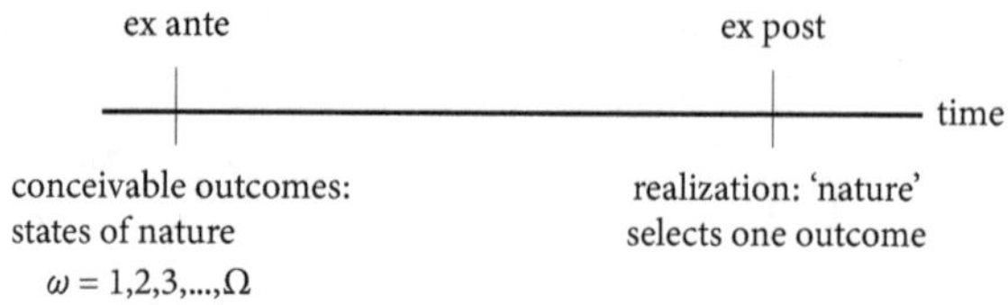

Figure 5.1 Uncertainty and its realization

states of nature capture all conceivable outcomes. It follows that the event 'any one of the Ω states' will be realized with certainty, implying that

$$\Sigma_{\omega=1}^{\Omega} \pi_\omega = 1,$$

1 being the probability of a certain event. Ex post, a force beyond any player's control, call it *nature* for lack of a better word, selects a single outcome. At that point this state becomes a description of the world as it is, while all others become past-time speculations that have never materialized.

5.3 The Market for Risk

In Chapter 1 we show that one can trade future deliveries through future contracts. The mechanism for trading a delivery conditional on the realization of a certain event is through a contract *contingent* on that state of nature. Such contracts are well known from everyday life. For example, fire insurance is a contract that states 'player *A* (the insurer) would pay player *B* (the insured) £*X* in case *B*'s house is destroyed by fire (and zero otherwise)'. To facilitate the application of the competitive model, we abstract the analysis from three common characteristics of the insurance industry. First, while insurance contracts are usually bought from specialized intermediaries, in our model they are traded on competitive markets.[1] We can justify the abstraction on grounds that the risk is ultimately born by the intermediary's shareholders, who can trade their shares on the stock market, making the intermediary just a go-between between the insured and the market. Second, we split the amount X units of income above to X contracts, each delivering one unit of income in the event (and zero otherwise). To be precise, fire insurance is obtained by trading multiples the X^f contract, which pays, across states of nature:

$$x_\omega^f = \begin{cases} 1 & \text{if} \quad \omega = f \\ 0 & \text{if} \quad \omega \neq f \end{cases}, \tag{5.2}$$

[1] It is implied that the payment can be collected by any player who bought the contract on the market, so that the wording of the contract, above, changes from 'pay player *B*' to 'pay the bearer'.

f being the state of nature 'B's house is destroyed by fire'.[2] This abstraction is immaterial. Third we abstract from enforcement costs, including the insurer's default to comply with the term of the contract.

Now consider player B. In case state of nature f is realized, she is left with a much diminished income, y_f, and therefore consumption, relative to a benchmark standard-of-living that she aims to maintain across states of nature. We denote that benchmark by $\bar{c}$. As we shall see below, $\bar{c}$ is actually the standard of living that she can afford to maintain across all states of nature could she trade at particular market prices, called *fair prices,* that would allow her to spread out all the risks that she faces and maintain a stable standard of living in an uncertain environment. (The last sentence takes it for granted that she is risk averse.) Notice that $\bar{c}$ is fixed across states of nature (it has no ω index) but may change across players: some can afford a standard of living higher than others in all states of nature.

Figure 5.2 plots the player's ex-ante subjective valuation of an extra unit of f-contingent income. In line with arguments in Chapters 1 and 4, that DUSV curve is also the demand curve for f-contingent contracts. As the subjective value of an extra unit of income at y_f is higher than the market price of the f-contingent contract, p_f, she would buy $c_f - y_f$ such contracts, bringing her state-f consumption up to c_f. Since $c_f < \bar{c}$ we say that the player is still *exposed* to the risk of fire, though buying insurance, she managed to decreased her exposure—to some extent. Had the price of insurance been sufficiently low, she would buy *full insurance*, to bring her state-f consumption up to the benchmark level, $\bar{c}$. Figure 5.2 also marks the amount spent on buying insurance and the player's surplus from being able to access the market for insurance.

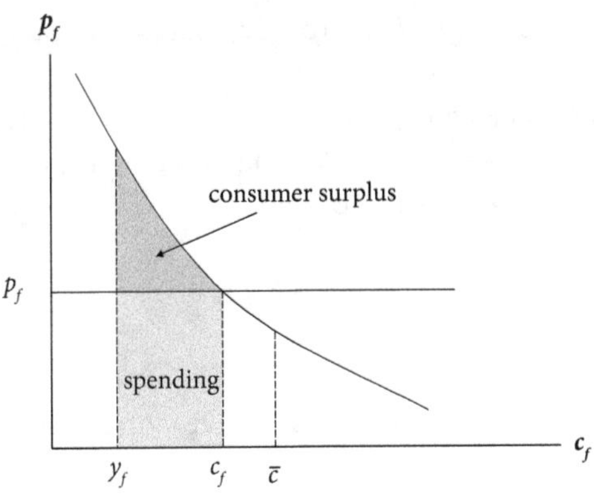

Figure 5.2 The market for fire, event f, insurance contracts

[2] The reader should not be alarmed by the fact that the letter 'f' is used to denote the number of a certain state of nature.

5.3.1 Linear Demand Functions

In the spirit of Chapter 1, we parameterize the demand function using a linear specification. One advantage of the linear function is that it provides a reasonably good approximation to many other non-linear functions. Another important advantage is that it is easy to estimate: just two data points will do; see Section A.2 of the Mathematical Appendix.

Next, we add the probability of the event into the specification. Since a higher likelihood of a state of nature must be associated with a higher subjective valuation of an extra unit of income (at any level of consumption), we write:

$$v_\omega = \pi_\omega (a - b \times c_\omega). \tag{5.3}$$

Notice that the coefficients a and b are fixed across states of nature. That is, ex ante, players differentiate states of nature on grounds of just two variables: probability and the level of consumption.

The arguments above leads us towards one additional assumption:

$$a - b \times \bar{c} = 1. \tag{5.4}$$

To see why, consider a player who is not exposed to any risk (i.e. consumes the benchmark $\bar{c}$ in each and every state of nature). Now consider a 'basket' with Ω contingent contracts, one contract of each state of nature. How would the player evaluate such basket? Clearly, since the basket delivers one unit of income, unconditionally, its value must be, simply, one unit of income:

$$1 = \Sigma_\omega \pi_\omega (a - b\bar{c}) = (a - b\bar{c})\, \Sigma_\omega \pi_\omega = (a - b\bar{c}).$$

It follows that, for any state-contingent contract, the graph of the demand function is a straight line with a slope of $-b\pi_\omega$, passing through the point $(\bar{c}, \pi_\omega)$. It follows that b and $\bar{c}$ already dictate the value of a at:

$$a = 1 + b \times \bar{c}.$$

5.3.2 Risk Aversion and the Demand Function

Intuitively, the more risk-tolerant a player is, the flatter is his demand curve. That is, he is more sensitive to the price of insurance, willing to take on greater risks as the price of insurance increases. Indeed, we can establish a direct relationship between the coefficient of risk aversion as defined in Chapter 1 and the slope of the demand curve for contingent contracts.

Consider a player with a base-level of consumption, $\bar{c}$, facing risk modelled as a random variable, $\tilde{\varepsilon}$, taking values $(-\varepsilon, +\varepsilon)$, 'good' and 'bad' realizations, each with a probability of $\frac{1}{2}$, so that $\tilde{\varepsilon}$ has a zero mean and a variance:

$$\sigma_{\tilde{\varepsilon}}^2 = \frac{1}{2}\varepsilon^2 + \frac{1}{2}(-\varepsilon)^2 = \varepsilon^2. \tag{5.5}$$

Remember that, in Chapter 1, we defined the coefficient of risk aversion as

$$\theta = \frac{S}{\sigma^2/2}, \tag{5.6}$$

where S is the maximum premium that the player is willing to pay in order to dispense with the entire $\tilde{\varepsilon}$ risk. Structured in terms of Equation (5.2) contracts, the player pays an amount S in return for ε contracts contingent on the bad state, but also handing over ε contracts contingent on the good state.

Let us use our model in order to calculate S. Notice that since, for both states of nature, $\pi_\omega = \frac{1}{2}$, the subjective valuation function for a unit of state-contingent consumption is the same for both the good and the bad state: a straight line through the point $(\bar{c}, \pi_\omega)$ with a slope of $-b \times \pi_\omega$. The only difference between the two states is the player's income in the good and bad states: $\bar{c} + \varepsilon$ and $\bar{c} - \varepsilon$, respectively; see Figure 5.3.

While exposed, the player's ex-ante well-being is measured by the a area (namely the combined $a\prime$, $a\prime\prime$ and $a\prime\prime\prime$ subareas) for the bad state and $a + b + c$ for the good state (where b and c are similarly split into primed sub areas). Once the risk is removed, he has the same consumption, $\bar{c}$, in both states of nature, with the same ex-ante level of well-being, $a + b$. It follows that the maximum insurance premium that he is willing to pay for an arrangement that would fully dispense of the $\tilde{\varepsilon}$ risk is:

$$S = 2(a + b) - (2a + b + c) = b - c = b\prime\prime$$

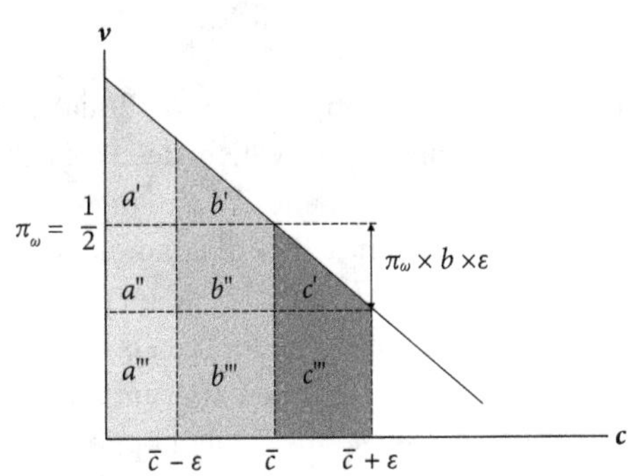

Figure 5.3 Calculating S from consumer surplus

(linearity implies $b' = c'$). The b'' rectangle has a base of ε and a height of $b \times \pi_\omega \times \varepsilon$ (because the ratio between the height and the base of the c' triangle is $b \cdot \pi_\omega$). It follows that, using Equation (5.5)

$$S = area\,(b'') = \frac{b\varepsilon^2}{2} = \frac{b\sigma^2}{2}. \tag{5.7}$$

Comparing Equations (5.6) and (5.7) it follows that:

Proposition 5.1. $\theta = b$, *so that the slope of the demand curve for* ω*-contingent contract is* $-\theta\pi_\omega$.

5.4 Insurance and Investment

Superficial detail often obscures the inherent commonality shared by certain phenomena. Abstracting from that detail allows for the development of a unified conceptual framework, a gain in clarity as well as simplicity and analytic efficiency.[3] Such is the case of investment and insurance, both being driven by a single behavioural motive—risk aversion. The following results highlight this statement. Using

Definition 5.1. A contract is said to be *fairly priced* if $p_\omega = \pi_\omega$,

we can now derive two important results:

Proposition 5.2. *Offered fair insurance, a player would purchase full insurance whether she is highly or lowly risk averse.*

Proposition 5.3. *Offered an investment opportunity at a price below the fair price, both a highly risk averse and a lowly risk averse player would 'take a position' and expose themselves to some risk, albeit the latter invests more aggressively and exposes herself to more risk relative to the latter.*

Proposition 5.2 is an immediate implication of Equations (5.3) and (5.4). For Proposition 5.3 consider Figure 5.4, which describes the demand for an e-contingent contract by two players, Ph and Pl, with high and low coefficients of risk aversion, respectively, and the same $\bar{c}$. The diagrammatic implication of a high risk aversion is a steep demand curve, namely a tendency 'not to take on too much risk' and stay close to $\bar{c}$. A state-e contingent contract is traded at a price, $p_e < \pi_e$, below the fair price. We interpret the selected consumption levels, $c_e^{Pl} > c_e^{Ph}$, as 'more aggressive trading on a high-yield investment opportunity'.

[3] By analytic efficiency I refer to Ockham's famous razor.

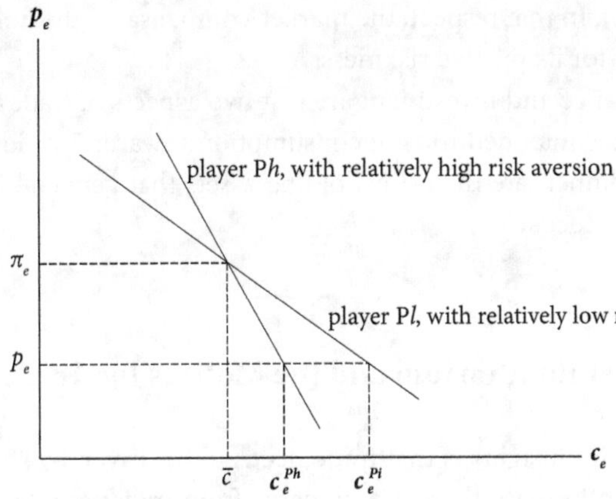

Figure 5.4 Insurance and investment by risk aversion

In the traditional finance literature there is a certain preference for expressing prices in terms of rates of return and treating them, explicitly, as random variables. Doing so we can derive some of the basic intuition for the asset-price results below. As our basic building block is the contract (5.2), the gross rate of return on such a contract is the cash flow that it bears over its market price, namely the random variable,

$$1 + \widetilde{r^e} = \begin{cases} \dfrac{1}{p_e} & \text{if} \quad \omega = e \\ 0 & \text{if} \quad \omega \neq e \end{cases} .$$

Calculating the mean of that random variable we get:

$$E\left(1 + \widetilde{r^e}\right) \begin{cases} > 1 & \text{if} \quad p_e < \pi_e \\ = 1 & \text{if} \quad p_e = \pi_e \\ < 1 & \text{if} \quad p_e > \pi_e \end{cases} . \tag{5.8}$$

Clearly, a high expected rate of return on a state-e contingent contract encourages players to buy an asset that is risky in the sense that it generates income when income is relatively less valued. (Alternatively, it fails to generate income when income is relatively highly valued.) The main business of this chapter is to reverse this logic so as to analyse the determination of $\widetilde{r^e}$, in equilibrium, as a function of the risk that is embedded in state-of-nature e. Obviously, this is just an instance of the common reversal of roles between individual-players' problems, where market prices are taken to be exogenous, and equilibrium problems where the environment is exogenous and the price is endogenized. Hence, high income in state e drives a high supply of e-contingent contracts, resulting in relatively low (high) p_e (expected $\widetilde{r^e}$). In that respect, the market 'compensates' the holder of the e-contingent contract for its relative riskiness.

To conclude, insurance and investment are just two aspects of trade in contingent claims, the former intended to take consumption towards $\bar{c}$ in low-income states, the latter to compensate them for holding assets that generate income in states where income exceeds $\bar{c}$.

5.5 Market Equilibrium and the Motives for Trade

One of Chapter 4's main insights is that trade needs to be driven by some differences across players, otherwise there are no gains from trade; see, for example, the analysis of trade between two countries driven by differences in productivity. Trade in risk is driven by three possible motives: differences in exposure, differences in risk aversion, and differences in beliefs regarding the likelihood of various events.

5.5.1 Trade Driven by Differences in Exposure

Consider an economy with two types, with the same coefficients of risk aversion, each having the same *beliefs*[4] about the likelihood of event e, π_e. We also assume that the two types have the same levels of wealth and, as a result, the same benchmark level of consumption, $\bar{c}$, against which they measure their exposure to risk. Types differ in their initial exposure: type 1 has a high event-e income in comparison to type-2's event-e income: $y_e^{P1} > y_e^{P2}$. Suppose that there is one player of each type, who, nevertheless, behaves as competitive price taker. (Increasing the number of players of each type so as to make the price-taking assumption more credible would result with more cumbersome notation, with no analytical gain.) To analyse the equilibrium, we draw the market demand by horizontal summation of individual demand curves. For convenience, we describe the market in per-capita terms. Since both types have the same demand curves for e-contingent contracts, per-capita demand is the same as the individual demand curve, see Figure 5.5. As for supply, we assume that in this *exchange economy*, so that both y_ω^{P1} and y_ω^{P2} do not result from any production activity; they are just 'manna from heaven', varying across states of nature independently of players' actions and, therefore, not responsive to market prices. Hence, players can sell e-contingent contracts to the extent that they are able to deliver them. (Remember that we do not allow default in this

[4] The distinction between beliefs and expectations is made clearer in Chapter 8.

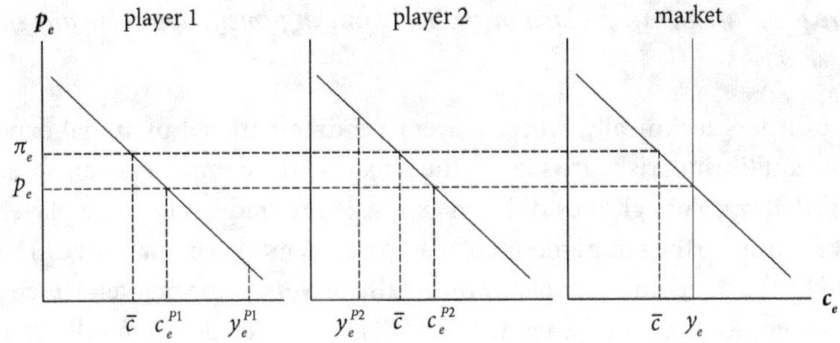

Figure 5.5 Trade due to different exposure

chapter.) It follows that market per-capita supply of state-e contingent contract is just per capita income, which, as it happens, is greater than $\bar{c}$:

$$y_e = \frac{y_e^{P1} + y_e^{P2}}{2} > \bar{c}.$$

Hence, although the e state of nature is 'bad' from $P2$'s point of view, on aggregate, e is a state of affluence. As a result, the equilibrium price, p_e, is below the fair price. A diagrammatic description of the market is provided in Figure 5.5.

Several observations are worth making. First, given that both types have the same demand functions and face the same equilibrium price, they also end up with the same level of state-e consumption. Second, that level of consumption is independent of y_e^{P1} and y_e^{P2} but does depend on aggregate per-capita income, y_e. In fact, $c_e^{P1} = c_e^{P2} = y_e$. Third, trade is motivated by the players' different exposure to risk. Fourth, the gain from trading state contingent contract is in *risk sharing* some of the exposure.

Proposition 5.4 states the result slightly more generally, allowing for any number of players and using some additional commonly used terminology:

Definition 5.2. Let $y_e - y_e^j$ be player j's idiosyncratic risk exposure and let $y_e - \bar{c}$ is the economy's systemic, or macro, risk.

Proposition 5.4. *Consider an economy where all players have the same coefficient of risk aversion, θ, the same beliefs about the likelihood of event e, and the same benchmark against which they measure risk, $\bar{c}$. Then: i) idiosyncratic risk has no effect on the equilibrium price. ii) Through risk-sharing, players eliminate the entire exposure to the idiosyncratic risk. They share, equally, the systemic risk: $c_e^j = y_e$. iii) Where $y_e > \bar{c}$ ($y_e < \bar{c}$) state-e contingent contracts are traded below (above) fair price, a reflection of state-e scarcity of income. iv) In case there is no systemic risk, namely $y_e = \bar{c}$, contracts are fairly priced at $p_e = \pi_e$. v) Since heterogeneity disappears in equilibrium, each player can 'represent' the* *entire population, in equilibrium. vi) The same argument applies to any state of nature ω.*

To put it less technically, where players are differentiated by initial exposure alone, in equilibrium risks are shared, the idiosyncratic component vanishes, or is *diversified away*. Though they differ in exposure pre trade, post trade players are equally exposed to the same amount of macro risk. A market of that sort can be *represented* by the demand curve of any one of the players in the market, which gives rise to a common, yet confusing, manner of speech such as 'the market believes that ...' or 'the market values ...', as if the market has a personality of its own.

5.5.2 Trade Driven by Different Attitudes towards Risk

Different attitude towards risk will cause players to deviate from equal risk sharing, in equilibrium. Consider a market with two players, the first being more risk averse than the other, so that $\theta^{P1} > \theta^{P2}$. Yet, the two types evaluate risk against the same benchmark, $\bar{c}$, and they share the same beliefs about the likelihood of state *e*. It follows that both players' demand curves should be drawn via the point $(\bar{c}, \pi_e)$, albeit the *P*1's is steeper relative to *P*2's; see Figure 5.6. We also assume that the players are not exposed to any idiosyncratic risk, $y_e^{P1} = y_e^{P2} = y_e$, though they are exposed to a certain state-*e* macro risk. Clearly, in equilibrium, *P*2, the more risk tolerant, takes on more of the macro risk relative to *P*1. This is in spite of the fact that equal risk-sharing is feasible. To put it a bit more generally:

Proposition 5.5. *Consider an economy where all players share the same view about the likelihood of state e, and use the same benchmark against which they evaluate risk, $\bar{c}$. They differ, however, by their attitude towards risk: some are more risk averse than others. Then, in equilibrium, the more risk averse would bear less of the macro risk relative to the less risk averse.*

Notice that no single player can represent market in this case.

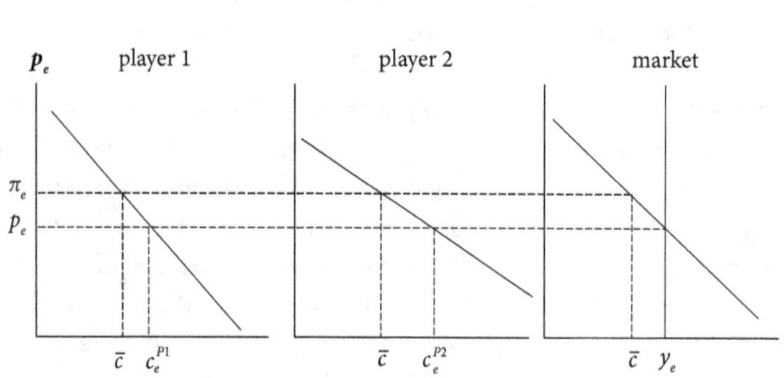

Figure 5.6 Trade due to different risk aversion

5.5.3 Trade Driven by Different Beliefs

Disagreements about the likelihood of an event would drive players away from equal risk sharing, with those players who believe that the event is more likely taking a bet on its realization. Hence, consider an economy with two types, with the same risk aversion, having the same benchmark against which to evaluate risk, but different beliefs: player 1 assigns a higher probability to state-e compared with player 2, so that $\pi_e^{P1} > \pi_e^{P2}$. To highlight the role of differences in beliefs, we also assume away macro risk, $\bar{c} = y_e$, so that without the diversity of beliefs, full insurance for both players is the equilibrium outcome. But given the diversity of beliefs, the demand curves for state-e contingent contracts are drawn via points $(\bar{c}, \pi_e^{P1})$ and $(\bar{c}, \pi_e^{P2})$, the former curve being steeper than the latter; see Figure 5.7. Now, equilibrium price lies in between π^{P1} and π^{P2}. To see why, check whether π_e^{P1} can be an equilibrium price: $P1$ has no desire to trade as at a price of π_1 he is already satisfied with $c_e^{P1} = \bar{c}$, which equals his income; in contrast, at such a high price $P2$ would like to sell off state-e contingent contracts, so the market is in a state of excess supply. It follows that the equilibrium price is below π_e^{P1}. By a similar argument, the market is in excess demand at π_e^{P2} and, therefore, the equilibrium price must be above π_e^{P2}. It follows that in equilibrium, player 1 trades to a point where $c_e^1 > \bar{c}$ while player 2 trades to the point where $c_e^2 < \bar{c}$. Less technically, player 1 bets on event e, bidding the price up to a level that tempts player 2 to trade out of the state $\bar{c}$. As we have assumed, neither is initially exposed to idiosyncratic risk, that is $y_e^{P1} = y_e^{P2} = y_e$, $P1$ would buy e-contingent contracts and $P2$ would sell them – in equilibrium. More generally,

Proposition 5.6. *Even in the absence of systemic risk, but with players having different beliefs regarding the probability of state e, players deviate from full insurance, those who assign higher (low) probability to event e increase (decrease) their consumption by buying (selling) state-e contingent contracts—in equilibrium.*

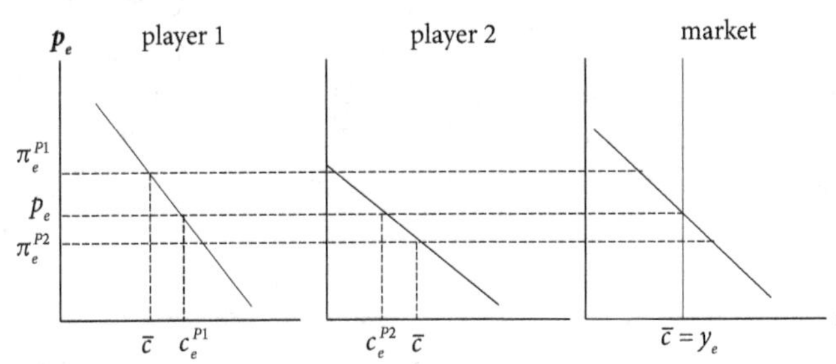

Figure 5.7 Trade driven by differences in beliefs

5.6 Normative Analysis

Regarding economic efficiency, our analysis is both obvious and surprising: all the normative results of Chapter 4, particularly the First Welfare Theorem and Second Welfare Theorem apply. Hence, it is conceivable that competitive financial markets can achieve economic efficiency without any regulation. The only policy that is required is to avoid any restrictions on trade in state-contingent contracts and to enforce any written contract to the last iota. As we shall see in the next three chapters, this conclusion strongly depends on the frictionless nature of the kind of economy described in Chapter 4; in particular, on the assumption that *markets are complete*, so that every commodity has a market in which it can be traded; every commodity is priced. In terms of this chapter, there are Ω markets to trade contracts contingent on each and every state of nature. Notice that there is no requirement that contracts actually change hands; an equilibrium price that generates a zero volume of trade qualifies for the requirement that 'there is a market to trade ...'. For example, in case where $y_{\omega}^{P1} = y_{\omega}^{P2} = \bar{c}$, and where players are homogeneous in their beliefs and their attitude to risk, the equilibrium price is π_e, but there is no active trade; the *volume of trade* is zero. In fact, the equilibrium price is that which removes any motive to trade out of the full-insurance point, $\bar{c}$, as there is no economic motive to justify a departure from this allocation, which happens to be Pareto efficient to begin with.

As we shall see below, completeness is a very strong assumption that is not very likely to hold in reality. Yet, at least from an analytical point of view, the observation that economic efficiency in financial market is conceivable under some, albeit highly unrealistic assumptions, is a very useful idea, providing a benchmark against which real-world arrangements can be evaluated.

5.7 Empirical Tests of Risk Sharing

In his seminal paper, Robert Townsend (1994) suggests a test of risk-sharing and applies it to three tiny, very poor, villages in North India, Aurepalle, Shirapur, and Kanzara, each having less than 50 households. Each village is treated as a mini economy. The only reason for selecting these villages is that during the period 1970–1980s, a non-profit research institute, ICRISAT, had laboriously collected detailed consumption data for the households living in these villages.

Poor agricultural communities are highly exposed to natural risks such as weather, animal, or crop disease. Crucially, there is no reason to think that such risks equally affects each and every household in the village. For example, high precipitation can flood lowlands fields but may be a blessing to elevated plots. Households specializing in animal farming are not exposed to crop disease but are exposed to animal disease. On top of this, there are the ordinary idiosyncratic risks, such as illness of the family's breadwinner, fire etc. It follows that there are as many risk-sharing opportunities within such a village community as there are in a developed economy with specialized financial market.

Proposition 5.4 offers a benchmark for the analysis of the data. Needless to say, competitive markets in state-contingent contracts are unlikely to exist in such small and underdeveloped communities. However, here we draw upon Second Welfare Theorem: since any Pareto-efficient allocation can be implemented by a competitive equilibrium, we can use our competitive model in order to hypothesize the characteristics of a Pareto-efficient risk allocation. We can then test the hypothesis that risk is efficiently shared, whether the data originates in a competitive market or some other social organization based on say, custom or familial bondage.

Fortunately, under the assumptions of Proposition 5.4, the characteristics of the Pareto-efficient allocation are remarkably easy to derive: macro risk is equally shared by all members of the community, while idiosyncratic risk has no effect on individual consumption. More accurately, under the null hypothesis of efficient risk sharing, player (household) j's consumption in period t, c_t^j, equals period-t per-capita income, y_t, where $j = 1, 2, \ldots, J$ is an index that runs across the members of each community. (Obviously, y_t has no j index.) At the same time, an individual's own income, y_t^j, should have no effect on the her consumption. We can therefore run, for each player separately, the linear regression:

$$c_t^j = \alpha^j + \beta^j y_t + \gamma^j y_t^j + \varepsilon_t^j,$$

and test the hypothesis:

$$H_0 : \qquad \beta^j = 1, \qquad \gamma^j = 0.$$

Prior to the execution of a regression analysis, it is always useful to look at the raw data. Figure 5.8 provides a three-dimensional plot for one of the villages, Aurepalle (taken from Figures 1 and 3 in Townsend (1994)). The 'floor' of the box

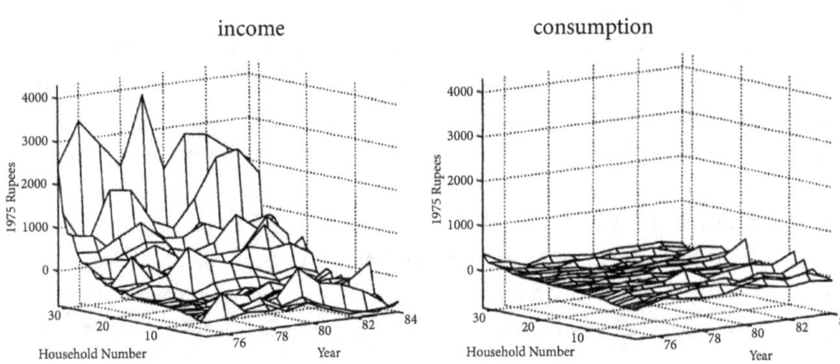

Figure 5.8 Townsend's data, income, and consumption for Aurepalle

Table 5.1 Townsend's test of risk sharing

village	N	for which H_0 cannot be rejected	
		$\beta = 1$	$\gamma = 0$
Aurepalle	44	38	32
Shirapur	45	35	31
Kanzara	44	34	33

has the year and the household index number on the axes, while the vertical axis has income and consumption, measured in inflation-adjusted Rupees. Hence, each of the solid lines 'floating' above the floor of the box is a plot of a certain household's income and consumption—over time. It takes no complicated statistical analysis to notice the very substantial 'smoothness' of consumption relative to income, over time and across households.

Table 5.1's results are based on formal regression analysis (taken from Tables IV and V in the published paper). It reports the number of households for which the null hypothesis could not be rejected at the 5% significance level. It turns out to be the majority in all three villages. Some evidence in the paper is consistent with the idea that landless households are more likely to be excluded from risk sharing compared with land-owning families. As already hinted above, it is likely that risk sharing is obtained via customary arrangements such as gift-giving to villagers who fall on hard times. Landless households may be excluded from the social networks that manage such relationships.

One may dismiss Townsend's evidence as irrelevant to the understanding of a sophisticated market economy. Alternatively, one may emphasize that diversity in social organizations may obscure a commonality of purpose: to provide a hedge against risk. To put it differently, abstracting from 'cultural' detail, these Indian villages may have developed effective institutions, less sophisticated in their legal and financial structure compared with a developed market economy, yet remarkably suitable to the economic conditions of these villages.

To demonstrate the general applicability of Townsend's method we present, in Table 5.2, another application, by Obstfeld (1994), to test the amount of cross-country risk sharing (based on Table 6 in the published paper). Many of the β^j coefficients are surprisingly close to 1, though the standard errors, in parentheses, are quite high. A '∗' symbol indicates that the parameter differs from 1 at the 5% significance level. It is worth noting that applied on a macro level, the technique is a test of the risk-sharing efficiency of the financial system as a whole—bonds, stocks, derivatives, and foreign exchange markets—rather than each component separately. Indeed, the question whether each component is efficient on its own is meaningless.

Table 5.2 Obstfeld's test of cross-country risk sharing

Country	1951–1972	1973–1988
Canada	1.29 (0.34)	0.84 (1.02)
France	0.55 (0.27)	0.63 (0.26)
Germany	0.06 (0.51)	1.14 (0.37)
Italy	0.13* (0.44)	0.68 (0.47)
Japan	0.45 (0.58)	1.45 (0.36)
UK	1.00 (0.47)	1.77 (0.49)
US	1.77* (0.22)	1.53* (0.20)

5.8 Arbitrage, Arrow-Debreu Securities, and Complex Securities

The idea of arbitrage was already presented in Chapter 1: if lending and buying a future contract are two, perfectly substitutable methods of acquiring a future delivery, then their prices should be tightly linked, otherwise there will be an opportunity for infinite profit. This simple idea is used extensively by financial practitioners so as to 'price' new, not presently traded, financial instruments—*financial innovations.* The basic idea is that market prices of existing instruments already contain a very substantial amount of information about the market valuation of risk. If only we can decompose these prices to more primitive building blocks, we may be able to reassemble them in the pricing of any financial innovation.

Financial markets are characterized by an extraordinary diversity of financial instruments, some of which may be highly complex. Yet, provided that our Ω states of nature indeed capture all conceivable realizations, even the most complex security can be described, simply, by listing the income that it generates in each state. Let x^s_ω be the income that security s generates in state of nature ω. Hence,

$$X^s = (x^s_1, x^s_2, x^s_3, \ldots, x^s_\Omega),$$

is a general formulation of any conceivable *complex security* whether it is already used, considered as an innovation or, perhaps, will never be traded.

Definition 5.3. Like the fire-insurance contract in Equation (5.2), an Arrow-Debreu Security, (ADS) pays one unit of income in state ω and zero otherwise. Its general formula is, therefore, $(0, 0, \ldots, 1, \ldots, 0, 0)$. An economy that has a full set of Ω ADSs, a contract for each and every state, is called a *complete-markets* economy. In such an economy, any risk has a price tag. It is not implied that there is active trade in each and every one of the Ω markets.

No extra notation for the price is required: p_ω is, simply, the price of the ADS that pays one unit of income in state ω and zero in all other states. ADSs are named in honour of Kenneth Arrow and Gerard Debreu, winners of the 1972 and 1983 Nobel Prize in Economics, respectively.

In such an economy, a complex security X^s can be priced, by arbitrage:

$$q^s = \Sigma_{\omega=1}^{\Omega} p_\omega \times x_\omega^s.$$

That is, the complex security is viewed as a basket of ADSs, where the delivery of x_ω^s units of income by the s security in state of nature ω is viewed as the income delivered by x_ω^s state-ω ADSs. Since the state-ω ADS has a market price of p_ω, the ex-ante value of the delivery is $p_\omega \times x_\omega^s$. Repeating the operation for all states of nature, from 1 to Ω and adding up we derive the price of the entire basket, that is the complex security s. In that respect, the job of pricing a complex security is no different, in principle, than the job of cashier who needs to add up the values of the goods in a supermarket trolley.

Obviously, ADSs do not exist in reality; only complex securities do. So what does it mean to price by arbitrage 'as if' the ADSs exist? The answer is that we think of ADSs as the small particles, the atoms, of the financial system, from which all other structures are assembled, even though these atoms cannot be observed in isolation. Likewise, many chemical elements do not exist in nature in pure form, only as parts of more complex molecules. Notwithstanding, the observation that all the 'stuff' that exist in nature is made of just 94 simpler building blocks is an amazing insight of the science of chemistry, of great theoretical and practical value.

5.9 Some Classic Results

The following are some of the most famous results in financial economics. They are described in many finance textbooks in greater detail but, often, in a way that mars the fundamental economic argument that deliver them. We try to fill in this gap using the framework developed above.

5.9.1 The Modigliani–Miller Theorem

Debt and equity are the most common complex securities; see Chapter 3. Denote their cash flows by d_ω and e_ω, respectively. Suppose that all of the company's income, x_ω, is distributed (to both external and internal investors) via these two contracts:

$$x_\omega = d_\omega + e_\omega.$$

Now let D and E be the market value of the company's debt and equity. Then, the value of the company, that is the sum of all the claims against the cash flow that it generates, is:

$$\begin{aligned} D + E &= \Sigma_{\omega=1}^{\Omega} p_\omega \times d_\omega + \Sigma_{\omega=1}^{\Omega} p_\omega \times e_\omega \\ &= \Sigma_{\omega=1}^{\Omega} p_\omega (d_\omega + e_\omega) \\ &= \Sigma_{\omega=1}^{\Omega} p_\omega x_\omega. \end{aligned}$$

Proposition 5.7. *The value of a company is independent of its capital structure, namely the distribution of its cash flow, x_ω, across debt and equity payments.*

In fact, the proof makes no use of the structure of debt and equity, as described in Chapter 3. It could apply to any two (or even more) assets that absorb the company's income. Notice that the linear approximation of the ADS price as a function of players' equilibrium consumption is not necessary in the derivation of the result. The above is just a simple exercise in arbitrage pricing.

It is sometimes argued that the Theorem presents a 'puzzle': how come a decision that is considered critical by so many real-world companies is deemed irrelevant by financial theory? A benign answer is that the competitive, frictionless, complete-markets model may not be suitable for the analysis of the capital-structure problem. In fact, Chapter 3's discussion of the Hart and Moore (1998) model already demonstrates that a friction that keeps certain contingencies out of a debt contract would affect the value of the firm. A more structured analysis is presented in Chapter 7.

Section 5.11, below, presents, and comments on, the response of the traditional finance literature: that capital structure is determined by the trade-off between the tax advantage of debt against its disadvantage of exposing the company to the hazard of bankruptcy.

5.9.2 Derivative Pricing

Standard derivative-pricing techniques are another important application of arbitrage arguments, though the standard text-books tend to emphasize arguments that do not involve ADSs. To demonstrate the point, we take one such text-book example, from chapter 20 in Brealey and Myers (2002), and reformulate it into the current setting.

Consider a share that currently trades at a price of 85. It is anticipated that in the next period the price will either drop to 68 or will increase to 106.25. No extra information about the probability of these events is required, though it is assumed that such information is already 'priced into' the current price. (Remember that although the current price is 'much closer' to the down price than to the up price, state prices reflect the scarcity of income in the state, as well as its probability.) It is worth informing the reader, who may doubt the practical relevance of a formulation that includes only two states, up and down states, u and d respectively, that using such binomial distributions repeatedly over multiple periods can provide quite a realistic description of the evolution of share prices over time, at least in times when the markets are 'not in turmoil'. However, the technical detail of such dynamic multi-period modelling lies well out of the scope of this book.

Consider a *call option* on the said share, namely a contract the gives the bearer the right to buy (not an obligation to buy!) the share, next period, at a certain *exercise price* of 85. That right is worthless in the d state since no one would buy a share for 85 when it can be bought on the open market for 68. In contrast, exercising the option is profitable in the u state, when the market price is 106.25, leaving the bearer with a profit of 106.25 – 85 = 21.25. It follows that the option is equivalent to 21.25 ADSs that deliver one unit when $\omega = u$ and zero otherwise.

The information provided so far is not sufficient in order to extract two ADS prices, p_d and p_u. Although it follows from the above analysis that the share is just a basket with 68 (106.25) d (u) ADSs, from which it follows that the current price of 85 must be:

$$85 = 68 \times p_d + 106.25 \times p_u, \tag{5.9}$$

this single equation, which is not sufficient in order to solve out two unknown prices. However, just one additional complex security, say a riskless bond, will do. Suppose that the riskless interest rate is 2.5%. Then, a bond priced at 1 must be discounting the same cash flow, 1.025, across both the u and the d states of nature:

$$1 = 1.025 \times p_d + 1.025 \times p_u. \tag{5.10}$$

Together, Equations (5.9) and (5.10) allow us to solve out for two ADS prices. The rest is just algebra:

$$p_u = \frac{85 - \frac{68}{1.025}}{106.25 - 68} = 10.36$$

and

$$q_{\substack{\text{call option} \\ \text{exercise price}=85}} = 21.25 \times p_u. \tag{5.11}$$

Notice that, again, the linear approximation of the ADS price as a function of players' equilibrium consumption is not necessary in the derivation of the result. Notice, also, that for this calculation we ignore all the other securities that are traded in the market, with the many states of nature that affect them. That might be justified on grounds that the option is just a *derivative*, namely a security that is derived by writing a contract on another security, in which case 'most of the information' that is relevant to the derivative's price must be contained in the *underlying contract*. How well this assumption works in practice is more a matter of experience than economic theory.

It is worth commenting that the competitive model 'works much better' for derivative pricing than for capital structure. It is an additional reminder, if one is necessary, that no single economic model can answer all our questions, and that even a model that provides good answers to one question may not perform that well in answering some other questions.

5.9.3 The Capital Asset Pricing Model (CAPM)

Consider a finance practitioner who is asked to assess the value of an unlisted company, s, towards a *listing* of its shares for trading on the stock exchange, an *initial public offering* (IPO) in finance lingo. The company is unique and cannot be priced by comparison to similar companies. (Say, this is an hypothetical IPO of a privatized London Underground System.) Unlike in the previous case, it is no longer plausible that the IPO price,

$$q^s = \Sigma_\omega p_\omega x^s_\omega, \tag{5.12}$$

can, somehow, be reduced to just two states of nature, u and d. However, progress can be made by making stronger assumptions: that, as in Proposition 5.4, players differ just by their initial exposure. As we have seen there, in equilibrium, perfect risk sharing washes away all idiosyncratic risk, so that equilibrium state prices are determined by per-capita (macro) income alone:

$$p_\omega = \pi_\omega \left(a - \theta y_\omega\right). \tag{5.13}$$

In fact, linearity decreases the number of parameters to just two: a and the coefficient of risk aversion, θ. If, in addition, we have information about the statistical properties of the two random variables, x^s and y, then we can price the IPO.

To estimate two parameters, just two securities are sufficient. For that purpose, better select two securities that trade at a high volume, so that their market is liquid enough to minimize random fluctuations in the price. The two natural candidates for the job are riskless (government) bonds,

$$1 = \left(1 + r^f\right) \Sigma_\omega p_\omega \tag{5.14}$$

(since r^f is constant across states it can be factored out of the summation), and the entire market,

$$q^m = \Sigma_\omega p_\omega y_\omega, \tag{5.15}$$

'the market' being, simply, the claims against the entire economy. The rest is just algebraic manipulation: solve out for a and θ, substitute into Equation (5.12) and price the IPO. It is worth mentioning, however, that in practice, unlike in Section 5.5.1, stock markets trade claims against a certain part of the economy but not its entirety, in which case one needs to limit the interpretation of y_ω accordingly, but we can ignore this technical detail at the current level of abstraction.

Some of this algebra is interesting enough to deserve our attention. Using the state prices (5.13) in Equations (5.12) and (5.14), replacing the summation operators by statistical notation and using some of the covariance rules from Section A.3.2 of the Mathematical Appendix,[5] we get:

$$q^s = [a - \theta E(\widetilde{y})]\, E(\widetilde{x}^s) - \theta \times Cov(\widetilde{x}^s, \widetilde{y}),$$

and

$$1 = \left(1 + r^f\right)[a - \theta E(\widetilde{y})],$$

which, combined, yield the basic pricing equation:

$$q^s = \frac{E(\widetilde{x}^s)}{\left(1 + r^f\right)} - \theta Cov(\widetilde{x}^s, \widetilde{y}). \tag{5.16}$$

Notice that the use of probabilistic notation, $\widetilde{y}$, say, instead of the longer '$y_1, \ldots, y_\Omega$ with probabilities $\pi_1, \ldots, \pi_\Omega$' does not change the substance of the model. Notwithstanding, it is an important step in the direction of operationalizing it, showing how to reduce the bewildering complexity of a world with Ω possible realizations into data with concrete statistical interpretation.

Equation (5.16) has a simple and intuitive interpretation: the value of the IPO is expected cash flow of company s, discounted using the riskless rate, minus a risk-adjustment term, which is increasing in the risk-aversion coefficient of the representative player and in the covariance between the cash flow of company s and the consumption of the representative player. That is, comparing two IPOs that generate the same expected cash flows, the first turning high cash flows in 'good times', and the second turning high cash flows in 'bad times', the first would generate a lower IPO price—a direct implication of the DUSV assumption and, therefore, of risk aversion. The intuition for the result is derived straight from Proposition 5.2.

[5] Particularly, that for any random variables x and y,

$$Cov(\widetilde{x}, \widetilde{y}) = E(\widetilde{x} \times \widetilde{y}) - E(\widetilde{x}) \times E(\widetilde{y}).$$

Noting that Equation (5.16) applies to any asset, including the market itself, and using another statistical result from Section A.3.2 of the Mathematical Appendix,[6] we get

$$q^m = \frac{E(\widetilde{y})}{(1+r^f)} - \theta \times Var(\widetilde{y},\widetilde{y}). \quad (5.17)$$

The last step in the derivation of the CAPM formula is purely technical: we express prices in terms of rates of return and, then, solve out for θ by dividing Equation (5.16) by Equation (5.17):

$$E(\widetilde{r}^s) = r^f + \beta^s\left[E(\widetilde{r}^m) - r^f\right], \qquad \beta^s = \frac{Cov(\widetilde{r}^m,\widetilde{r}^s)}{Var(\widetilde{r}^m)}, \quad (5.18)$$

with the detail relegated to this chapter's appendix. The basic intuition of the formula, is already included in the discussion of Equation (5.8). The formula served generations of financial practitioners in order to answer questions such as the pricing of an IPO, by estimating an s-specific risk adjustment factor, β^s, and using it in order to derive a risk-adjusted interest discount rate for company s.

5.9.3.1 CAPM and Idiosyncratic Risk

It is quite clear why, under Section 5.5.1's complete-markets assumption, idiosyncratic risk is not priced: because that risk is eliminated in equilibrium. In practice, many idiosyncratic risks are hardly insurable; for example unemployment, personal circumstances such as divorce, or certain medical conditions. One may think that these risks should have a big effect on traders willingness to hold risky securities and, thereby, on security prices. Somewhat surprisingly, this is not the case: idiosyncratic risk 'is not priced', only macro risk does. To be precise, even when idiosyncratic risk is present, we can still use state prices as specified in Equation (5.13), substituting in the economy's aggregate per-capita income, y_ω, ignoring the fact that players' incomes actually deviate from the aggregate by idiosyncratic risks.

To see why, consider a player with the following DUSV function for state-e contingent commodity:

$$v_e = \pi_e(a - \theta c_e).$$

Suppose that the price of the e-contingent security is p'_e, to which the player responds by trading to the point where his state-e consumption is c'_e. Now, suppose that we expose the player, in state e, to an additional risk[7], $\widetilde{\varepsilon}$, with outcomes of $\pm\varepsilon$ (good, bad), each with a probability of $\frac{1}{2}$. No insurance against the $\widetilde{\varepsilon}$ risk is

[6] That for any random variable, $\widetilde{x}$, $Cov(\widetilde{x},\widetilde{x}) = Var(\widetilde{x})$.

[7] Strictly speaking, this is an abuse of terminology since the extra risk splits the e event into two states of nature; we use it for simplicity of exposition.

available, so that the market is incomplete. Notice that due to idiosyncratic nature of the extra risk,

$$E(\tilde{\varepsilon}|\omega = e) = 0.$$

To see how the extra risk affects the demand for e-contingent securities, compute the subjective valuation of an e-contingent contract at the c'_e level of state-e consumption:

$$v'_{e,\tilde{\varepsilon}} = \frac{1}{2}\pi_e \left[a - \theta\left(c'_e + \varepsilon\right)\right] \tag{5.19}$$

$$+ \frac{1}{2}\pi_e \left[a - \theta\left(c'_e - \varepsilon\right)\right]$$

$$= v'_e. \tag{5.20}$$

Clearly the extra risk has no effect on the valuation of the e-contingent security at the c'_e level of consumption (or at any other level consumption). It follows that the player trades the same amount of e-contingent contracts, with and without the extra risk, $\tilde{\varepsilon}$. Needless to say, due to incompleteness, there is an unsatisfied demand for $\tilde{\varepsilon}$-contingent contracts, but that demand cannot be satisfied by trading extra e-contingent contracts, as the $\tilde{\varepsilon}$ is independent of event e.

The argument modifies, somewhat, for another risk term, $\widetilde{\varepsilon''}$, with outcomes $\pm\varepsilon$, and a probability of $\frac{3}{4}$ for the bad outcome, so that

$$E\left(\widetilde{\varepsilon''}|\omega = e\right) = -\frac{1}{2}\varepsilon;$$

clearly, $\widetilde{\varepsilon''}$ is not an idiosyncratic risk.

Substituting the probabilities of $\widetilde{\varepsilon''}$ in an equation similar to (5.19) it is clear that the demand for e-contingent contract is affected: the curve is shifted upwards. Intuitively, given that, in state e, a bad realization of the idiosyncratic risk is more likely than the good realization, the player increases his demand for the e-contingent contracts—as a hedge.

We can actually calculate an extra amount, Δ, of e-contingent contracts that the player buys at the p'_e price:

$$p'_e = \frac{1}{4}\pi_e \left[a - \theta\left(c'_e + \Delta + \varepsilon\right)\right]$$

$$+ \frac{3}{4}\pi_e \left[a - \theta\left(c'_e + \Delta - \varepsilon\right)\right]$$

or, collecting terms, which solves out:

$$\Delta_e = \frac{1}{2}\varepsilon.$$

It follows that

$$E\left(c_e' + \Delta_e + \widetilde{\varepsilon''}\right) = \frac{1}{4}\left(c_e' + 1\frac{1}{2}\varepsilon\right) + \frac{3}{4}\left(c_e' - \frac{1}{2}\varepsilon\right) = c_e'.$$

That is, after trading away that part of $\widetilde{\varepsilon''}$ that is correlated with event e, the player is left with an idiosyncratic residual, which has no pricing implications. Notice that Δ_e is independent of θ.

The good news is that our pricing results are resilient to certain forms of market incompleteness. (The careful reader will notice that the linearity of the DUSV function plays an important part in that conclusion.) At the same time, it is also important to notice that this applies just to pricing but not to welfare. Idiosyncratic risk still diverts consumption from the complete-markets consumption level, c_e' by $+1\frac{1}{2}\varepsilon$ in the 'good' outcome and $-\frac{1}{2}\varepsilon$ (for the $\widetilde{\varepsilon''}$ case, after the extra Δ trading).

5.9.3.2 Selling Short

It is easy to get carried away with the mathematical elegance of the argument and forget that the derived statistical expressions are generated by securities markets, operated by humans, affected by behavioural factors, as well as by trading frictions. To highlight the point, we provide a brief and preliminary analysis of one of the more common of these frictions, a restriction on short sales.

So far, we have made no distinctions between buying and selling contingent claims. For example, in Figure 5.5's analysis, player 1 sells e-contingent contracts and player 2 buys them; to put it differently, player 2 traded a positive amount of contracts while player 1 traded a negative amount. Mathematically, there is nothing particularly interesting in the distinction between positive and negative numbers. (Similarly, to Chapter 1, where we have argued that in a perfect debt market, the difference between lending and borrowing is just the ± signs.)

In practice, selling securities that one does not have is not straightforward. Yet, traders buy (sell) securities whose random cash flows they evaluate, subjectively, above (below) market price. They might want to sell such a security even if they don't have it. To do so, they borrow the security, sell it, and buy it again when the obligation to return the security is due. While in debt of that security, the obligation to deliver the security is, effectively, a negative position in the security, *going short* in finance lingo.

It is often the case that short sales cannot be executed due to either high transaction costs or a regulation that prohibits the trade. The full analysis of such restrictions in the market for complex securities lies well beyond the scope of this book. But we can provide a preliminary idea by looking at the effect of an imposed short-sell constraint in the market for state-e contingent contracts as in Figure 5.5.

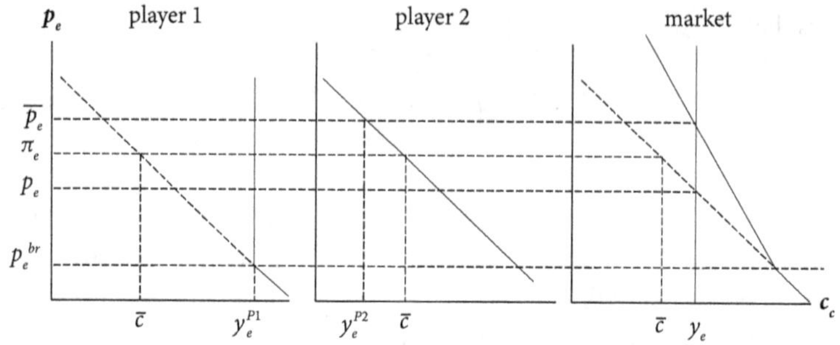

Figure 5.9 The effect of short-sale restrictions

Clearly, the constraint directly affects player 1, who has high event-e income and, therefore, sells e-contingent claims in the unrestricted equilibrium. But facing a restriction on selling short, his demand curve turns vertical at prices higher than p_e^{br}, where his demand turns negative. Pre-restriction demand is marked with a broken line; see Figure 5.9. That would affect the market demand as well, which breaks, becoming steeper at prices higher than p_e^{br}. Clearly, short-sale restrictions increase the equilibrium price, from p_e, without the restriction, to $\overline{p_e}$ with the restrictions. Notice that once player 1 cannot sell state-e contingent contracts, player 2 has no one to buy them from. It follows that the equilibrium price, $\overline{p_e}$, is determined so that player-2's demand for the security is zero.

5.10 The Equity-Premium Puzzle

Useful as the CAPM formula is for the financial practitioner, it is somewhat unsatisfactory for the financial economists. The argument, as presented above, was to solve out for a and θ so as to price the IPO. Doing so, we 'cancelled out' θ in the last stages of the derivation of the CAPM formula. However, doing so, we have ignored an important economic question: are securities prices actually explained by the behavioural parameter that was driving the whole analysis, namely the coefficient of risk aversion?

To be more specific, in that last stage of the derivation, the financial practitioner calculates the *premium* on the value of the s company, $E(\tilde{r}^s) - r^f$, and the premium on the market, $E(\tilde{r}^m) - r^f$, then uses β^s in order to express the ratio between the two; see the more detailed calculations in this chapter's appendix. Finding that company s is β^s times more risky than the market is sufficient for the discounting of the company's cash flows. That θ cancels out is a blessing for the financial practitioner, who is not interested in the explaining market prices.

In contrast, the financial economist's main interest is in testing whether the amount of risk that players are allocated in equilibrium explain the equilibrium price, given their risk aversion. Surprisingly, financial economists ignored this important question for a long time, until Mehra and Prescott (1985)[8] (the latter is the winner of the 2004 Nobel Prize in Economics) have gone back to the basic pricing formulas (5.16) and (5.17) and discovered, to the amazement of many, that the theory is rejected by the data: risk aversion and the actual level of risk exposure do not explain the risk premium as observed in the stock market.

Mehra and Prescott focus their analysis on the equity premium, $E(\tilde{r}^m) - r^f$, namely the premium that equity holders collect 'in return' for holding the entire portfolio of risky stock-market traded securities. Though they test the model using a multi-period model, we can get the essence of the argument from an adapted Equation (5.17). In such a multi period framework, the main risk facing investors is an economy-wide 'slow down' and, as a result, a stock-market 'crash'. If so, we have to adjust Equation (5.17) so that the risk of a drop in next-year's income is measured against this year's income, y_0, which is normalized to one.[9] We relegate the technicalities to this chapter's appendix, but notice that in the adapted formula,

$$E(\tilde{r}^m) - r^f = A_0 \theta Var(\tilde{g}_y), \tag{5.21}$$

risk is measured in terms of the economy's growth rate

$$\tilde{g}_y = \frac{\tilde{y}}{y_0} - 1$$

(the detail of the derivation are relegated to this chapter's appendix). A_0 is a constant, roughly equal to one and, therefore, ignored in the rest of the discussion. That, in the adapted formula, risk is measured by the entire economy's growth rate, is a direct implication of Section 5.5.1's assumption: since players trade away all idiosyncratic risk, what is left over is just the risk of the entire economy.

Table 5.3 presents the data, all adjusted for inflation. The risk premium during a sample almost a hundred years long, including two world wars and the Great Depression, is about 6%. The standard deviation of the economy's growth rate is 3%, implying a variance rounded up to just 0.1% (one-tenth of a percent, 0.03^2). It follows that only a θ of around 60 could reconcile the data and the theory. In fact, most empirical studies of the insurance market find a coefficient between 1 and 10, with the majority of the estimates closer to one. Hence the Equity Premium Puzzle, a dramatic rejection of the theory.

Most disappointingly, the result does not originate in some incomprehensible mathematical argument. To the contrary: it actually captures some remarkably

[8] Relying on earlier work by Lucas (1978).

[9] Implied by this argument is the need to measure risk in relative terms, to account for changes in y_0 over the years. In fact, a coefficient of relative risk aversion is used by Mehra and Prescott, a fact that can be glossed over in our static presentation.

Table 5.3 Mehra–Prescott data, US 1889–1978

	Mean	Standard Deviation
Growth rate of per-capita consumption	1.83%	3.57%
Rate of return on a risk-free security	0.80%	5.67%
Rate of return on the S&P 500	6.98%	16.54%
The risk premium	6.18%	16.67%

simple and intuitive considerations. While idiosyncratic risk can be traded away, the representative player has no one to whom she can 'sell' the macro risk: all other traders already bear, in equilibrium, the same amount of that risk and are not willing to take on any extra—at the equilibrium prices. The very definition of risk aversion (already in Chapter 1) implies that could she insure herself, she would be willing to pay a premium equal to her risk aversion times (one half) the variance of that risk. In fact, this is the kind of a premium that she pays for fire or automobile insurance, which generate the data from which Mehra and Prescott estimation θ in the first place. Since the risk of stock-market securities cannot be traded away, the prices of these securities need to be adjusted so that the representative player is willing to bear it. By how much? Obviously by the same premium as measured in the insurance market. In theory, a premium of an order of magnitude $\theta Var(\tilde{g}_y)$ should be sufficient, removing away any desire to sell the risk off. Essentially, the puzzle is: why are investors so much more sensitive to stock-market risk than they are to fire risk?

However, it is important to recognize that Mehra and Prescott reject an hypothesis that is derived from a model that makes very strong assumptions regarding complete markets, absence of trading frictions, full information, as well as linear subjective-valuation functions. Obviously, 'something' important is missing from this model. Financial economists have experimented with many candidates for 'the' missing link; although some success has been registered, it is fair to say that no professional consensus has risen—yet.

5.11 A Note on the Tradeoff Theory

It is a fact of life that corporate income tax is levied on profit but not on interest payments. Let corporate income tax rate be τ.[10] Hence, in states of nature where the company is solvent, it pays its bond-holders a fixed amount, R, and its equity holders $(x_\omega - R)(1 - \tau)$. Hence, payments to creditors are tax exempt while payments to

[10] We abstract from personal income taxes. Alternatively, interpret τ as the tax advantage of debt finance after accounting for the income tax that the debt holder pays on interest income.

equity holders are not. That gives the company a strong incentive to avoid equity finance. To balance off this effect, it is argued that debt has the disadvantage of increasing the likelihood of bankruptcy, which has a fixed cost, b. Hence, the company chooses its capital structure so as to balance off these effects.

To see how that works, consider a company with state-contingent cash flows (gross of debt payments and bankruptcy costs) labelled (just for the ease of exposition) so that

$$x_1 < x_2 < \ldots < x_\Omega.$$

Let ρ be the threshold solvency state so that the company is bankrupt in states of nature $\omega = 1, 2, \ldots, \rho - 1$ and solvent in states of nature $\omega = \rho, \rho + 1, \ldots, \Omega$. In which case it sets the fixed debt repayment, R, just below x_ρ, so as to maximize the tax exemption for the ρ state of nature. We therefore read the expression,

$$R = x_\rho,$$

as: R is set just below x_ρ. Hence, the value of the company is[11]

$$V^\rho = \left[\Sigma_{\omega=1}^{\rho-1} p_\omega (x_\omega - b) + R \Sigma_\rho^\Omega p_\omega\right] + \left[\Sigma_\rho^\Omega p_\omega (x_\omega - R)(1 - \tau)\right],$$

the expression in the left (right) bracket being the value of its debt (equity). Collecting the solvency terms we get

$$V^\rho = \left[\Sigma_{\omega=1}^{\rho-1} p_\omega (x_\omega - b)\right] + \Sigma_\rho^\Omega p_\omega \left[R + x_\omega - R - (x_\omega - R)\tau\right].$$

Cancelling R across debt and equity holders[12] within the right-hand brackets, substituting in $R = x_\rho$, and collecting x_ω term in both debt and equity payments, we get:

$$v^\rho = V - b\Sigma_{\omega=1}^{\rho-1} p_\omega - \Sigma_\rho^\Omega p_\omega \left(x_\omega - x_\rho\right)\tau, \tag{5.22}$$

where

$$V = \Sigma_{\omega=1}^{\Omega} p_\omega x_\omega.$$

That is, the value of the company is its Modigliani–Miller value (so to speak) minus the cost of bankruptcy, minus taxes, all evaluated at state prices.

It is quite common for finance textbooks to graph the value of the company, that is Equation (5.22), as concave function of its capital structure, already assuming

[11] Suppose $x_1 \geq b$.

[12] Notice that an investor in the company can be both a debt holder and an equity holder.

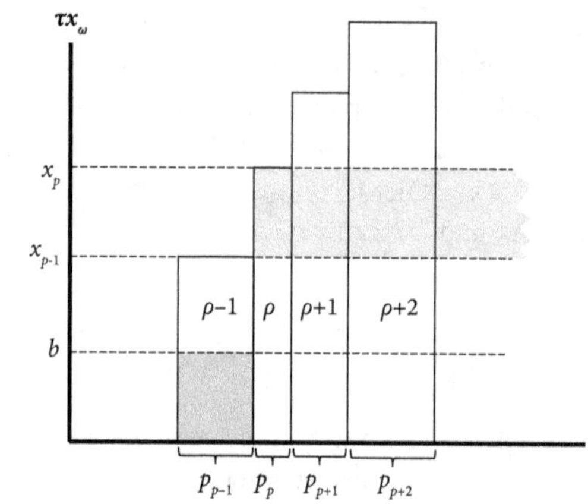

Figure 5.10 Cost and benefits of increased leverage

a single peak, away from the corners of a debt structure that is either 100% debt or 100% equity. To check the validity of this assumption, define the incremental change of making state ρ fully tax exempt, at the cost of driving state $\rho - 1$ into bankruptcy:

$$\Delta^{\rho} = v^{\rho} - v^{\rho-1} = -bp_{\rho-1} + \Sigma_{\rho}^{\Omega} p_{\omega} \left(x_{\rho} - x_{\rho-1}\right) \tau.$$

Figure 5.10's bar chart provides a diagrammatic exposition. The cost of state $\rho-1$, b, is evaluated at the state price $p_{\rho-1}$; hence the darker, bottom left shaded rectangle. At the same time, the benefit of increasing tax exemption from $x_{\rho-1}$ to x_{ρ}, which affects all states of nature $\omega \geq \rho$ is also evaluated at the relevant state prices; hence the lighter top right shaded rectangle.

Now, a single-peaked concave shape for the function (5.22) requires that $\Delta^2 > 0$ (i.e. Δ for $\rho = 2$) and $\Delta^{\Omega} < 0$ and that in between, the Δs decrease monotonically, that is $\Delta^{\omega-1} > \Delta^{\omega}$. Clearly, that would require quite strong, not necessarily plausible assumptions. Indeed, Miller (1977) argues that it is quite plausible that the tax benefit of debt dominates the cost due to bankruptcy, driving the company towards heavy reliance on debt. Kraus and Litzenberger (1973) demonstrate that the graph of Equation (5.22) against capital structure may not be concave, so that a multitude of local peaks is possible. Given that the empirical literature on capital structure struggles to find strong patterns in data, that may be more than just a theoretical speculation.

Three other points are worth making. First, to the extent that b is a 'real' cost, associated with legal and other administrative expenses, it could be avoided through a debt write-down, as indicated in the analysis of debt restructuring in Chapter 2. Particularly in a complete-markets setting, as assumed in this chapter, it is hard to see what could prevent this cheap way out of bearing the cost of bankruptcy. Second, to the extent that 'real' bankruptcy costs cannot be avoided, the analysis highlights the distortionary nature of corporate taxation: real resources are being wasted as companies try to decrease their tax liability. Third, the idea that debt is just a means of tax avoidance, with no positive economic role, does not provide a satisfactory theory of debt, as contractual solution that mitigates trading frictions as, for example, in the Hart-Moore model that was presented in Chapter 3. Additional 'positive' theories of debt are presented in Chapters 6 and 7.

5.12 Conclusions

In this chapter we apply the frictionless competitive model of Chapter 4 to the analysis of the market for risky securities, perhaps the most elegant application of the competitive model. Analytical elegance apart, the model provides a unifying framework for the analysis of insurance and securities markets. Some of its applications are widely used in practice. Nevertheless, the Mehra–Prescott rejection is disappointing. Evidently, the work of financial economics is far from being completed.

Appendix

As for CAPM, multiply both sides of the basic pricing equation (5.16),

$$q^s = \frac{E(\widetilde{x}^s)}{(1+r^f)} - \theta Cov(x^s, y),$$

by $(1+r^f)$, divide both sides by q^s; also multiply and divide the covariance term by q^m. Using covariance rules from Section 5.3.2 of the mathematical appendix [13], we get:

$$1 + r^f = \frac{E(\widetilde{x}^s)}{q^s} - (1+r^f)\, q^m \theta Cov\left(\frac{\widetilde{x}^s}{q^s}, \frac{\widetilde{y}}{q^m}\right). \tag{5.23}$$

Remember that asset returns, as defined in Equation (5.8) is:

$$\frac{E(\widetilde{x}^s)}{q^s} = 1 + E(\widetilde{r}^s).$$

[13] For any constant k and for any random variables $\widetilde{x}$ and y, $kCov(\widetilde{x},\widetilde{y}) = Cov(k\widetilde{x},\widetilde{y})$; remember that q^s and q^m are not random variables.

Using another covariance rules from Section A.3.2 of the Mathematical Appendix,[14] we get:

$$E(\tilde{r}^s) - r^f = (1 + r^f)\, q^m \theta Cov(\tilde{r}^s, \tilde{r}^m). \tag{5.24}$$

The same applies to the market:[15]

$$E(\tilde{r}^m) - r^f = (1 + r^f)\, q^m \theta Var(\tilde{r}^m). \tag{5.25}$$

Dividing Equation (5.24) by Equation (5.25) and cancelling $(1 + r^f)\, q^m \theta$ we get the CAPM formula, (5.18).

Take similar steps to derive the Mehra-Prescott equity-premium formula. Starting with market pricing formula (5.17):

$$q^m = \frac{E(\tilde{y})}{(1 + r^f)} - \theta \times Var(\tilde{y}),$$

multiply both sides by $(1 + r^f)$, divide both sides by q^m and then multiply and divide the variance term by covariance term by the squared base level of income, y_0. We get:

$$1 + r^f = \frac{E(\tilde{y})}{q^m} - (1 + r^f)\frac{E(\tilde{y})}{q^m}\frac{y_0}{E(\tilde{y})} y_0 \theta var\left(\frac{\tilde{y}}{y_0}\right),$$

where

$$\frac{\tilde{y}}{y_0} = 1 + \tilde{g}_y$$

is the growth rate of income. Using the same covariance rules as above we get

$$E(\tilde{r}^m) - r^f = \frac{(1 + r^f)[1 + E(\tilde{r}^m)]}{1 + E(\tilde{g}_y)} y_0 \theta Var(\tilde{g}_y).$$

Since r^f, $E(\tilde{r}^m)$ and $\tilde{g}_y$ are all 'close to zero' numbers, we can approximate,[16]

$$\frac{(1 + r^f)[1 + E(\tilde{r}^m)]}{1 + E(\tilde{g}_y)} \approx 1 + r^f + E(\tilde{r}^m) - E(\tilde{g}_y).$$

[14] For any constant k and for any random variables $\tilde{x}$, $Cov(k + \tilde{x}, \tilde{y}) = Cov(\tilde{x}, \tilde{y})$.
[15] Remembering that for any random variable $\tilde{x}$, $Cov(\tilde{x}, \tilde{x}) = Var(\tilde{x})$.
[16] For example, for close-t-zero constants w and z,

$$\frac{1 + w}{1 + z} = \frac{(1 + w)(1 - z)}{(1 + z)(1 - z)} = \frac{1 + w - z - zw}{1 - z^2} \approx 1 + w - z,$$

z^2 and zw being 'even closer to zero' and $\approx$ standing for 'approximately'.

Since y_0 is set up to one,

$$E(\tilde{r}^m) - r^f = A_0 \theta Var(\tilde{g}_y)$$

where A_0 is a number 'reasonably close' to one, that can be ignored 'in practice'.

References

[1] Brealey, Richard A. and Stewart C. Myers (2000). *Principles of Corporate Finance*, Sixth Edition, McGraw-Hill.

[2] Kraus Alan and Robert H. Litzenberger (1973). *Journal of Finance*, Vol. 28, No. 4, pp. 911–922.

[3] Lucas, Robert E. Jr. (1978). 'Asset Prices in an Exchange Economy', *Econometrica*, Vol. 46, No. 6, pp. 1429–1445.

[4] Lucas, Robert E. Jr. (1980). 'Methods and Problems in Business Cycle Theory', *Journal of Money Credit and Banking*, Vol. 12, No. 4, pp. 696–715.

[5] Mehra, Rajnish and Edward C. Prescott (1985). 'The Equity Premium Puzzle', *Journal of Monetary Economics*, Vol. 15. 145–161.

[6] Miller, Merton H. (1977). 'Debt and Taxes' *Journal of Finance*, Vol. 32, No. 2, pp. 261–648.

[7] Obstfeld, Maurice (1994). 'Are Industrial-Country Consumption Risks Globally Diversified?', in Leiderman, Leonardo and Assaf Razin (eds), *Capital Mobility: The Impact on Consumption, Investment, and Growth*, pp. 13–44, Cambridge University Press.

[8] Townsend, Robert M. (1994). 'Risk and Insurance in Village India', *Econometrica*, Vol. 62, No. 3, pp. 539–591.

6
Market Failures

6.1 Introduction

An important accomplishment of the analysis in Chapters 4 and 5 is in providing an accurate meaning to the notion of a frictionless economy: one where *complete markers* and *perfect competition* deliver First and Second Welfare Theorems. By reference to Chapter 2's analysis, it could be anticipated that not having a market where a certain trades can be executed (and priced) would result in economic inefficiency. Yet, a comprehensive analysis of *missing markets*, as well as *imperfect competition*, was deferred to this chapter. To some extent, the analysis highlights the power of the competitive model as it can serve as a platform for the analysis of at least some frictions.

Two additional themes are highlighted in this chapter. First, the competitive model has a very simple structure: supply, demand, equilibrium, etc. It is therefore easy to point out various aspects in which some (perhaps most) real-world markets deviate from the theoretical construct: only few competitors, some information is missing, etc. It is much more difficult to assess whether the deviation completely undermines the applicability of the competitive model or, alternatively, that the competitive model is still applicable although (perhaps because) it abstracts from quite a few realistic attributes.

Second, as markets get further away from the perfect-competition abstraction, other forms of organization appear: relationships, contracts, companies, intermediaries, etc. Are these forms of organization an impediment to the efficient operation of the market or, alternatively, an endogenous reaction to some underlying frictions, innovated by the players who operate within the market so as to recover lost trading opportunities? The question has some highly practical implications: should regulators try to break down the alternative modes of organization so as to force the market closer to the idealized competitive model, or should they celebrate the creative power of market participants who manage to overcome these frictions spontaneously?

6.2 Imperfect Competition

A perfectly competitive market is characterized by price-taking behaviour by all participants. The assumption is often justified on grounds of the 'atomistic' size

The Economics of Financial Markets and Institutions. Oren Sussman, Oxford University Press. © Oren Sussman (2023).
DOI: 10.1093/oso/9780192869739.003.0007

of the players. Though most industries are populated with numerous firms, they are sizable enough to resist the atomistic description. We start this section with a more detailed discussion of the determinants of a firm's size and, therefore the determination of the number of firms in a competitive industry.

6.2.1 Perfect Competition in More Detail

Under Chapter 4's HP derivation of supply and demand curves, firms had only one factor of production, labour, of which they employed no more than one unit. Here, we refine the modelling in two ways: the scale of production is no longer fixed to one unit of input, and there is an explicit reference to capital expenditures. It is useful (though not essential) to preserve the HP interpretation of the consumer side of the market.

6.2.1.1 Cost Structure of Firms

We distinguish *fixed costs* from *variable costs*, F and $c(q)$, respectively, q being the output of the firm or, alternatively, the scale of its production. F includes buildings, overheads, fixed assets, etc. and remains constant as scale changes, while $c(q)$ includes labour and other factors of production that vary with the scale of production; see the left-hand-side panel of Figure 6.1. The fixed and the variable cost add up to *total cost*, $F + c(q)$. The extra cost of increasing the scale of production by just one additional unit is called the *marginal cost*, *MC*.[1] It is represented by the slope of graphs of either the total-cost or the variable-cost functions.[2] The assumed

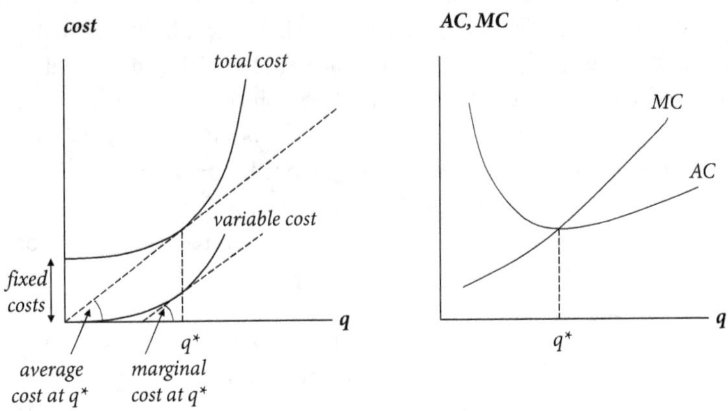

Figure 6.1 Cost structure of a competitive firm

[1] Similar to Chapter 4's unit cost, $\frac{w}{y}$, but, unlike there, unit cost changes with the scale of production.

[2] Since the graph of the total-cost function is just a vertical shift in the graph of the variable-cost functions, both have the same slope.

convexity of $c(q)$ implies that the marginal cost is increasing with scale: the more the firm produces, the more it costs to produce one extra unit. The *average cost of production*, AC, is defined as $[F + c(q)]/q$. The average cost is represented by the slope of a ray, from the origin to the relevant point on the total-cost function. Hence, both the average cost and the marginal costs vary with q; hence the $MC(q)$ and $AC(q)$ functions. The following properties deserve special attention.

***Claim* 6.1.** Average costs are minimized at the point q^* of Figure 6.1, defined by the tangency of a ray from the origin and the graph of the total-cost function. Clearly[3], average costs are higher than $AC(q^*)$ both to the right and to the left of q^*. Hence, q^* is the scale where the average cost of production is the lowest; we call q^* the firm's *effective scale*. It follows from the tangency property that defines q^* that average costs equal marginal costs at that point: $AC(q^*) = MC(q^*)$, both of which are represented by dashed lines in the left panel of Figure 6.1. It also follows from that panel that the marginal costs are higher (lower) than the average cost for any point to the right (left) of q^*. Hence, on the right-hand-side panel of Figure 6.1, the graph of $MC(q)$ intersects with the graph of $AC(q)$ at point q^*, from below.

***Claim* 6.2.** The firm's effective scale is increasing in the firm's fixed costs: higher fixed costs increase the effective scale, q^*.

***Claim* 6.3.** For a competitive firm, the marginal cost curve is also the supply curve. For any q such that MC is lower (higher) than some market price, p', it is profitable to expand (contract) production. Now consider a point q' where $p' = MR(q')$. To the left of q' it is profitable to scale production up, and to the right of q' it is profitable to scale production down. It follows that q' is the profit-maximizing scale given p' and, hence, that a price of p' a profit-oriented firm would choose to supply the quantity q'. Since this argument is valid for any market price, the graph of $MC(q)$ is the firm's supply curve. We define the firm's *economic profit* $p' \times q' - AC(q') \times q'$. If profits are negative and the firm is 'losing money', it should stop operating. It may delay shut-down if, for example, its fixed costs are already sunk and cannot be recovered. But it will not renew its investments and, so, shut down eventually.

***Claim* 6.4.** The firm's *economic profit* differs from its *accounting profit*. For example, suppose that F is just capital expenditure, and the firm is 100% equity financed. Then, the firm's *accounting profit* is, by standard definitions, just $p' \times q' - c(q')$, to be distributed to the firm's owners. In contrast, for the purpose of economic accounting, $p' \times q' - [F + c(q')]$, where F should include not

[3] The reader is advised to check the validity of this statement, and the other below, by drawing a graph and plotting the relevant rays or tangents.

just the owners' out-of-pocket expenditure on buying the firm's capital, but also the opportunity cost of the capital that they have provided, against the alternative of 'putting their money in the bank'. Moreover, that cost of capital should be adjusted for the risk born by the owners, along the lines of the Chapter 5 analysis. It follows that a firm may be profitable by the accounting definition of profit and, at the same time, bearing negative economic profit, in the sense that its (accounted) profit fails to generate the owners an adequate return on the capital that they have provided—adjusted for the risk that they bear. Alternatively, a firm that makes positive economic profits actually earns the owners a rate of return in excess of the money-in-the bank option. For that reason, economic profits are sometimes called *above-normal profits*. It follows that a firm that makes zero economic profits is actually a perfectly healthy firm.

6.2.1.2 Competitive Structure in the Short Run and in the Long Run

Consider a competitive industry with n_0 firms with identical cost structures. We derive the industry's supply curve through a horizontal summation of individual supply curves across the n_0 companies that serve the market, initially. Market demand curve is given by D, implying a *short-term equilibrium* price p', above the average cost at the implied scale, $AC(q')$, so that firms are making positive economic profits; see Figure 6.2. The above-normal profitability of the industry attracts entry of new firms, so that the number of companies active in the industry start to increase above n_0. As a result, the short-term supply curve, S^{SR}, shifts to the right and prices start falling, gradually. This process carries on until the market price falls to $p^* = AC(q^*)$, the effective cost of production, where economic profits fall to zero, so that new entrants are no longer attracted into the industry. It follows that a flat line at a price of p^* is the industry's long-term supply curve, S^{LR}. The number of firms in that long-run equilibrium is $n_1 \times q^*$ that satisfies the demand at the long-term price, p^*.

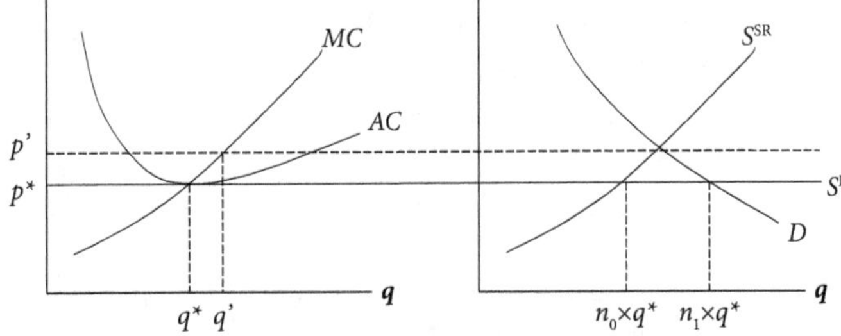

Figure 6.2 Entry, competitive industry

6.2.2 Monopoly

A monopoly is an industry served by one firm only. The monopolist is not a price taker. Rather, profit-seeking implies that it takes into consideration the effect of its own scale on the market price: the higher the scale the lower the price. This point apart, the monopolist's profit considerations are similar to that of a competitive firm: expand the scale of production as long as the extra revenue per extra unit (called the marginal revenue, *MR*) exceeds the cost of producing that extra unit (namely, the marginal cost, *MC*). The only difference is that for a competitive firm, the marginal revenue equals the market price, p, which a competitive firm takes as given, but the monopolist does not.

The graph of the marginal revenue function is always below the graph of the demand function, *D*, from which it is derived. To see why, consider a monopolist who expands some arbitrary scale, q', by one unit, which decreases the price that it can charge form $p(q')$ to $p(q' + 1)$. While the extra unit generates a revenue of $p(q')$, the monopolist also needs to consider the negative price effect. It follows that:

$$MR(q') = p(q') - q' \times [p(q') - p(q' + 1)] < p(q'). \tag{6.1}$$

Since this argument is valid for any quantity, the entire graph of the $MR(q)$ function lies below the graph of the demand function. Figure 6.3 describes the special case of a linear demand function, where the $MR(q)$ is also a linear function, twice steeper than the demand curve,[4] the two graphs intersecting at $p(0)$, as implied by Equation (6.1). It follows that the marginal revenue curve intersects with the horizontal axis half way between the origin and the point where demand curve intersects with the horizontal axis.

Clearly, the monopolist's production scale, q^m, falls short of the scale of a competitive industry with the same cost structure, q^c: the monopolist cuts down the scale of production so as to benefit from higher prices, p^m instead of p^c. Doing so, it undermines economic efficiency. To see why, consider the following policy: let the monopolist keep on servicing the existing clientele at the scale[5], q^m, and the same price, p^m, but offer the good to the rest of the population at the competitive price, p^c, expanding scale by $q^c - q^m$. The existing clientele is not worse off. The rest of the population is better off since players with subjective valuation between p^m and p^c can buy the commodity. Adding up the surplus of these new clients yields the pale shaded area in Figure 6.3. Indeed, even the monopolist is better off by the dark shaded area, since the price at which it sells to the new clients is higher than his marginal cost. Such outcome can also be implemented by a policy that prohibits

[4] To demonstrate this point, use high-school calculus or just use Excel to simulate revenue for different quantities, then deriving marginal revenue.

[5] Remember that, in Chapter 4, we have demonstrated that, under the HUSV derivation of demand, each point on the demand curve maps to a player with a certain subjective valuation of the commodity.

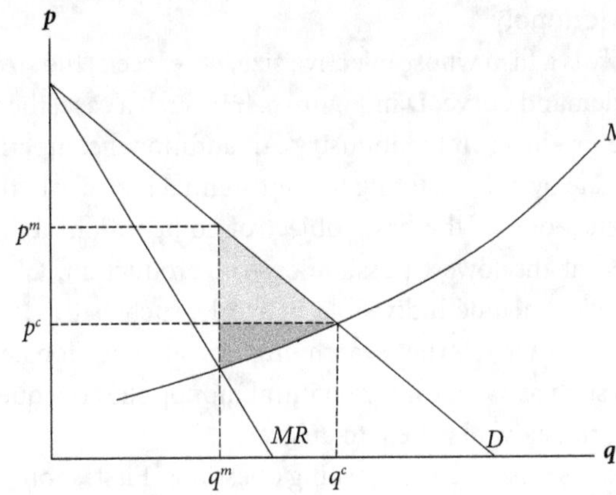

Figure 6.3 Monopoly

the monopolist from charging a price above p^c, but compensating it with a transfer, $(p^m - p^c) \times q^m$, funded by a lump-sum tax on buyers with subjective valuation higher than p^m to the monopolist.

Proposition 6.1. *A monopolist produces a lower quantity and charges a higher price relative to a competitive industry with the same cost structure. The monopolistic outcome is Pareto dominated by the competitive outcome.*

It is worth noting that the economic argument against monopolies differs from the popular one, namely that the monopoly rips off its customers: the argument above demonstrates how it is possible to design a policy that would Pareto improve on the monopolistic outcome, namely make all players, including the monopolist, better off.[6] Notice, however, that the welfare-enhancing policies suggested above make some strong assumptions regarding the power of the regulator: to discriminate across buyers, to lump-sum tax and to have perfect information about the monopolist's cost structure (where the monopolist has a strong interest in reporting higher costs than the actual ones).

6.2.3 Causes for Monopolization

Why do monopolies exist in the first place? We discuss three possible reasons. The first relates to a special cost structure that favours a single production facility. The other two, political favouritism and exclusive ownership of a production technology are discussed in Sections 6.2.5.2 and 6.2.5.1, respectively.

[6] It does not follow from the above that we recommend that the monopolist is compensated; as in previous chapters, we remain mute on matters of redistribution.

6.2.3.1 Natural Monopoly

A natural monopoly is a firm whose effective size, q^*, exceeds the size of its market as defined by the demand curve, D in Figure 6.4. In such a case, there is 'no room' for more than one producer in the industry. An additional competitor would cut the monopolist's scale by half, resulting in a substantial increase in the cost of production, which defies one of the basic object of competition: to guarantee that markets are served at the lowest possible cost of production. Classic examples of natural monopolies include indivisible networks such as the London Underground network. Whether internet search engines such as Google or computer operating systems such as Windows are natural monopolies is a question that the analytical framework below may help to answer.

Natural monopolies raise a few interesting questions. First, should the regulator aim at setting the price at p^z, where the demand curve intersects with the average cost curve, AC, or to p^o where the demand intersects with the marginal cost curve, MC? The former price brings the monopolist's profit down to zero, but the latter is the Pareto efficient price. To see why, consider the following policy: keep on selling q^z units of the commodity to the existing clientele at a price of p^z, while offering the commodity to the rest of the population at a price of p^o, resulting in extra production of $q^o - q^z$. That would be a Pareto improvement: the existing clientele is not worse off while the rest of the population is better off as players with subjective valuation between p^z and p^o can buy the commodity. Adding up their individual surpluses yields the pale shaded area. Indeed, even the monopolist is better off at the price p^o, profiting from extra producing, $q^o - q^z$.

Second, is the natural monopolist actually immune to competition? Indeed, the monopolist has no competitor within its own market, but may face competition from a new entrant that would try to replace it and take over the entire market.

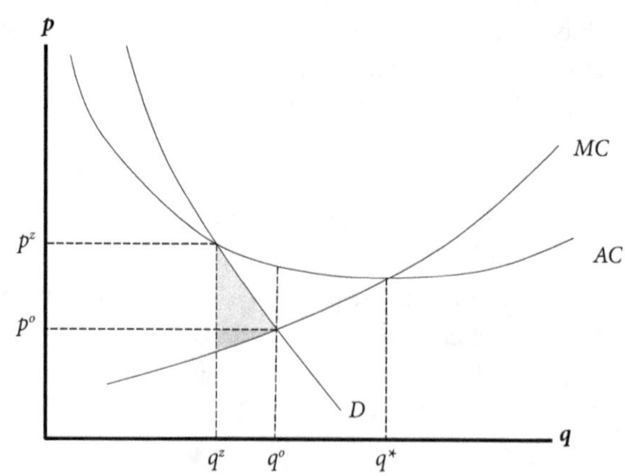

Figure 6.4 Natural monopoly

The incentive to enter is particularly strong if the price is above p^z, generating a handsome economic profit, so that an entrant could offer a lower price while capturing the entire market. Some have argued that a single-firm industry *threatened by entry* is as competitive as an industry with several acting competitors. That may be the case in industries like airlines, where costly fixed costs are easy to reallocate from one market to another.

Third, since the main reason for the existence of a natural monopoly is the magnitude of its effective scale, q^*, and since an important determinant of the effective scale is the magnitude of the fixed cost (see Claim 6.2), how sensitive is the natural monopoly to technological innovations that decrease the fixed cost? For once the effective scale falls short of the market size (half the market size, to be precise), production efficiency no longer implies a single production facility. A good historical example is the telephone landline industry. In the old days, the land-line grid was immensely costly, allowing its owner to monopolize the market. But then, new microwave and cellular technologies appeared, providing close if not a better substitute, making the industry highly competitive. Given concerns that regulators would be captured by industry (see Section 6.2.5.2 below), Friedman (1962) suggests that leaving monopolies to face such technological challenges may prove a more effective competition policy than regulation, at least in the long run.

6.2.4 Oligopoly

A pure monopoly is a rare phenomenon. Most real world deviations from perfect competition are oligopolies, namely industries served by a small number of firms. We discuss, below, two famous oligopoly theories, the first by Bertrand and the second by Cournot. For the sake of simplicity, we analyse the case of a duopoly, a special case of an oligopoly, with just two firms. Both theories highlight the force of competition even within an oligopolistic market. Economists who are sceptical of regulation emphasize this result: competition may be more effective than regulation in diminishing monopoly power.

6.2.4.1 Bertrand Duopoly

Consider a duopoly with two identical firms; for simplicity, assume that each has a fixed marginal cost of production, c, and no fixed costs. Market demand is expressed by the decreasing function, $q(p)$. Each player chooses a price and, then, satisfies whatever demand it faces. Notice that it is in the joint interest of both companies to collude on the monopolistic price, p^m, and then split the market among themselves.

Our first observation is that any price, $p' > c$, is not a Nash Equilibrium. Table 6.1 explains why. Consider a unilateral deviation, by player 1, from the collude strategy: by undercutting the price by a small amount, ε, she slightly decreases

Table 6.1 Bertrand oligopoly

		player 2	
		collude	**cheat**
player 1	collude	$\left[(p'-c)\times\frac{q(p')}{2},(p'-c)\times\frac{q(p')}{2}\right]$	$[0,(p'-\varepsilon-c)\times q(p'-\varepsilon)]$
	cheat	$[(p'-\varepsilon-c)\times q(p'-\varepsilon),0]$	$\left[(p'-2\varepsilon-c)\times\frac{q(p'-2\varepsilon)}{2},\ (p'-2\varepsilon-c)\times\frac{q(p'-2\varepsilon)}{2}\right]$

the joint profit of the duopoly from $(p'-c)\times q(p)$ to $(p'-\varepsilon-c)\times q(p'-\varepsilon)$, but, selling at a lower price she can capture the entire market. Notice that the gain due to an increased market share is always substantial, while ε can be made arbitrarily small, so that undercutting is always a profitable policy. Our second observation is that there is no incentive to undercut at the competitive price $p=c$, for that would push the profit down from zero to a negative amount. Hence, the conclusion from the Bertrand model is that any industry with more than one company actually behaves like a competitive industry.

6.2.4.2 Cournot Duopoly

In the Cournot-duopoly model, each player chooses a quantity (rather than a price as in the Bertrand model), with the price being determined by the market-clearing condition. The results go in the same direction as the Bertrand model, but reach a less extreme conclusion.

Consider a duopoly serving an industry with a linear demand curve,

$$p=6-\frac{q}{100},$$

its graph being a straight line from the point $(0,6)$ to the point $(600,0)$. Assume, for simplicity, that the cost of production is zero. Joint profits are maximized at the monopolistic quantity, 300, and the market price is 3. Under a collusive arrangement, each duopolist produces 150 and collects a profit of 450.

We now check whether each duopolist has the incentive to compete with the other duopolist and, if so, how 'hard': softly, by producing 200, or aggressively by producing 250. Table 6.2 derives the payoff matrix with the profit level associated with each combination of the three strategies.[7] It is easy to see that the monopolistic

[7] For example, if player 2 plays the monopolistic strategy of 150 and player 2 plays the soft deviation of 200, the price drops to 2.5, generating a profit of 500 for player 1 and 375 for player 2. If player 2 competes aggressively at 250, the price drops to 2 yielding payoffs of (500, 300).

Table 6.2 Cournot oligopoly

			player 2	
			compete	
		monopoly	softly	aggressively
player 1	monopoly	(450, 450)	(375, 500)	(300, 500)
	softly	(500, 375)	(400, 400)	(300, 375)
compete	aggressively	(500, 300)	(375, 300)	(250, 250)

strategies, though (by definition) generating the highest joint profit, is not a Nash Equilibrium: if player 2 sticks to the monopolistic strategy, player 1 can increase her profit by 'stealing' some of her market share. Table 6.2 confirms that a 'soft' competition with both players producing 200 (each) is a Nash Equilibrium (indeed, the only symmetric Nash Equilibrium) while a production scale of 250 (each) is not a Nash Equilibrium.

To summarize:

Proposition 6.2. *Both Bertrand and Cournot models of oligopoly predict that the monopolistic outcome is not stable due to the players' strong incentive to compete one with another on market share. The models have a different prediction regarding the strength of competition.*

Why does a seemingly technical difference in the specification of the two games, one in price strategies and one in quantity strategies, has a substantial difference on results? It seems that the critical difference is in the speed at which firm scale can be adjusted. Under Bertrand, a firm undercuts a (monopolistic) price and promptly increases scale in order to expand market share at the expense of its competitor and, thereby, its own profits. Under Cournot, scale adjustment is slow, which can be used in order to commit not to compete too aggressively; competition is 'softened'. Kreps and Scheinkman, (1983) model the argument into a two-stage game where firms build up production capacity in the first stage, and compete (Bertrand) in the product market in the second stage. Most economists would probably agree that the prediction of the Bertrand model is too optimistic. At the same time there is wide agreement that competition puts pressure on any oligopolistic price-fixing scheme.

6.2.4.3 A Note on Oligopoly and Product Differentiation

In both the Bertrand and Cournot models, the members of the oligopoly produce exactly the same good. In most real world situations, each player has a brand that is slightly differentiated from the other's. The formal analysis of so called *differentiated product* markets is beyond the scope of this book. We do point out, however, a practical problem that is raised in many antitrust cases: by definition, each producer of a differentiated product is a monopolist in the market that it serves. At the same time, it is clear that its monopoly power is substantially diminished if another competitor produces a close substitute. Hence, many antitrust cases are ultimately decided on the definition of the market: the more substitutes are recognized, the weaker is the monopolistic case against the accused firm.

It is worth consolidating some of the results above:

Proposition 6.3. *An industry's competitiveness is not a mechanical implication of the number of firms in the industry; rather, an industry's competitiveness is affected (among other factors) by the threat of entry, by the nature of competition (Bertrand versus Cournot), and the presence of close substitutes.*

6.2.5 More Regulation-Sceptical Arguments

There are two additional, famous arguments against the regulation of monopolistic industries.

6.2.5.1 Schumpeter: Monopoly and Technological Innovation

Consider Figure 6.2, and a single company that could develop a technology that would decrease the costs of production. The development cost is a fixed amount, but the new technology can be emulated by any other competitor. That would drive prices down, perhaps after a while, to a new zero-profit level. Possibly, the innovator's short-term above-normal profit is not sufficient to cover the cost of developing the new technology.

Schumpeter (1934) argued that the 'static' loss of economic efficiency due to monopolistic power may be dominated by the 'dynamic' advantage generated by new technologies developed by monopolistic firms. Notice that the argument becomes redundant when the economy has a well functioning patenting system, which grants the patent holder monopoly power, temporarily, thereby balancing the need to protect innovation against the need to promote competition.

The Schumpeter analysis carries a more general lesson. An innovator's inability to retain a property right in a new technology undermines the incentive to innovate and causes a loss of welfare. By itself, lack of competition also undermines social welfare. Yet, the combined welfare-loss of these two effects is not the sum of the two welfare effects on their own. Hence:

Proposition 6.4. *Market organization is often complex; it deviates from the competitive-market abstraction in more than one respect. A welfare evaluation of the structure must take into consideration the interaction between the various respects rather than add them up.*

6.2.5.2 Regulatory Capture

So far, we viewed the state as an instrument for the implementation of policies that promote efficiency and (perhaps) fairness. We have ignored the simple fact that policies are implemented through a political process. In a seminal paper, Stigler (1971) develops the idea that:

> political systems are rationally devised and rationally employed, which is to say that they are appropriate instruments for the fulfillment of desires of members of the society. This is not to say that the state will serve any person's concept of the public interest: indeed the problem of regulation is the problem of discovering when and why an industry (or other group of like-minded people) is able to use the state for its purposes, or is singled out by the state to be used for alien purposes.
>
> (Stigler, 1971, p. 4)

Hence, industries can use the state for the purpose of enhancing their monopoly power by preventing entry:

> A central thesis of this paper is that, as a rule, regulation is acquired by the industry and is designed and operated primarily for its benefit.
>
> (Stigler, 1971, p. 3)

For example:

> The Civil Aeronautics Board has not allowed a single new trunk line to be launched since it was created in 1938. The power to insure new banks has been used by the Federal Deposit Insurance Corporation to reduce the rate of entry into commercial banking by 60 percent.
>
> (Stigler, 1971, p. 5)

Stigler's ideas have inspired a wealth of empirical work. The work by Blanes-i-Vidal, Draca, and Fons-Rosen (2012) is a good example. Using a sample collected over the years 1998 to 2008 they study the operations of politically connected Washington lobbyists. It turns out that 42% of them were formerly employed by the government, of which more than half are ex-congressional staffers. The mean revenue generated by a revolving-door lobbyist is $310, 000. These facts are consistent with the existence of an active market where political connections are traded for money, in line with the idea of regulatory capture. At the same time, the facts are also consistent with more benign explanations, like a short supply of high-quality political specialists, for whose services government and private sector compete, resulting in a certain degree of labour mobility across government and lobbying. To rule out at least some of these benign explanations, the authors focus on the subset of lobbyists who were ex-congressional staffers during the sample period and compare the revenue that they generated before and after exit of the congressman with whom they were connected. (Exit is related to various reasons: retirement, death, electoral defeat, etc.) They find that exit of a Senator results in a 21% to 24% loss of revenue to the lobbyist (with high statistical significance), while an exit of a Representative results in a 7% to 10% loss of revenue (with low or no statistical significance). When the connection is narrowed down to powerful congressional committees the effect is stronger. For example, exit of a member of the Senate's Finance Committee results in a 36% loss of revenue.

Regulatory capture is more than a statement about 'some corrupt politicians'. It points out that political institutions, just like markets, have inherent structural weaknesses that cause them to fail, sometimes. It is fair to say that the claim that 'as a rule' industry captures regulators (rather than regulators restraining industry) is not conclusively substantiated, empirically, at least so far. Neither is the policy implication, hinted by Stigler and explicitly elaborated by Friedman (1962), that since regulation might prolong monopoly power, society is better off without it. At the same time, it is an important reminder that the remedy to the failure of the market cannot be evaluated against a hypothetical, perfect, political system. Rather, any intervention has to weigh the benefit of eliminating a market failure against the risk of suffering from a political failure. Whether we accept the Friedman–Stugler view, or not, the idea that regulation might have its own failures, adds another layer of complexity to that already stated in Propositions 6.3 and 6.4.

6.3 Missing Markets

We develop the argument through a sequence of examples.

6.3.1 The Textbook Case: Emission

Suppose, for simplicity, that an industry that releases a polluting substance, for example carbon dioxide, can be represented by just one firm. The amount pollutants released is directly related the firm's scale of production: the higher the scale the more it pollutes. We suggest that the firm's valuation, per-unit of pollution released, is a decreasing function its scale; see Figure 6.5. Close to the origin, the release of an extra unit is highly valuable simply because unit costs of production are low, so profitability is high. As the scale of production goes up, the value of releasing an extra unit of pollution falls, because production is less profitable. At q^u, the value of releasing just one extra unit of pollutants is zero, simply because the firm reaches the maximum-profit scale of production. Since it has no interest in expanding production, it has no interest in extra pollution. By an argument that is, by now, already well rehearsed, once the industry has to buy a licence for each

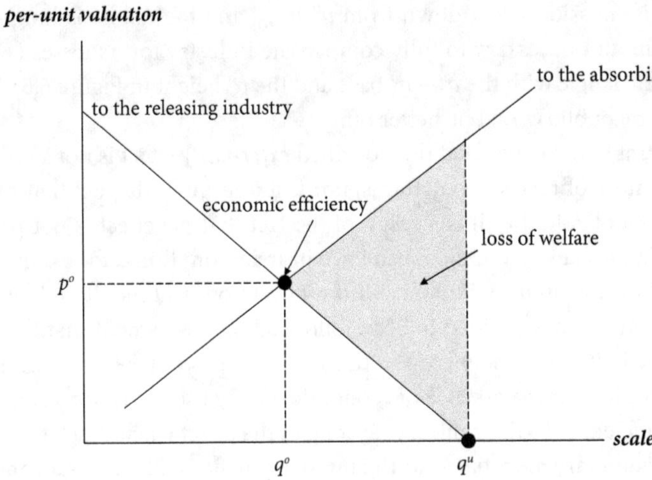

Figure 6.5 The market for emission

unit of pollutant released, this unit-valuation graph becomes the demand curve for such licences: the firm would buy an extra licence as long as the unit value of the released pollutants exceeds the price of the licence.

On the other side of the market there is a 'public' that absorbs the pollutants. (This collective entity gets a more rigorous treatment—below.) For either aesthetic or material reasons, say damage to wildlife, health hazards or concerns about global warming, the public's subjective valuation of the damage caused by pollution is increasing in the amount of pollution. Probably, at low levels of pollution, an extra unit hardly makes a difference, while at high levels of pollution an extra unit might tip off the entire ecological balance. By the same well-rehearsed argument, once the public gets the power to issue pollution licences, this upwards sloping unit-valuation curve becomes the supply curve for such licences: the public would issue an extra licence as long as the price exceeds the subjective value of the unit absorbed.

The first implication of the above considerations is that there exists a price, p^o, where the two curves intersect. This price defines the economically efficient amount of pollution, q^o. At q^o, the public would only be willing to absorb an extra unit of pollutants at a price that exceeds the industry's valuation of the release. By the standard argument, at any $q' < q^o$ ($q' > q^o$) increasing (decreasing) emission by one unit would cause more good than harm which makes q^o economically efficient in the Pareto sense.

The second implication is that where the market for licences *is missing*, so that the industry is emitting without being charged, the unregulated amount of emission, q^u, is excessive. We can also identify the amount of welfare lost as the shaded area in Figure 6.5. That is, any amount that is emitted above q^o generates more (subjective) damage on the public's side than profit on the industry's side. To put it differently, if emission is cut down from q^u to q^o and the public is lump-sum taxed by an amount necessary to fully compensate industry for its losses (which the un-shaded triangle with the $q^u - q^o$ base and the p^o height in Figure 6.5), both industry and the public would be better off.

It is important to recognize that this so-called *externality* effect is not a result of the harmful nature of released pollutants, nor is it a result of the fact that industry affects the public. Rather it is a result of the fact that the effect is not priced. Many things in life cause pain, inconvenience or irritation; think, for example, of the noise and dust caused by builders who renovate one's home. It is, however, an irritation that one has decided to bear, following the assessment that the benefit exceeds the irritation. The mere fact that a certain player takes an action that affects another player is the essence of economic life. By itself, it is not a source of economic inefficiency. To the contrary: as long as the effect (including associated payments) is voluntary, negotiated to the mutual benefit of all parties, economic efficiency is enhanced. The only reason why the release of pollutants is a market failure is because the effect of the industry on the public is external to the market and, thus, has not been priced; the industry has failed to *internalize* the *social cost* of pollution and, as a result, have produced too much of it.

6.3.1.1 Policy Responses

The solution to the externality is simple (in theory): to levy a tax on emission at the level of p^o per unit. In some cases, the government may be in a better position by auctioning off q^o licences and 'let the market determine the price'. In fact, where the exact shape of supply and demand are known, the two policies are equivalent.

It is important to note that once the emission is efficiently priced, there is no need to regulate any related markets. For example, when carbon emissions are not priced, air-fairs are too low, which encourage excessive air travel. Yet, a carbon tax would be passed through to the commercial aviation market. Once carbon tax restores the level emission to its economically efficient level, the volume of air travel is aligned accordingly.

6.3.1.2 Social Valuation

We discuss, above, somewhat vaguely, the valuation that the public, collectively, assigns to emissions. A more careful derivation of this social valuation is required for completeness, but also for a better understanding of the reasons behind the market's failure.

In the ordinary case of a private commodity, each player values the commodities that he buys and consumes. In the case of emission, the entire amount released spreads out, so that the environment in which each and every member of the public lives is affected to the same extent. Notwithstanding, players may have different subjective attitudes to the quality of the environment. Measuring the social cost of

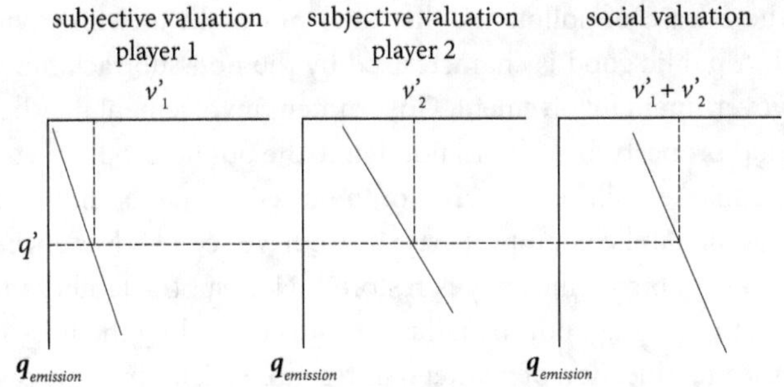

Figure 6.6 Deriving supply of absorption capacity

pollution, namely value assigned collectively by the public, requires an approach that differs from the one used in the case of private commodities.

To make the point more accurately, consider an economy with two players who are exposed to a certain level of pollution, q'. Although the two players are equally exposed to q', they relate to it differently. Figure 6.6 plots their subjective valuations on a clockwise-rotated graph (the rotation is for graphical convenience only, so that the graphs better fit into a single page). Clearly, player 2 is more averse to pollution than player 1: she requires a higher compensation, v'_2, relative to player 1's, v'_1, in order to absorb an extra unit: $v'_2 > v'_1$. It follows that, at a q' level of emission, the amount required in order to compensate both for the exposure to one extra unit is $v'_1 + v'_2$. Notice that the result is valid for any level of emission other than q'. More generally:

Proposition 6.5. *Unlike a private good, the social valuation of non-subtractable commodities is derived through vertical, rather than horizontal, summation of per-unit subjective valuation functions.*

6.3.1.3 Public Goods

Section 6.3.1.2's analysis highlights a fundamental difference between *public goods,* like a (relatively) pollution-free environment, and private goods; hence the *subtractability* property of private goods. That is, a player who consumes a private good, say a loaf of bread, subtracts the amount consumed from the amount that is available to other players. Or, to put it differently, the entire amount of the commodity has to be distributed across the players in the market, each player benefiting from the amount of the commodity that is allocated to her. Public goods are characterized by non subtractability.

A few points need to be emphasized here. First, a public good is not characterized by the fact that the government is involved in its production. If the government decides to take over the production of, say, automobiles, that does not make automobiles a public good. Conversely, if the government decides not to regulate the release of pollutants, that does not make a clean environment a private good. A public good is characterized by the non-subtractability property rather than government involvement. Government involvement may be a result of the public good property, but it does not define the public good.

Second, the market failure is a result of the missing market, not by any physical property of the public good property: as we have seen above, once the public good is priced, economic efficiency is restored. Non-subtractability may explain why the market is missing, but the failure itself is caused by the missing market. That makes the identification of market failures more tricky. In some cases, a commodity seems to have the physical characteristics of a public good, but a market, or an alternative arrangement, has risen spontaneously, eliminating (or at least moderating) the extent of economic inefficiency. In other cases, a market is missing although the commodity does not seem to have the physical characteristics of non-subtractability.

A missing market is, therefore, a more general and more accurate way of characterizing a market failure. An additional advantage is that the explanation offered for missing-market inefficiency and the policy that is required in order to restore efficiency are somewhat similar to those offered in Chapters 2 and 3. In both cases, the root problem is that trade has failed to materialize. It was already mentioned, there, that some commodities, by their very physical characteristics, resist bilateral trading; a clean environment is an important example.

6.3.2 The Identification of Market Failures

The following are two famous examples where one might expect that a market failure but, actually, a market or an alternative institutional arrangement has risen spontaneously, by no means a perfect market, yet with certain competitive characteristics, capable of ameliorating the inefficiency caused by the missing market.

6.3.2.1 Lighthouses

On first inspection, lighthouses could serve as paradigmatic examples of a market failure: potentially affected parties benefit (perhaps to a different extent) from the existence of the same ray of light. The ray is not subtractable: it is impossible to break it to parts that would be allocated, for a charge, to the users through a market mechanism, to each user according to her subjective valuation. Indeed, some textbooks have used the lighthouse as a paradigmatic example of a public good. Coase (1974) cites a long list of very eminent economic authors, from J. S. Mill to P. A. Samuelson, who took it for granted. According to the latter:

> Take ... [the] case of a lighthouse to warn against rocks. Its beam helps everyone in sight. A businessman could not build it for a profit, since he cannot claim a

> price from each user. This certainly is the kind of activity that governments would naturally undertake. ...even if the operators [of the lighthouse] were able—say, by radar reconnaissance—to claim a toll from every nearby user, that fact would not necessarily make it socially optimal for this service to be provided like a private good at a market-determined individual price. Why not? Because it costs society zero extra cost to let one extra ship use the service; hence any ships discouraged from those waters by the requirement to pay a positive price will represent a social economic loss-even if the price charged to all is no more than enough to pay the long-run expenses of the lighthouse.
>
> (Samuelson's 1965 famous textbook, cited by Coase 1974)

Coase studies the early history of English lighthouses (back to the sixteenth century) to reveal a more complicated and nuanced reality. Interested parties would

> obtain a patent from the Crown which empowered them to build a lighthouse and to levy tolls on ships presumed to have benefited from it. The way this was done was to present a petition from shipowners and shippers in which they said that they would greatly benefit from the lighthouse and were willing to pay the toll. Signatures were, I assume, obtained in the way signatures to petitions are normally obtained but no doubt they often represented a genuine expression of opinion. The King presumably used these grants of patents on occasion as a means of rewarding those who had served him. Later, the right to operate a lighthouse and to levy tolls was granted to individuals by Acts of Parliament.
>
> The tolls were collected at the ports by agents (who might act for several lighthouses), who might be private individuals but were commonly customs officials. The toll varied with the lighthouse and ships paid a toll, varying with the size of the vessel, for each lighthouse passed. It was normally a rate per ton ... for each voyage. Later, books were published setting out the lighthouses passed on different voyages and the charges that would be made.
>
> (Coase, 1974, pp. 364–365)

The crucial insight here is that when markets fail, (semi) decentralized arrangements are sometimes developed in order to replace them. It is fairly obvious that these institutions may operate in a way that is different from a competitive market and may not deliver the entire benefit that a competitive market would deliver (could it operate). Some intermediaries may be called in order to organize the relevant parties to write the petition, lobby the Crown to grant the patent, manage the construction of the lighthouse itself, and then organize the collection of tolls from vessels while they visit ports. Then, once the petition is granted, the lighthouse becomes a natural monopoly. It would thus set the price higher than the marginal cost, which would decrease the amount of traffic below the socially optimal level (as noted by Samuelson). Yet, it is conceivable that this practical arrangement delivers an outcome that is not that inferior to the one prescribed by the abstract concept of perfect competition. Or, to put it differently, can any other practical arrangement get any closer to economic efficiency?

Coase (1974, pp. 374–375) concludes with a sarcastic note regarding the writers before him:

> how is it that these great men have, in their economic writings, been led to make statements about lighthouses which are misleading ... and which, to the extent that they imply a policy conclusion, are very likely wrong? The explanation is that these references by economists to lighthouses are not the result of their having made a study of lighthouses or having read a detailed study by some other economist. ... The lighthouse is simply plucked out of the air to serve as an illustration.

It is worth noting that, as in some of the monopoly cases above, technological progress may change the nature of the public good problem. Nowadays, ship navigation can be assisted by chargeable encrypted signals, so that a market may be able to operate, albeit making the service a natural monopoly, with a very substantial fixed cost and next to zero variable cost.

Perhaps a deeper point is that faced with trading frictions, which prevent them from trading in a competitive manner, the players who operate in relevant market may develop, spontaneously, institutions that would help them overcome these trading frictions. In which case, it is not obvious whether a non-competitive market organization is an impediment to economic efficiency or an attempt to organize so as to get outcomes that are closer to the competitive benchmark. For example, in the case of the lighthouse, are the intermediaries that collect tolls from vessels, a monopoly or a mechanism to provide a public good? More generally, and in the same spirit as Proposition 6.4 above:

Proposition 6.6. *Market organization is often an endogenous reaction to some underlying trading friction. Hence, without detailed analysis, it is impossible to determine whether a non-competitive market organization is causing or ameliorating economic inefficiency.*

6.3.2.2 The Fable of Bees

Cheung (1973) explores another textbook example of an externality leading to a market failure:

> Suppose that in a given region there is a certain amount of apple-growing and a certain amount of bee-keeping and that the bees feed on the apple blossom. If the apple-farmers apply 10% more labour, land and capital to apple-farming they will increase the output of apples by 10%; but they will also provide more food for the

> bees. On the other hand, the bee-keepers will not increase the output of honey by 10% by increasing the amount of land, labour and capital to bee-keeping by 10% unless at the same time the apple-farmers also increase their output and so the food of the bees by 10%.... We call this a case of an unpaid factor, because the situation is due simply and solely to the fact that the apple-farmer cannot charge the beekeeper for the bees food.
>
> (J. E. Mead as cited by Cheung 1973, p. 12)

Applying the subtractability test, one might speculate that bee-collected apple nectar is a public good. In fact, the relationship between bee-keepers and apple-growers is two sided: apples provide nectar to bees, but bees provide apple groves with essential pollination. It turns out that a market does exist for both sides of the relationship. Namely, apple-growers buy pollination services from bee-keepers and bee-keepers buy the access to apples for nectar. In the case of apples, it seems that pollination is relatively more scarce then nectar. As a result, it is mostly the apple-growers who pay the bee-keepers.

Pollination contracts are fairly elaborate and detailed. They include, in addition to the rental fee, clauses regarding the required strength of the colonies as well as the time of delivery and removal of beehives (it is common to transfer beehives from one grove to another over the season). There are also clauses that protect bees from farmers spraying pesticides. Other issues involve relationships between farmers where one may benefit from beehives placed by his neighbour. To resolve potential conflicts, '"a social rule, or custom of the orchards, takes the place of explicit contracting: during the pollination period the owner of an orchard either keeps bees himself or hires as many hives per area as are employed in neighboring orchards of the same type. One failing to comply would be rated as a "bad neighbor," it is said, and could expect a number of inconveniences imposed on him by other orchard owners'.

The following (fictional) numerical example is aimed at sharpening Cheung (1973) insights. In particular, it shows how to measure the welfare gains that are generated by the introduction of a market for pollination services. It also shows that when a market is opened there will be winners and losers, though the gains dominate the losses. We assume:

- Pollination is essential for apple-growing, each beehive generating 10 units of apples. Apple nectar is not essential in the production of honey as nectar found in the wild is (almost) a perfect substitute to apple nectar.
- A beehive produces 10 units of honey and costs £40 to set up. There is free entry of bee-keepers into the industry.
- The demand for honey is

$$p_{honey} = 10 - \frac{q_{honey}}{100}.$$

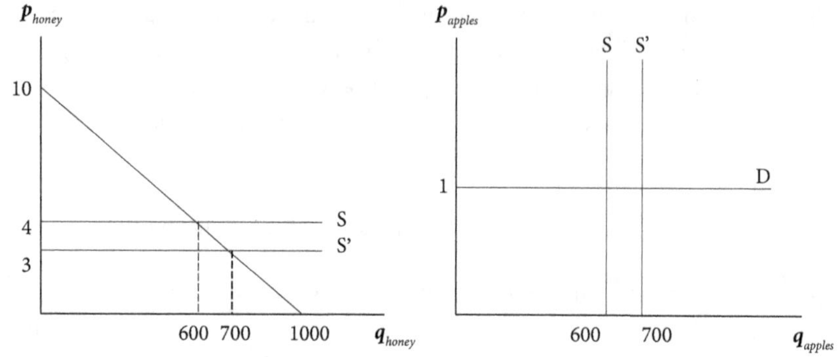

Figure 6.7 The market for pollination

The demand for apples is horizontal at a price of £1 per unit of apples; see Figure 6.7.

We start by analysing the equilibrium in a missing market case, where farmers don't pay bee-keepers for pollination services. Entry to the bee-keeping industry is determined by the bee-keepers' zero-profit condition, from which a price of honey is derived:

$$10 \times p_{honey} = 40.$$

It follows that the equilibrium price is £4 per unit of honey, and the equilibrium quantity of honey is 600 units. Since each beehive generates 10 units of honey, the equilibrium number of beehives is 60. Since each beehive generates 10 units of apples, the supply of apples is fixed at 600 units. At a price of £1 per unit and in absence of any other cost, an apple grower makes a profit of £600. The surplus of honey consumers is

$$surplus_{honey} = \frac{(10 - 4) \times 600}{2} = 1,800.$$

Once a market is opened, bee-keepers relocate their beehives to the highest-bidding grove. Competition then drives the price that apple growers pay bee-keepers for locating their beehives nearby up to £10. That would affect the bee-keepers' free-entry condition to

$$10 \times P_{honey} + 10 = 40,$$

dropping the price of honey to £3 per unit. The production of honey increases to 700, the number of beehives increases to 70, with apple production increasing

Table 6.3 Bee-keepers' and apple growers' welfare (numerical example)

change in bee-keepers' welfare	0
change in honey consumers' welfare	2,450 – 1,800 = 650
change in apple growers' welfare	−600
change in apple consumers welfare	0
net welfare effect	+50

to 700, accordingly; in Figure 6.7 the new supply curves are labelled with prime. Now, the surplus of honey consumers is

$$surplus'_{honey} = \frac{(10-3)\times 700}{2} = 2,450.$$

Table 6.3 accounts for parties' changes in welfare due to the creation of the market. Notice that the welfare of the bee-keepers does not change, since they operate on their zero profit condition both before and after the opening of the market. At the same time, the apple growers are worse off in spite of the expanded production, because a free commodity, pollination, has become a transacted commodity, with the fees eating up their entire profits. Apple consumers are not affected, as they keep on buying apples at a price equal to their subjective valuation, with zero surplus. It follows that the consumers of honey grab the entire surplus. The net welfare effect is still positive, 50, but with sizable distributional consequences.

6.3.3 Information as a Public Good

Information seems to be the paradigmatic non-subtractable commodity: when an additional player gains access to existing information, the players who already use that information do not have less of it (although their ability to extract a monopolistic rent out of that information might be diminished). Arrow (1963), in a seminal paper that uses medical care as an example, was among the first to point out the far-reaching implications of that observation.

6.3.3.1 Health Care

The medical-care industry seems to be particularly vulnerable to missing-markets problems, due to externality effects generated by contagious disease, new technologies that are difficult to patent, complicated eventualities that are difficult to write into insurance contracts, etc.. Above all, so much of the industry's 'output' is information, which by its very nature cannot be turned into a traded commodity;

see the Chapter 3 discussion of trade in test-drilling results. Most importantly, the role of institutions is to remedy trading frictions:

> when markets fail ... society will ... recognize the gap [and] ... non-market social institutions will arise attempting to bridge it. Certainly, this process is not necessarily conscious; nor is [it] uniformly successful ... [I contend] here that the special structural characteristics of the medical-care market are largely attempts to overcome ... non-marketability... [T]he government ... is usually implicitly or explicitly held to function as the agency which substitutes for the market's failure. I am arguing here that in some circumstances other social institutions will step into the optimality gap
>
> Arrow (1963, p. 947)

6.3.3.2 Costly State Verification

The theory of Costly State Verification (CSV), developed by Townsend (1979) and Diamond (1984), provides a simple explanation for the piece-wise linear structure of the debt contract[8] and, also, for the prevalence of intermediaries in financial markets. Both the contract and the intermediary emerge, spontaneously, as a market reaction to an informational trading friction.

Consider an owner-manager player, call him the *entrepreneur*, with no resources of her own but with an exclusive access to a project, which requires funding, I. If started up, the project would generate a random cash flow, y_ω, across $\omega = 1, 2, ..., \Omega$ states of nature, with probabilities π_ω. For simplicity, we number the states such that $y_1 < y_2 < y_3 ..., y_\Omega$. Funding can be supplied by an external investor. Both players are risk neutral; at this stage we don't call them debtor and creditor as the shape of the contract is not-yet determined. Competition for investment opportunities drives the investor to his 'break even' point so that, in expectations, he earns a zero economic profit beyond the opportunity cost of his funds, which is the riskless rate, r^f. The outcome of the project is known to the entrepreneur only. Nevertheless, the investor can find out the outcome through ex-post *monitoring*, an audit that would reveal the outcome, at a cost of $c < y$. A contract is, thus, a repayment schedule, $R_\omega \leq y_\omega$ and a monitoring policy, m_ω such that $m_\omega = 1$ implies monitoring and $m_\omega = 0$ implies no monitoring. Though, in reality, monitoring is a matter of discretion, we assume that the investor is committed to implement it, ex post, exactly as agreed in the contract. We can therefore write the ex ante break-even condition as

$$\Sigma_\omega R_\omega \pi_\omega - c\Sigma_\omega m_\omega \pi_\omega = I\left(1 + r^f\right).$$

[8] See the Chapter 3 discussion.

A crucial insight of the CSV model is that the investor need not monitor the entrepreneur in all eventualities. For example, if the entrepreneur declares the y_Ω realization, then there is no point in wasting resources on monitoring her: since, by itself, monitoring generates no value, its incidence should be restricted to the minimum that sustains the relationship. Clearly, the entrepreneur would declare such high repayment state only if she cannot declare another state with lower payment where she isn't monitored and, therefore, is not caught cheating. That is, a contract that allows for states h and l, $R_l < R_h$, such that $m_l = 0$, creates an incentive to cheat. Excluding such contracts implies that[9]

$$\text{if } m_\omega = 0, \text{ then } R_\omega = R \qquad \text{(a constant)},$$

$$\text{if } R_\omega < R, \text{ then } m_\omega = 1.$$

Lastly, it makes sense to set repayments as high as possible in the monitored states so as to set R as low as possible; a higher R might bring in more states into the set of monitored states. It follows that

$$\text{if } R_\omega < R, \text{ and } m_\omega = 1, \text{ then } R_\omega = y_\omega.$$

Calling the $m_\omega = 1$ states 'bankruptcy' and the flat-repayment states 'solvency', we have thus specified a standard debt contract.

To make things less abstract, consider the following numerical example: $I = 80$, $y_\omega = 0, 110, 200$, $\pi_\omega = 0.2, 0.6, 0.2$, $c = 20$, $r^f = 0$. Clearly, the debtor must be monitored when she declares zero income; otherwise she would always declare that state. For the opposite reason, there is no point monitoring the debtor when she declares an income of 200. The question is whether we can set the fixed repayment below 110. Let's try:

$$0.8 \times R - 20 \times 0.2 = 80,$$

which solves at $R = 105 < 110$. Hence, with a fixed repayment of 105 the entrepreneur can avoid default at the two higher states, which would limit the incidence of monitoring to the case where $y_\omega = 0$, with the sole purpose of deterring cheating in that state.[10]

[9] In Chapter 7, where we provide a more rigorous analysis of such agency problems, we call such conditions 'incentive compatibility constraints'.

[10] Careful readers may notice that the investor's break-even condition can also be satisfied by setting $R = 150$ and $m_1 = m_2 = 1$, that is monitoring in both states 1 and 2. We dismiss such a contract on grounds that it is Pareto dominated, as it implements the same expected payoff to the investor, 80, at an expected cost of monitoring higher by £12 ($20 \times \Pi_2$) relative to $R = 105$ and only $m_1 = 1$. It follows that all monitoring costs ultimately fall on the borrower; see Chapter 7 for a more rigorous treatment of contract theory.

Now consider the situation where the project is too big for a single lender. How should the many lenders who come together to fund the project organize the audit? Clearly, a separate audit by each and every one is wasteful. Why? Because the audit generates information, which is a public good. As such, the benefit that the information generates for one lender does not diminish the benefit that it generates to others. Just like in the case of pollution or the lighthouse, an efficient production of the public good requires collective action on the part of the lenders. They should thus appoint one of them to be the *delegate monitor*, to audit the investor on behalf of them all. We interpret the delegate monitor as the bank.

How can the non-monitoring lenders be sure that the delegate monitor is reporting honestly to them? If the delegate monitor holds a diversified portfolio so that the return on her portfolio is hardly random, it removes the need to 'monitor the delegate monitor'. That makes the bank interpretation of the delegate even more attractive. It may also require some government involvement in monitoring the rare event of a failure of the delegate monitor, which is typically the case when a bank fails.

6.3.3.3 Some Empirical Evidence

On July 1984, Continental Illinois Bank (CIB), at the time the seventh largest commercial bank in the United States, was, for all intents and purposes, insolvent. On 23 July, quite unexpectedly, the Federal Deposit Insurance Corporation (FDIC), the US bank regulator, announced that it would bail out CIB.[11] Slovin, Sushka, and Polonchek (1993) have used that event to test some of the predictions of costly state verification theory.

Plausibly, through a lending relationship, a bank can gain a certain familiarity with the client's business. That familiarity allows the bank to benefit from a lower cost of monitoring, c, relative to any potential competitor. It is also plausible that the client can use this fact in order to bargain with the bank so that part of the cost advantage is passed through to herself. The client can thus price the relationship as if it was an ordinary asset that generates cash flows. However, this asset would vanish once the bank goes bankrupt. That is, unlike a tangible asset, familiarity is just information, for which a market does not exist. Hence, a testable hypothesis that is consistent with the costly state verification theory is that the pending bankruptcy of CIB had a negative effect on the market value of its clients, and the surprise rescue had a positive effect on their value.

The authors manage to identify 53 publicly listed companies (for which there is a stock-price data that can be used to measure the client's value), who had a borrowing relationship with CIB. Of these, 29 had a strong relationship with CIB in the form of either a direct lending relationship or in the form of CIB being the lead manager in a syndicated loan (a loan funded jointly by several banks, one of

[11] This event is considered by many as the birth of the 'too big to fail bank' practice in the US.

Table 6.4 CIB bankruptcy/rescue and client's characteristics

	3 days before rescue		upon rescue	
characteristics	**coefficient (%)**	***t*-statistics**	**coefficient (%)**	***t*-statistics**
AGENT	−5 to −7	−2.6 to −4.1	2.2 to 3.6	1.9 to 2.9
LEVERAGE	−2	−2.9 to −3.5	1.7 to 2	5.5 to 6.0
OTHER	8	3.7	3.9 to 4.2	2.8 to 3.3
NOBOND	−0.03	−0.02	3.6	3.4
R^2	0.16 to 0.44		0.11 to 0.66	

Source: Slovin, Sushka and Polonchek (1993)

whom is the agreed upon leader). Changes in valuation are estimated, over and above changes in the value of the entire market.

It turns out that on average, the 29 companies with a strong relationship to CIB lost 4.2% of their value in the three days prior to the surprise FDIC rescue and gained 2% of their value upon rescue (with statistical significance of 1% and 5%, respectively). The authors then correlate the change in the client's value to its characteristics for all 53 companies. The characteristics that are included are the following (see Table 6.4): AGENT is a dummy variable that takes the value of 1 in case the company has a strong relationship with CIB (in the sense above) and 0 otherwise, LEVERAGE is the ratio of company's debt to its market value, OTHER is a dummy variable that takes the value of 1 in case the company has a relationship with another bank and 0 otherwise and NOBOND is a dummy variable that takes the value of 1 in case the company has no access to the bond market and 0 otherwise. Clearly, the hypothesis is not rejected.

6.3.3.4 The 'Hirshleifer Effect'

One may be tempted to conclude that additional information would necessarily ameliorate the missing-market problem. Hirshleifer (1963) shows that this is not the case. Consider, again, the case described in Chapter 5, Section 3.2. A player has an income $\bar{c}$ and is exposed to the risk, $\tilde{\varepsilon}$, with outcomes $\pm\varepsilon$, each having a probability of 1/2. We have demonstrated, there, that the risk decreases his welfare by $\theta\varepsilon/2$ where θ is the coefficient of risk aversion.

Now suppose that the player is offered 'fair insurance': a risk neutral insurer is willing to 'take over' $\tilde{\varepsilon}$ risk, both the upside and the downside, at a fair price—that is zero. Clearly, the execution of such a transaction is a Pareto improvement.

Suppose, alternatively, that the outcome of the $\tilde{\varepsilon}$ is revealed before the player and the insurer could complete the transaction. Clearly, the transaction is no longer viable: it is refused by the player in case the outcome is $+\varepsilon$ and by the insurer if the outcome is $-\varepsilon$. In general, an early revelation of information destroys insurance markets.

In recent years, concerns have been raised that sophisticated diagnostics technology, which can identify an hereditary disease, would disable medical insurance contingent on such a disease. For it would be in the best interest of insurance buyers to show their insurer test results, but only if the result indicates that they are free from the disease. A failure to show such test results would be treated by the insurer as a sign that the buyer is affected by the disease.

6.3.4 Liquidity

Upon first examination, liquidity, that is the storage of fungible resources for a case of emergency,[12] does not raise any concerns regarding frictions or market-failures. Hence, it may come as a surprise that financial economists often argue that 'liquidity is a public good'. Indeed, in a seminal contribution, Diamond and Dybvig (1983)[13] have demonstrated that due to a missing market in personal insurance, there is a shortage of liquidity, at the level of the entire economy. The following simplified example captures the essence of their argument.

Consider an economy with three periods, $t = 0, 1, 2$ and 1000 players. At $t = 0$ each player receives 1 unit of wealth, which she needs to invest in order to fund future consumption (there is no need to consume at $t = 0$). Two assets are available: liquidity, essentially a storage technology, which preserves value from one period to the next but bears no return. The other is a long-term capital investment that yields a return of 100% if held to maturity (at $t = 2$), but loses all its value if discontinued at $t = 1$. The timing of consumption is uncertain: there is a 25% (75%) probability that, at $t = 1$, the player will discover that she derives zero subjective valuation from $t = 2$ ($t = 1$) consumption, so that she must concentrate all her consumption at $t = 1$ ($t = 2$). We call the former event an 'emergency'. There is no $t = 0$ indication which player is more likely to suffer an emergency; they are ex-ante identical, from their own as well as others' point of view. The players are 'very highly' risk averse, so their preferred policy is to smooth consumption perfectly across the two consumption eventualities, above.

It is quite clear that hedging the risk of an emergency on one's own (i.e. without sharing the emergency risk with other players), by building a portfolio of l units of liquid assets and k units of capital,

$$l + k = 1,$$

[12] See Chapter 8 for another interpretation of this illusive concept.

[13] Douglas Diamond and Philip Dybvig, together with Ben Bernanke are the winners of the 2022 Nobel Prize in Economics. Their paper is equally famous for its analysis of bank runs. A simple version of the idea is already presented in Chapter 2, applied to the creditors of a company rather than the depositors of a bank.

is highly inefficient, for in state of emergency, capital is useless. Perfect consumption smoothing requires investing in liquid assets alone, consuming one unit (namely just the initial wealth) under both eventualities.

In order to share the emergency risk, consider a competitive insurance industry that charges a $t = 0$ premium of 1 (namely the players' entire initial wealth) and provides, in return, a personal-insurance contract that pays a $t = 1$ compensations to players who face an emergency. The payoff, to the 250 players who face an emergency,[14] is paid out of a liquid inventory, l^o per capita. The rest can be invested, long term, in productive capital, k^o, per capita, with $t = 2$ earnings distributed to players who suffer no emergency. The very high risk-aversion assumption implies that players value insurance contracts that deliver the same level of consumption, c^o, under both eventualities; competition drives insurers to supply such contracts. Competition also drives them towards zero profit; insurers bear no operational costs.[15] Hence, the competitive equilibrium is:

$$\begin{aligned} 250 \times c^o &= 1000 \times l^o, \\ 750 \times c^o &= 2 \times 1000 \times k^o, \\ 1 &= l^o + k^o. \end{aligned}$$

solving out these three equation in three unknowns yields $c^o = 1.6$ and $l^o = 0.4$, $k^o = 0.6$. By First Welfare Theorem the equilibrium is Pareto efficient. It assumes, however, that the emergency event is verifiable by the insurer, who pays the $t = 1$ compensations only after confirming that a player, indeed, faces a state of emergency.

What if the state of emergency is not verifiable? We consider a 'market-oriented' approach, whereby players manage their own portfolios, but have access to a $t = 1$ market where they can sell (buy) capital if they do (don't) face an emergency. To make the example more exciting suppose that the capital stays put so that only titles to capital change hands in this 'stock market'. Let the $t = 1$ equilibrium price of capital be q^m and let the equilibrium portfolio in this economy be (l^m, k^m). Since there is no macro risk, q^m can be perfectly anticipated already at $t = 0$. Upon which, the following contingent consumption plan can be devised:

$$\begin{aligned} c_1^m &= l^m + q^m k^m, \\ c_2^m &= 2 \times \left(\frac{l^m}{q^m} + k^m \right). \end{aligned}$$

[14] For the sake of simplicity, we assume that the realized number of players who face an emergency is always 250, exactly, so that insurers bear no risk.

[15] Alternatively, the return on capital is net of such expenses.

We demonstrate, below, that the equilibrium price is $q^m = 1$, implying that $c_1^m = 1$ and $c_2^m = 2$. Though at $q^m = 1$ players' portfolios have no effect on their consumption, we assume that they hold portfolios that would clear the market, so that $250 \times c^o = 1000 \times l^m$. It follows that $l^m = 0.25$. That is, in the stock-market economy, liquidity is under-provided relative to its amount in the Pareto-dominating equilibrium, $l^o = 0.4$.

But why is it that $q^m = 1$ in a stock-market economy? Suppose, by way of contradiction, that $q > 1$. It is easy to see that in this case there is no incentive to hold any liquidity. By moving, say, a fraction δ of the portfolio from liquid assets to long-term investment, a player would increase his consumption for both the event of emergency and the event where there is no emergency:

$$\Delta c_1 = -\delta + q\delta = (q-1)\,\delta > 0,$$

$$\Delta c_2 = 2 \times \left(\frac{-\delta}{q} + \delta\right) = 2 \times \left(1 - \frac{1}{q}\right) \times \delta > 0.$$

It follows that in this case players select a 'corner solution' with portfolios of long-term investments only. No liquidity is held by any player. But then, desperate players in a state of emergency would be willing to sell their investment at any price, as low as it gets, for they need to consume at $t = 1$ and cannot wait for their investments to mature. It follows that $q > 1$ cannot be an equilibrium price. A similar argument can be constructed to rule out an equilibrium with $q < 1$ (albeit with the inverse portfolio implications).

Perhaps an easier way to see the result is by calculating the event-contingent rate of return vector on liquidity and capital:

$$r^l = \left(1, \frac{2}{q^m}\right) = \frac{1}{q^m} \times (q^m, 2),$$

$$r^k = (q^m, 2).$$

Namely, a unit of liquidity provides 1 unit of consumption in case of a $t = 1$ emergency; otherwise, the holder can use it to buy $1/q^m$ unit of capital and hold them to maturity when each would yield 2 units of consumption. Likewise, a unit of capital can be sold for q^m of consumption in case of $t = 1$ emergency; otherwise, it can be held to maturity when it would yield two units of consumption. Evidently, for any price other than 1, one asset dominates the other, which implies an arbitrage opportunity, as demonstrated in the previous paragraph. Figure 6.8 demonstrates the point for the $q^m > 1$ case, where capital dominates liquidity for both eventualities.

Clearly, the stock market delivers an inferior outcome: a 'very highly risk-averse' player values his contingent consumption plan $c_1^m = 1$ and $c_2^m = 2$, according to the worse-case consumption level, namely 1, compared with $c^o = 1.6$ provided by the

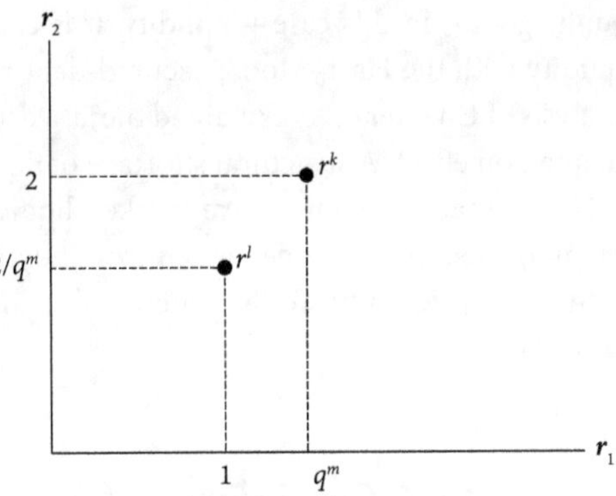

Figure 6.8 Conditional return on liquidity and capital, $q^m > 1$.

insurance industry. Evidently, the stock market cannot resolve the informational friction of the non-verifiable emergency events.[16] The competitive incomplete stock-markets equilibrium is characterized by a low level of liquidity, only l^m = 0.25 in comparison to l^o = 0.4 complete-markets insurance equilibrium. That is, as a result of the missing-market problem, the economy suffers a shortage of liquidity at the level of the entire market. In other words, liquidity is a public good, under provided in a competitive stock-market equilibrium. Notice that a subtractability test would not reveal the problem; only careful modelling would. As already emphasized above, it is not for any physical characteristic that a commodity turns into a public good; rather it is due to a friction that prevents certain trading opportunities from being materialized.

Moreover, in our example, the very use of the stock market for the purpose of hedging personal risk is an indication of a missing market. In the complete-markets version, liquidity is held by insurance companies and is distributed out via settlements of personal insurance contracts. In contrast to popular perceptions, a more active stock market is not an indication of a 'more developed' or 'more sophisticated' financial system; quite the opposite. To put it slightly differently, the more concentrated management of the economy's liquidity in the hands of (relatively) few insurance companies is not an indication that the 'market is not working'.

The result that liquidity is a public good seems to be robust to changes in the detail of the modelling: across models, liquidity tends to be under provided in a competitive equilibria where individual risks are hedged via trading. Interestingly, the result seems to be embedded in central-banks policy: to top-up liquidity in financial markets at times of turbulence, thereby dampening price volatility. Like other organs of the state, central banks can be understood as agencies tasked with

[16] We leave the question whether, given the friction, the market equilibrium constrained Pareto efficient, see the Chapter 3 definition, unanswered.

the provision of public goods, in this case—liquidity. It is common to associate the demand for liquidity with the Hart–Moore secured-debt model of Chapter 3 and the fire-sales analysis of Chapter 4. As explained there, a drop in collateral values could create a contagion effect. A structural shortage of liquidity would much amplify this effect. Notice that in a competitive market, liquidity is provided by speculators who are motivated by profits generated from buying cheap fire sales, ignoring the value that extra liquidity would generate for financially distressed companies; hence the externality.

6.4 Conclusions

Drawing the line between well functioning and failed markets is the main business of modern economics. Presently, there seems to be a broad consensus that markets fail sometimes and 'work well' in many other cases. Most economists would agree that pollution is a textbook example of a market failure, while ordinary industrial activity can, in many cases, be left unregulated. The grey area in between still attracts a heated debate. In this chapter we have presented the main concepts, but have also tried to explain why their application can be quite difficult in practice.

Financial markets are information intensive and, thus, particularly sensitive to potential market failures. The financial crisis of 2008 made the point abundantly clear, to professional and laymen alike. Yet the policy debate is not resolved. Some argue that too-light regulation is the root problem, while others argue that the crisis was a result of badly structured regulation. Both sides could agree (perhaps) that neither markets nor regulators are perfect, but disagree about which friction should be targeted by public policy.

One insight that this chapter provides is that resolving these debates requires a detailed analysis of institutional structures that emerge in imperfect markets. In the coming chapters we progress the analysis in this direction.

References

[1] Arrow, Kenneth J. (1963). 'Uncertainty and the Welfare Economics of Medical Care', *The American Economic Review*, Vol. 53, No. 5, pp. 941–973.

[2] Blanes-i-Vidal, J., M. Draca, C. Fons-Rosen (2012). 'Revolving Door Lobbyists', *American Economic Review*, Vol. 102, No. 7, pp. 3731–3748.

[3] Cheung, Steven N. S. (1973). 'The Fable of the Bees: An Economic Investigation', *Journal of Law and Economics*, Vol. 16, No. 1, pp. 11–33.

[4] Coase, R. A. (1974). 'The Lighthouse in Economics', *Journal of Law and Economics*, Vol. 17, No. 2, pp. 357–376.

[5] Diamond, Douglas, W. (1984). 'Financial Intermediation and Delegated Monitoring', *Review of Economic Studies*, Vol. 51, pp. 393– 414.

[6] Diamond Douglas, W. and Philip H. Dybvig (1983). 'Bank Runs, Deposit Insurance, and Liquidity', *The Journal of Political Economy*, Vol. 91, No. 3, pp. 401–419.

[7] Friedman, Milton (1962). *Capitalism and Freedom*, University of Chicago Press.

[8] Hirshleifer, Jack (1971). 'The Private and Social Value of Information and the Reward to Inventive Activity'. *The American Economic Review*, Vol. 61, No. 4, pp. 561–574.

[9] Kreps, David M. and Jose A. Scheinkman (1983). 'Quantity Precommitment and Bertrand Competition Yield Cournot Outcomes', *The Bell Journal of Economics*, Vol. 14, No. 2, pp. 326–337.

[10] Schumpeter, Joseph Alois (1934). *The Theory of Economic Development*, Oxford University Press.

[11] Slovin, Myron B., Marie E. Sushka, and John A. Polonchek (1993), 'The Value of Bank Durability: Borrowers as Bank Stakeholders', *The Journal of Finance*, Vol. 48, No. 1, pp. 247–266.

[12] Stigler, George J. (1971). 'The Theory of Economic Regulation', *The Bell Journal of Economics and Management Science*, Vol. 2, No. 1, pp. 3–21.

[13] Townsend, Robert, M. (1979). 'Optimal Contracts and Competitive Markets with Costly State Verification', *Journal of Economic Theory*, Vol. 21, pp. 265–293.

7
Trading with the Better Informed

7.1 Introduction

In spite of numerous references to 'information frictions' and to institutional arrangements intended to ameliorate their effect, no systematic treatment of the subject is offered so far. Some questions have remained unanswered. For example, in Chapter 3, in the analysis of the Hart–Moore model, we demonstrate that the failure to make debt repayments contingent on cash flows that are observable by both the lender and the creditor (but not the court) results in loss of value. Yet, it is not entirely clear whether the loss could be avoided by more sophisticated contracts that would incentivize the players to reveal, truthfully, that information to the court.

In this chapter we offer a preliminary, though systematic, treatment of trade under conditions of *asymmetry of information*. Namely, trade where one party 'knows something' about the object that is being traded that the other party does not.

7.2 Asymmetric Information: Taxonomy

There are two sorts of asymmetric-information problems: *adverse selection* and *moral hazard* or, more intuitively, *hidden type* and *hidden action*, respectively. In both cases players trade an item that one party is materially better informed about than the other; the broken lines in Figure 7.1 connect the attributes of the item, which the uninformed cannot observe. In the adverse-selection case, 'nature' randomly selects the type, θ_i ($i = 1, 2$), of the informed player's item. Though the uniformed player cannot observe θ_i, she knows the incidence of each type in the population, π_i, and forms expectations about her trading partner's type, accordingly.

In the moral-hazard problem, an uninformed player, called the *principal*, delegates a task to another player, called the *agent*. The agent may be more or less diligent in performing the task: the more *effort*, e_i, he puts in, the better is the outcome for the principal. Though the principal cannot observe the amount of effort that the agent puts into his task, she is fully aware of the agent's circumstances and, hence, is able to form an informed guess about his choice.

The Economics of Financial Markets and Institutions. Oren Sussman, Oxford University Press. © Oren Sussman (2023).
DOI: 10.1093/oso/9780192869739.003.0008

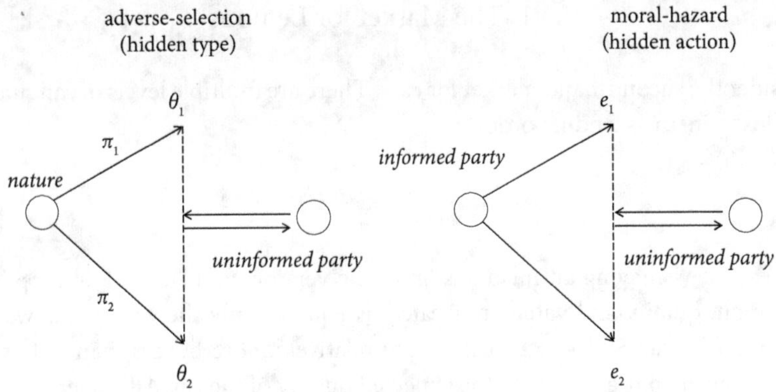

Figure 7.1 The taxonomy of asymmetric information problems

In both cases, the two players can communicate. Hence, the informed can tell the uniformed player about his type or his action, but there is no reason why the uninformed should believe such 'cheap talk'. Intuitively, players' mere suspicion that their trading partners are 'cheating' on them could undermine the prospect of reaching Pareto-efficient outcome. In line with arguments made in previous chapters, credibility is more likely to be achieved by action rather than by communication. Hence, in the hidden-type case, the question is whether the informed player can take an action that *signals* her type. Obviously, such a signal is credible to the extent that only one of the two types can bear the cost of sending the signal while the other cannot. In the hidden-action problem, the question is whether the principal and the agent can negotiate a contract that would *incentivize* the agent to take the action favoured by the principle as a matter of self interest.

7.3 The Hidden-Type Problem

In his 1970 path-breaking paper on the market for lemons (American slang for defective second-hand cars), George Akerlof provides the basic insights: in a setting where only vendors know whether the quality of the car is a lemon, lemons will drive good cars out of the market, to the point that the entire market breaks down. In an equally important 1976 paper, Michael Spence (who shared with Joseph Stiglitz and George Akerlof the 2001 Nobel Prize for contributions to information economics) extended the analysis to include signalling. In his example, university degrees have no intrinsic value; their only purpose is to allow graduates to signal employers a high quality. As we shall see, the applicability of their ideas extend well beyond the automobile or the education markets.

7.3.1 The Market for Lemons

Consider the second-hand market for cars. There are multiple levels of car quality, θ_i indexed in an ascending order,

$$\theta^1 < \theta^2 < \ldots < \theta^I,$$

with each class having an incidence π^i in the vendor population. For simplicity exposition, quality and value are treated as equals. Only the vendor knows the quality of the car. Suppose that there are relatively more buyers than sellers, so that the buyers bid the price to the expected quality of the car. All players are risk neutral.

It is common to start the analysis of an asymmetric-information problem by removing the information asymmetry so as to establish a clear benchmark against which one can assess its effect. In which case, there would be I markets, so that each type is traded in a separate market at a different price,

$$p^i = \theta^i.$$

By the First Welfare Theorem, the equilibrium is Pareto efficient.

Back to the asymmetric-information case, could a buyer pick a car at random from the vendor population, she would treat quality as a random variable, $\widetilde{\theta}$, and value the car at $E\left(\widetilde{\theta}\right)$. However, cars are not picked at random; it is up to the vendor to decide whether to put his car up for sale. At a price of $E\left(\widetilde{\theta}\right)$, it is in the best interest of the owner of the highest-quality car, θ^I, not to sell the car, since $E\left(\widetilde{\theta}\right) < \theta^I$. The buyer should take this fact into consideration and consider a valuation $E\left(\widetilde{\theta}|\widetilde{\theta} < \theta^I\right)$[1]. But now, it is in the best interest of the owner of the second highest-quality car, θ^{I-1} not to sell the car; the buyer should also take this fact into consideration and revise her valuation to $E\left(\widetilde{\theta}|\widetilde{\theta} < \theta^{I-1}\right)$. And so on. Eventually, only the lowest-quality owners could trade, so that the market is virtually shut down.

7.3.2 Education as a Signal

Consider a population of workers of varied productivity. The size of the population is normalized to one, by which we mean that rather than conducting the analysis in terms of number of workers we conduct it in terms of fractions (percentages)

[1] To be read: the mathematical expectations of $\widetilde{\theta}$ conditional on $\widetilde{\theta} < \theta^I$; see Section A.3.3 of the Mathematical Appendix.

of the population. Each member of that population is born with a certain level of productivity, θ^i, with $i = H, L$, high or low, respectively,

$$\theta^H > \theta^L > 0. \tag{7.1}$$

We think of productivity as, simply, the value of output, or cash, that an employee generates once employed. For simplicity, we assume that each firm can employ either zero or one worker, although the assumption is not essential. Productivity is due to innate ability, which workers cannot affect, neither through better training nor through their conduct on the job. We denote the percentage of H productivity workers in the population by π; the rest, $1 - \pi$, are of L type. We denote the wage rate by w^i. Both workers and firms are risk neutral.

The assumptions that we make about information are critical. Each worker knows his type, either H or L. firms cannot observe θ^i. At the same time they are fully aware of the heterogeneity across workers. Moreover, they know the value of π, precisely, so that could they randomly pick a worker out of the entire population, they would know for sure that, with a probability π, the worker is highly productive and with a probability of $1 - \pi$ that the worker has low productivity. Wages are negotiated at the beginning of the working period (a week or a month) and paid before the firm has an opportunity to observe the actual productivity of the worker. It is therefore impossible to condition the wage rate on (the eventual) output.

For simplicity, suppose that acquiring education, say a university degree, is a binary choice: $e = 0, 1$. Labour productivity is unrelated to the worker's level of education. Yet, acquiring education comes at a cost, c^i, of both money and effort. We assume that

$$c^L > c^H > 0, \tag{7.2}$$

so that the cost, particularly in terms of effort, is lower for the H type relative to the L type. It is implied that education does not generate any value.[2] Unlike type, education is observable. Crucially, the magnitude c^i is known to all, in particular to the firms. The main question is whether the acquisition of education can be used in order to signal type and, therefore, productivity.

Lastly, the labour market is competitive. Workers 'need money' so, although higher wages make them better off, as price takers, they would work for a low wage rather than not work at all: the supply curve of labour is vertical. The demand for labour by an individual firm is derived by profit maximization. There are 'many more' firms than workers, so competition drives wages up to the point that firms make zero profit; workers capture the entire surplus of the relationship.

[2] Alternatively, that c^i is the cost of effort net of the subjective value of the pleasure of being educated.

7.3.2.1 Full Information Benchmark

Consider, first, the full-information benchmark. That is, we make type observable to the firm. In which case the labour market splits according to type, each type being paid according to its own productivity. Profit-seeking behaviour implies that an individual firm's demand for labour is

$$\text{firm's labour demand} = \begin{cases} 1 & \text{if} \quad \theta^i \geq w^i \\ 0 & \text{if} \quad \theta^i < w^i \end{cases} . \tag{7.3}$$

Competition drives wages up to the productivity of labour; see Figure 7.2.

Since the acquisition of education comes at a cost but generates no benefit, no worker bothers to acquire it. That is, for both H and L types,

$$e^H = e^L = 0.$$

By First Welfare Theorem, this equilibrium is Pareto efficient. That is, goods that generate value, i.e. labour, are traded at a price that reflects their 'true value' while goods that don't generate value, i.e. education, are not even produced.

7.3.2.2 Separating Equilibria

So far, we have derived market equilibria by drawing supply and demand curves, then looking for an intersection point. This approach does not quite work here, for without knowing whether workers acquire education, we don't even know how to draw the curves, let alone how to cross them. So we take a slightly different approach: we hypothesize that equilibrium is either of the *separating* type or the *pooling* type. In the former case, high-ability workers do signal their type by acquiring education; in the latter case it is not in their best interest to do so. For each type of equilibrium, we write down a set of conditions that need to be satisfied, including conditions regarding the acquisition of education (or not). We

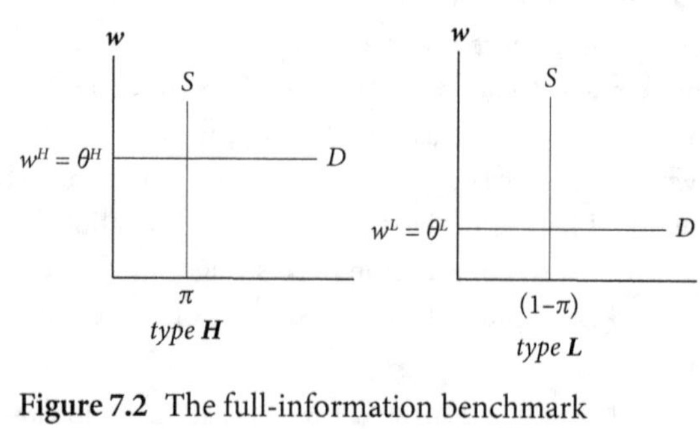

Figure 7.2 The full-information benchmark

then look for a combination of endogenous variables that satisfy all conditions—simultaneously. Notice that there is no guarantee that such a combination exist; equilibrium, of one type or another may not exist.

Consider a separating equilibrium, where the H-types signal their high productivity by acquiring education. If such an equilibrium exists, it needs to satisfy the following conditions. First,

$$prob\left(\theta = \theta^H \mid e = 1\right) = 1, \qquad \longrightarrow \qquad w^H = \theta^H. \tag{7.4}$$

To be read as follows: the probability that a worker is of high quality, conditional on that worker being educated, is 1. Once all firms make similar inferences, the equilibrium wage for educated workers is θ^H. Likewise,

$$prob\left(\theta = \theta^L \mid e = 0\right) = 1, \qquad \longrightarrow \qquad w^L = \theta^L. \tag{7.5}$$

For such inferences to be valid, two conditions must be satisfied. First, it is in the best interest of the H type to acquire education:

$$w^H - c^H > w^L. \tag{7.6}$$

That is, the H type, facing the choice between bearing the cost of acquiring education, c^H, in return for a high wage rate, w^H, or avoiding education in return for a low wage, w^L, prefers the former option. Notice that, within a separating equilibrium, in case a worker of type H avoids education, his low wage, w^L, is not a result of low productivity but, rather, of his decision not to signal his type in a credible manner. On the job he would actually generate a cash flow of θ^H, to the benefit of his employer.

Second, and more interestingly, it is in the best interest of the L type not to guise himself as an H type by acquiring education:

$$w^H - c^L < w^L. \tag{7.7}$$

That is, the L type, facing the choice between acquiring education at a cost of c^L and earning a high wage, w^H, or avoiding education and earning a low wage, w^L, prefers the latter option. Crucially, the L type avoids 'cheating' not because of a moral sense, not even because of the fear of being caught (under our assumption so far, fraudsters are never caught!) but, rather, because of a selfish reason: the pain of acquiring education is too high, and does not compensate for the benefit in terms of a higher wage rate.

If conditions (7.4) to (7.7) are satisfied, then there exists an equilibrium such that information is *fully revealed* and the asymmetry of information vanishes. To find out whether the equilibrium actually exist, we use Equations (7.4) and (7.5), express the wage rate, w^i, in terms of productivity, θ^i, substitute into conditions (7.6) and (7.7), and rearrange:

Proposition 7.1. *There exist a separating equilibrium if*

$$\frac{c^L}{\theta^H - \theta^L} > 1 > \frac{c^H}{\theta^H - \theta^L}. \tag{7.8}$$

The expressions on both sides of the inequality should be interpreted as the effective cost of signalling: the direct cost, c^i, adjusted by the productivity (and thus the wage) gain, $\theta^H - \theta^L$, is the cost of education per unit of extra income. Notice that the effective cost of education tends to infinity when the productivity differential tends to zero.

Figure 7.3 helps to identify those economies, within a wider *family* defined by the assumptions of our model, where a separating equilibrium exits. It differs from our earlier chapters' approach to a market analysis, which is to describe behavioural relationships, supply and demand, by drawing graphs of endogenous variables, prices against quantities, 'shifting the curves' in response to changes in the exogenous variables, say income or technology. The family of relevant economies is defined by a combination structural parameters: $\theta^H, \theta^L, c^H, c^L$, and π. Fortunately, the characterization of equilibrium in Proposition 7.1 reduces to just two combinations of these parameters, $\frac{c^H}{\theta^H - \theta^L}$ and $\frac{c^L}{\theta^H - \theta^L}$, which are plotted against the horizontal and vertical axis in Figure 7.3, respectively. Points below the diagonal violate condition (7.2), $c^L > c^H$ and are irrelevant to our analysis as they are not part of the investigated family of economies. The *parameter space* of the investigated family is therefore captured by an (open) cone above the diagonal and to the

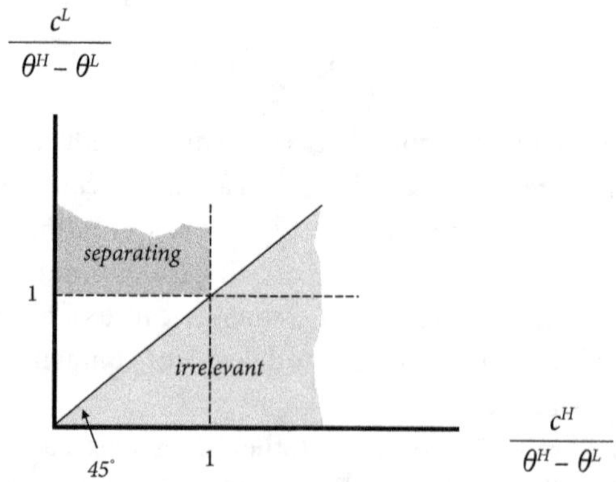

Figure 7.3 Condition for a separating equilibrium

right of the vertical axis, with each point within this area mapping to one member of the family.

Separating equilibria exist in the shaded, positive (open) rectangle to the left of the unit vertical line and above the unit horizontal line. Intuitively, the condition requires that the cost of signalling for the H type is relatively low, so that respective players have an incentive to acquire education and signal their type, while the cost of signalling for the L type is relatively high so that players do not have an incentive to guise themselves as a high type. The separating equilibrium breaks down if both types have a high cost of signalling because, then, even the H type avoids signalling. The separating equilibrium also breaks down if both types have a low cost of signalling because, then, even the L type has an incentive to 'dress up' as a high type.

7.3.2.3 Pooling Equilibria

In a pooling equilibrium the H type does not separate itself from the L type. It might be hoped that a pooling equilibrium exists whenever a separating equilibrium does not and, vice versa, whenever a pooling equilibrium exists a separating equilibrium does not. Unfortunately, things are somewhat more complicated. We take the same approach as above, starting by specifying a set of conditions that a pooling equilibrium must satisfy.

First, absent a signalling, workers' equilibrium wage, w^P, equals the expected productivity of a randomly selected worker:

$$w^P = \pi\theta^H + (1 - \pi)\,\theta^L; \tag{7.9}$$

See Figure 7.4.

Next, a pooling equilibrium only exists if it is in the best interest of the workers, particularly the H type, not to signal their type. Now, here comes the difficulty in the analysis of pooling equilibria. Any decision, whether to signal or not, depends on workers' beliefs, denoted by λ, about how their decision to acquire education would be perceived by employers once they look for a job:

$$\lambda = prob\left(\theta = \theta^H \mid e = 1\right).$$

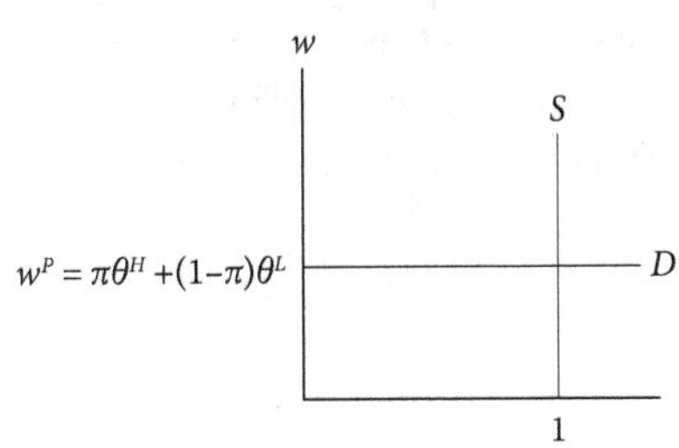

Figure 7.4 A pooling equilibrium

Unlike expectations, that can be formed on the basis of players experience with their environment, beliefs are about *counterfactuals*, that is 'things that don't happen'. Rather than facts, beliefs are derived from players speculations about environments of which neither them, nor anyone else, has any practical experience; see Chapter 8 for a more detailed analysis of expectations versus beliefs. At the same time, beliefs affect players' actions or, in our case, inaction. Given the difficulty of modelling them, we leave the question of their formation open—for the time being, and carry on:

$$w^b = \lambda\theta^H + (1-\lambda)\,\theta^L. \tag{7.10}$$

The rest is straightforward, as the two following conditions should be satisfied in equilibrium:

$$w^b - c^H < w^p, \tag{7.11}$$

$$w^b - c^L < w^p. \tag{7.12}$$

That is, both types can signal, gain a wage rate w^b and bear the cost of acquiring education, c^i, or settle for the pooled wage, w^p. In a pooling equilibrium, both H and L types prefer the latter option, which is not to acquire education. Substituting Equations (7.9) and (7.10) into Equations (7.11) and (7.12) and rearranging yields a condition for the existence of a pooling equilibrium:

Proposition 7.2. *There exists a pooling equilibrium if*

$$\frac{c^L}{\theta^H - \theta^L} > \frac{c^H}{\theta^H - \theta^L} > \lambda - \pi. \tag{7.13}$$

The disappointing implication of Proposition 7.2 is that without an economic mechanism to determine λ, 'everything is possible'. In particular, suppose λ equals π; that is, workers think that upon acquiring education, firms would still assign them with the population's probability of being of an H quality. In that case, condition (7.13) holds for any point in the parameter space. That is, for any member of the family of economies specified at the top of Section 7.3.2, whether a separating equilibrium exists or not, a pooling equilibrium exists. It even has an intuitive interpretation: since workers believe that no firm would take their decision to acquire education seriously, no one even tries.

Economic theorists have invested much effort in attempting to devise *refinements*[3] so as to eliminate at least part of this disappointing multiplicity of equilibria. For example, workers of the H type might acquire education and, then, try to

[3] The word is used in the same sense as in Chapter 2.

convince prospective employers that they would not have done so had they been of the L type. A detailed analysis of such arguments lies beyond the scope of the present book.

7.3.2.4 Economic Efficiency in Adverse Selection Models

With Chapter 6's observation in mind, that information is a public good, one is tempted to rush to the conclusion that the separating equilibrium must be economically more efficient than the pooling equilibrium. That would be a mistake. Consider an economy with structural parameters such that both a pooling and a separating equilibrium exists. Comparing the two, notice that:

- There is no gain of productivity in revealing the worker's type. The information that is revealed in a separating equilibrium has no use in, say, reallocating workers to more productive jobs or in providing better incentives. Regardless of the type of equilibrium, pooling or separating, all workers get a job where their productivity is, simply, the one they were born with. Building adverse-selection models with such allocation effects is possible, at a considerable cost of extra complexity.
- Education, per se, is a waste of resources as it generates no value, to the worker or the economy.
- Compared with a pooling equilibrium, a separating equilibrium increases the wage rate of the H type but decreases the wage rate of the L type. In that respect, even ignoring the cost of acquiring education, the two models cannot be ranked using the Pareto criterion. Had workers been assumed to be risk averse, there might even be some insurance value in the pooling equilibrium. In which case, and from an ex-ante point of view (that is before type is realized), the separation can be viewed as an example of Chapter 6's Hirshleifer effect, where the revelation of information undermines insurance opportunities.

7.3.3 Application: Debt and Equity

In spite of conceptual difficulties, the basic idea of adverse-selection theory is both sensible and extremely useful: that players whose type is hidden from their trading partners should try and signal that information, even when making the signal credible comes at a cost. A famous application of the idea to financial economics is due to Myers and Majluf (1984), who argue that firms can signal quality by prioritizing *information insensitive* debt over equity. The complete analysis of this argument involves technical difficulties (and some modifications) that go beyond the scope of this manuscript; see Noe (1988). We therefore limit ourselves, here, to the very basic idea.

Consider a market where each company is wholly owned by a risk-neutral owner-manager who already has some *assets in place* that generate a non-random cash flow, $\underline{y}$. Each firm has access to a project that requires an investment of one unit and generates some extra cash flow, y^i, i being the type of the project. That type is hidden ex ante, yet ex-post cash flow is verifiable. Since, currently, the company has no cash, if the owner decides that the project is worth investing in, she would have to fund it by selling debt or equity to risk-neutral external investors. Equity, in this case, is just a cash claim against the company, with no effect on the company's control structure, which remains in the hands of the original owner/manager.

There are only two types of projects, $i = H, L$, with $y^H > y^L$, their incidence in the population of companies being π and $1 - \pi$, respectively. For simplicity, we assume that the riskless rate is zero. The H project is NPV positive, $y^H - 1 > 0$, but, for the time being, we make no assumption regarding the NPV of the L project, whether positive or negative. As above, we assume that the external investors, though uninformed about the type of each company's project, are fully aware of model parameters, which are common knowledge.

Let $v^i = \underline{y} + y^i$ be the value of the company's cash flow to its owner (who knows y^i). We assume that for both types, $v^i > 1$. It follows that both types can fund the project by issuing default-free debt. In that sense, debt is *information insensitive*: regardless of type, the value of the firm's riskless debt equals to one. Clearly, the owner operates the project if and only if

$$v^i - 1 = \underline{y} + y^i - 1 > \underline{y},$$

so that only NPV-positive projects, with $y^i > 1$, are operated. They have no interest in operating a project with a negative NPV because that would eat into the cash generated by the assets already in place. From this point onwards we assume that L is NPV negative, $y^L < 1$, but not 'too negative' in a sense that is more accurately defined below.

The main result of the Myers–Majluf analysis is that the equity market shuts down. For a demonstration and by way of contradiction, suppose that there exists a pooled equity-market equilibrium where both types raise equity finance and operate the project. To do so, they 'float' a certain fraction of the company, α, on the market. The external share holders, from whom type is hidden, evaluate the equity on the expectation of its type. Hence, α is the share of the company that needs to be sold out in order to fund the project:

$$\alpha \left[\pi v^H + (1 - \pi) v^L\right] = 1,$$

or

$$\alpha = \frac{1}{\pi v^H + (1 - \pi) v^L}.$$

Notice that equity is information sensitive, as the value of the flotation depends on investors' expectations regarding the incidence of the H and L type in the population.

Unlike investors, owners who know the type of their project, evaluate the flotation at αv^i. In fact, this is their cost of funding: the share of the company that needs to be handed out to external investors in return for cash. Obviously, their objective is to bring the cost of funding down to a minimum. From the algebraic fact:

$$v^H > \pi v^H + (1 - \pi) v^L > v^L,$$

it follows that

$$\alpha v^H > 1 > \alpha v^L.$$

That is, the H type pays an excessive cost of funding as their flotation is under priced by investors who cannot separate them from the L type. For the same reason, the L get cheap funding as their flotation is over-priced by investors who assign a positive probability to them being of the H type. Notice that although Ls' projects are NPV negative,

$$y^L - 1 < 0,$$

due to the cheap funding that they get, investment is still profitable,

$$y^L - \alpha v^L > 0$$

(hence the assumption that L's NPV is not 'too negative').

However, this equilibrium does not exist. The reason is that it is in the best interest of the H type to deviate from this pooling equilibrium and issue riskless debt, lowering the cost of funding from $\alpha v^H > 1$ to 1. Since, under our simplifying assumptions, regardless of type, the cost of default-free debt is one, we need not bother with investors' beliefs about type conditional of the deviation. Once the H type leaves the equity market, type-L's flotation would no longer be over priced. Faced with the correct cost of debt, investment is no longer profitable. The equity market shuts down.

While the argument above concludes that no equity is issued at all, empirical work took the liberty of a more flexible interpretation: that by issuing debt companies signal their access to high-profit projects, while the issuing of equity signals the opposite. The market responds to news about debt and equity issuing accordingly, with a higher company valuation in the former case and lower valuation in the latter case. Mikkelson and Partch (1986) is just one of the many studies that have documented the phenomenon. Their study is based on a randomly selected sample of 360 US listed companies, which they have followed from 1972 to 1982. In spite of the fact that by 1982 only 221 companies have survived, the sample has more than three thousand *company years*.[4] The authors then search for external-funding events, important enough to be reported by news agencies such as the *Wall Street Journal*; they find 595 such events. Evidently, a funding event is less frequent than commonly perceived. To put it differently, '44% of the original sample did not engage in any publicly reported external financing', indicating a preference for internal funding rather than an engagement with any external-finance providers. At the same time, some of the companies in the sample engage in several rounds of external funding.

Table 7.1, based on Tables 2, 3, and 4 of the published paper, reports the incidence, the size of the deal, and the price impact. Only 13% of the events (80/595) involve straight equity, while an additional 8% involved hybrid debt/equity funding instruments (i.e. convertible debt or preferred stock). All the rest were debt transactions, of which only 37% (172/468) were public-market transactions. 235 (80 + 155) debt transactions were executed privately, mostly with banks or other financial institutions.

Further removed from the theoretical results is Myers' (1984) famous *pecking order theory* whereby the typical company 'prefers internal to external financing, and debt to equity if it issues securities ... [without having any] well-defined target [for] debt-to-value ratio'. That is, the company's first choice is internal funding, then debt, then equity. Needless to say, nothing in the Myers–Majluf analysis guides us towards such a formula. Indeed, more recent research has aimed at integrating the predicted signalling effect with Chapter 5's Trareoff theory; c.f.

Table 7.1 Incidence and consequences of funding events

Type of security	(1) Number of events	(2) Amount/value (%)	(3) Price impact (%)
Common stock issuance	80	15.1	−3.6*
Straight debt issuance	172	30.0	−0.2
Convertible debt	33	22.4	−2.0*
Preferred stock	14	25.6	−0.3
Privately placed debt	80	–	−0.6
Term loans	61	–	0.2
Credit agreements	155	–	0.9*

Columns (2) and (3) report means. In column (2), reports the value of the announced funding event, divided by the marketvalue of the listed equity. '*' implies statistical significance.
Source: Mikkelson and Partch (1986).

[4] Where the data tracks a company for several consecutive years, each data point is called a company year.

Frank and Goyal (2003). We make some additional comments on these matters in Section 7.4.6, below, while discussing an application of the hidden action theory.

7.4 The Hidden Action Problem

In finance applications of the principal–agent problem it is common to call the agent, the informed player: *entrepreneur*. Much like the Myers–Majluf owner-manager, the entrepreneur has exclusive access to an *indivisible* project that requires funding of 1 unit in order to start up. The entrepreneur's own wealth, to be used as internal funding, is only $w < 1$. The remaining funding is raised from an investor—the uninformed principal. Notice that could the investor buy and operate the project himself, the entire agency problem would vanish. The indivisibility assumption rules out the possibility that the entrepreneur would internally fund only a fraction, w, of the project. Both the entrepreneur and the investor are risk neutral. The opportunity cost of the funds is the market riskless rate, r. (For brevity, we depart from the r^f notation used in previous chapters.)

The technological characteristics of the project are as follows. The project is risky: it may either succeed or fail. If it succeeds it generates (in the next period) a cash flow of y. If it fails it generates zero cash. The probability of success, π^i, depends on the level of effort that the entrepreneur puts in, $i = H, L$, high or low, respectively, with $\pi^H > \pi^L$. That is, the more effort the entrepreneur puts in, the higher is the probability of success. Effort is measured in terms of its subjective cost to the entrepreneur, namely the opportunity cost of time spent in a more enjoyable manner. To simplify the notation:

$$e^H = e, \quad e^L = 0,$$

allowing the somewhat-loose usage of 'making an effort' and 'making no effort', below. Although effort is an expense in kind, its subjective valuation is fully accounted for in the entrepreneur's profit calculations:

$$y \times \pi^H - e - (1 + r) > y \times \pi^L - (1 + r) > 0, \tag{7.14}$$

so that even with low effort, the project is NPV positive. (It is convenient to express the problem in terminal rather than discounted values.) In Section 7.4.9 below we modify the assumption in Equation (7.14) so that only high effort is NPV positive.

Information is asymmetric: only the entrepreneur observes his own level of effort. Though the investor cannot observe the entrepreneur's effort, cash flow is verifiable, so that in case the project is successful, the cost of enforcing payments that are agreed upon ex ante is zero. Notice, however, that since both H and L effort generate the same level of cash, the event of success does not reveal the entrepreneur's level of effort; he might have made no effort and still, by sheer luck, be successful or might have made an effort and failed. The investor knows, precisely, all the parameters that affect the entrepreneur's decision: the subjective cost of effort, e, the probabilities of success, π^i, with or without effort making, and the magnitude, y, cash flow in case of success.

Ex ante, the two parties meet up and negotiate a contract: the investor advances funding in return for an enforceable promise to pay back certain amounts, contingent on outcomes. Our assumptions, above, simplify the contract considerably: the investor advances $1 - w$ funding and the entrepreneur pays back, $R \leq y$, in case of success. If the project fails, the entrepreneur goes bust, so he cannot pay anything. Had the entrepreneur been risk averse, the parties might have considered a certain 'subsistence' payment in case of failure or, alternatively, advancing ex ante more than $1 - w$, so that the entrepreneur has some resources left in case of failure.

To simplify the problem further, we assume that one party, the entrepreneur, takes the deal's entire surplus, while the investor just 'breaks even', so that she earns no more than the opportunity cost of the funds that she advances. This assumption can be motivated on grounds that the market for funding is competitive, so that there are fewer entrepreneurs than investors. It follows that, effectively, contract negotiations are aimed at maximizing the entrepreneur's income (net of the cost of effort) while, at the same time, making sure that the investor breaks even.

7.4.1 Full Information Benchmark

Imagine the entrepreneur and the investor meeting in order to negotiate a funding contract under conditions of full information. They must agree the level of effort the entrepreneur puts in and, accordingly, the repayment that the investor receives (if the project succeeds), R^i, in return for the funding that she provides, $1-w$. Since the investor breaks even:

$$R^H \pi^H = (1 - w)(1 + r), \qquad R^L \pi^L = (1 - w)(1 + r). \tag{7.15}$$

Clearly, $R^L > R^H$ so as to compensate the investor for the higher default risk.[5] The conditions in Equation (7.15) act as a constraint on the contract that the players can negotiate; failing to compensate the investor for the risk that she bears, funding is refused. We therefore call Equation (7.15) the *participation constraint* (*PC*).

Once it is understood that the investor breaks even, the negotiations should carry on to find the combination of R^i and e^i that deliver the highest-possible income to the entrepreneur. To put it more technically, the purpose of the

[5] The word 'default' carries the connotation of a debt contract; in fact, since our contract has only income-repayment point, it cannot be interpreted as specifically debt, equity, or any other contract.

negotiations is to find the contract that delivers the highest (maximum) value for the entrepreneur:

$$Max \quad \begin{cases} (y - R^H)\pi^H - e^H, & \text{funding} + H \text{ effort} \\ (y - R^L)\pi^L, & \text{funding} + L \text{ effort} \\ w(1 + r), & \text{no funding} \end{cases}, \tag{7.16}$$

subject to satisfying the *PC* as in Equation (7.15). To account for the opportunity cost of the entrepreneur's internal funding we give him a third option, which is to 'put his money in the bank' rather than operate the project.

Here comes an important observation:

Proposition 7.3. *Contracting is a maximization problem: to find a combination of contractible variables, i.e. funding effort and repayment, that deliver the highest value to the informed player subject to delivering enough to the uninformed player so that she is willing to participate in the contract. The agent values various feasible contracts using the objective function (16), subject to the participation constraint (15).*

Seemingly technical, Proposition 7.3 has important economic implications. Firstly, it differentiates the hidden-action problem from the hidden-type problem: while the former is a maximization problems, the latter is an equilibrium problem. For all intents and purposes, maximization problems have a solution, which is unique. As we have seen, it is sometimes the case that no equilibrium exists or, alternatively, that there is a proliferation of equilibria. Secondly, by definition, whatever the solution of the contract problem, it is, by construction, the best possible outcome; no other contract that can do any better. Unlike Chapter 3's incomplete contract, the solution of this problem is guaranteed to deliver the best possible, that is an *optimal contract.* By construction the optimal contract is constrained Pareto efficient. For once the parties to the contract find an arrangement that suits them best, it is hard to see how a regulator can make them better off.

To solve the contract problem (16), substitute the *PC* into the objective function to derive the entrepreneur's expected income, under the two possible levels of effort:

$$\begin{aligned} (y - R^H)\pi^H - e &= (\pi^H y - e) - (1 + r) + w(1 + r), \\ (y - R^L)\pi^L &= \pi^L y - (1 + r) + w(1 + r). \end{aligned} \tag{7.17}$$

By assumption (7.14), the contracting parties should select option *H*. The entrepreneur's outcome thus equals to the contract's cash flow, net of the cost of capital, plus the opportunity cost of the entrepreneur's own wealth. It follows that deciding between H and L, reduces to picking the option with the highest NPV. By this argument, it is also clear that operating the project dominates the money-in-the bank option, as it allows the entrepreneur to capture the project's entire NPV.

Though the analysis above is presented in terms of negotiations, it could also be presented in terms of a competitive market for effort-contingent funding. In which case the result is just a special case of the First Welfare Theorem: with complete markets, a competitive equilibrium is Pareto efficient. Although the investor bears some risk of default, once that risk is priced in, the entrepreneur internalizes the full consequence of his decision and opts for the one that is economically efficient. Notice that Equation (7.15) implies that the risk-adjusted cost of capital is always $(1 + r)$.

The result is also a special case of Chapter 5's Modigliani–Miller Theorem: though cash flow is now a function of the entrepreneur's effort decision, the entrepreneur always opts for highest NPV option. Then, the value of cash claims against the firm is:

$$\pi^H \left(y - R^H\right) + \pi^H R^H = \pi^H y.$$

That, is, regardless of the entrepreneur's wealth, the project is always operated at the high-effort level, and the value of the cash flow, for both the entrepreneur and the investor, adds up to $\pi^H y$. Notwithstanding, by Equation (7.17), the entrepreneur's final income is increasing in his initial wealth: the richer he is to begin with, the richer (in expectations) he is after investing in the project. Crucially, under the Modigliani-Miller Theorem, operational decisions, and hence corporate valuations, are independent of the distribution of wealth.

7.4.2 Hidden Effort: Incentive Compatibility

Now consider contract negotiations once effort is not observable. Similar to the argument made in Section 7.3.2 above, although the investor cannot observe the effort decision, through her knowledge of the parameters π^i, e^i and y, she can make an informed guess of the entrepreneur's behaviour. In fact, she can 'see through him', perfectly, and be entirely confident that her guess is correct. If so, effort levels can be part of contract negotiations, provided that the agreed level of effort is compatible with the entrepreneur's own incentives, which is to select an effort level that:

$$Max \quad \begin{cases} (y - R)\,\pi^H - e^H \\ \\ (y - R)\,\pi^L \end{cases} \quad \text{given } R\,. \tag{7.18}$$

(It should be clear by now that the money-in-the-bank option does not play a prominent role in the analysis.) In fact, the problem is remarkably similar to the full information problem (7.16), the main difference being that the i superscript next to R—vanishes. In order to appreciate the importance of the difference, consider contract negotiations with full information and without it. In the former case the entrepreneur is told: you may switch your effort level from H to L but doing so your repayment increases from R^H to R^L. In the latter case the entrepreneur is told: R is the repayment, though the investor cannot observe your effort decision, she knows what it is. A small difference but, as we shall see below—consequential.

Figure 7.5 provides a diagrammatic solution to the maximization problem (7.18). Repayment is plotted on the horizontal axis and the entrepreneur's expected income net of the cost of effort is plotted on the vertical axis, as a function of R. For $R = 0$, expected income for the high effort level is $y\pi^H - e$, which, by assumption (7.14), exceeds expected income for the zero effort, $y\pi^L$. For $R = y$, expected income for the L option is 0, where expected income for the H option is $-e$. It follows that the two graphs must cross at a certain repayment, $\underline{R}$. Hence, it is in the entrepreneur's best interest to make an effort only to the left of $\underline{R}$.

Hence our second key insight:

Proposition 7.4. *There is no 'cheating' in a moral-hazard relationship. The uninformed player knows, with confidence, what decision the informed player makes. However, deprived of the ability to directly observe and enforce an action on the informed player, the uniformed player must check that the action that is agreed in the contract is compatible with the incentives of the informed player. It follows that asymmetry of information adds an additional constraint to the full-information contract problem, called the incentive compatibility constraint (IC).*

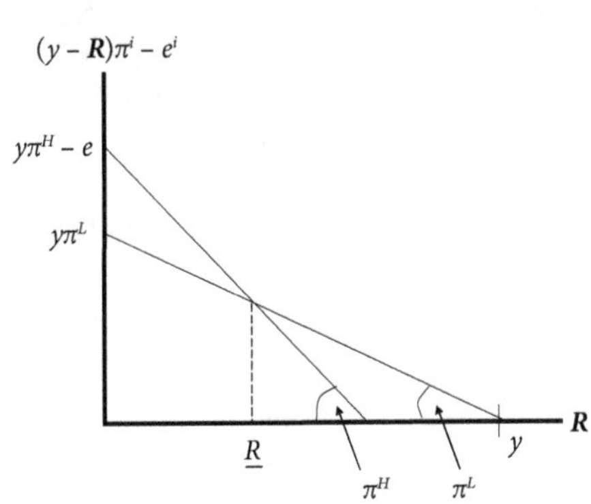

Figure 7.5 Entrepreneur's effort incentives

It is worth writing the *IC* in common mathematical format, similar to the way it appears in the academic literature:

$$i = argmax_i\,(y - R)\,\pi^i - e^i. \tag{7.19}$$

Equation (7.19) reads as follows: *i* is the argument, either *H* or *L*, that solves the entrepreneur's income-maximization problem, given *R*.

Before we carry on, a few words about the intuition behind the switch from high to low effort levels once *R* exceeds $\underline{R}$. Think of *H* as the safe option: by making an effort, the entrepreneur increases the probability of success from π^L to π^H, and the expected amount of cash from $\pi^L y$ to $\pi^H y$. However, the entrepreneur captures only part of the extra value, $(y - R)\,\pi^H$; the other part, $\pi^H R$, 'leaks out' to the investor: the higher π^i, the highest is the investor's expected payoff (holding *R* constant). However, the higher is *R*, the higher is the leakage. At some point the leakage is so great that effort is no longer worth making. Or putting it differently, though low effort implies a higher probability of failure, much of that risk is born by the investor. Hence, low effort is an act of *risk shifting*, from the entrepreneur to the investor.

7.4.3 Solving the Contract Problem with Hidden Effort

It follows from Proposition 7.4 that information asymmetry augments the maximization full-information benchmark with one additional constraint, the *IC*. Hence, the asymmetric-information contract problem is to find a combination of effort and repayment that maximizes the entrepreneur's income *subject to* two constraints, *PC* and *IC*:

$$Max_{i,R}\,(y - R)\,\pi^i - e^i \tag{7.20}$$

s.t.

$$\begin{aligned} PC:&\quad R\pi^i = (1 - w)(1 + r), \\ IC:&\quad i = argmax_i\,(y - R)\,\pi^i - e^i. \end{aligned}$$

For completeness, we notice the money-in-the-bank option:,

$$(y - R)\,\pi^i - e^i \geq w(1 + r), \tag{7.21}$$

which plays little role in the analysis given that the project is NPV positive even under low effort. As already noted above, the generic structure of a maximization problem is: maximize an objective function, with respect to certain variables (*i* and *R*), subject to (*s.t.*) certain constraints.

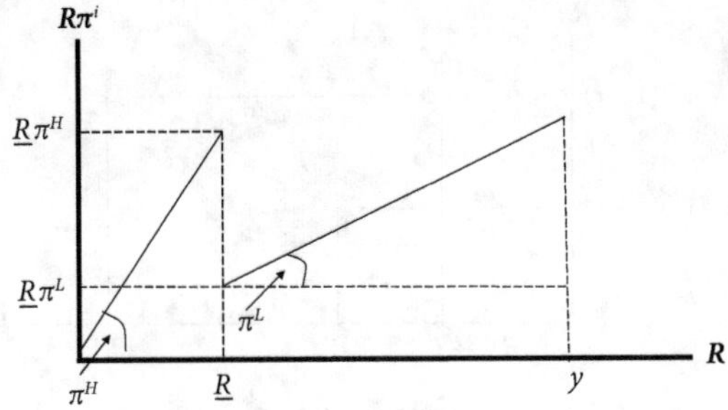

Figure 7.6 Investor's expected income

Now, the *IC* and the *PC* interact in a surprising manner. Figure 7.6 plots the function

$$R\pi^i, \qquad \text{such that } i \text{ satisfies the } IC.$$

Close to $R = 0$, $i = H$ so the probability of default is π^H. Moving rightwards but still staying to the left of $\underline{R}$, a one unit increase in R increases the investor's expected payoff by only $\pi^H < 1$ units. That relationship holds all the way up to $\underline{R}$. Then, approaching $\underline{R}$ from the left, the investor's expected income approaches $\underline{R}\pi^H$. But moving slightly to the right of $\underline{R}$, the investor's expected payoff drops to $\underline{R}\pi^L$, discontinuously. Further to the right, a one unit increase in R increases the investor's expected payoff by only $\pi^L < \pi^H$, so the curve become flatter. A payoff above y is not feasible.[6]

The next step is to find those (i, R) combinations that satisfy both the *IC* and the *PC*, Equation (7.19) and the investor's break-even condition:

$$(1 - w)(1 + r) = \pi^i R, \text{ such that } i \text{ satisfies the } IC. \tag{7.22}$$

Geometrically, we look for intersection of the Figure 7.6 graph with a horizontal $(1 - w)(1 + r)$ line; see Figure 7.7.

The last step is to find which intersection point, i.e. solutions to the problem in (7.22), delivers the highest value to the entrepreneur. There are two possible cases:

- When the entrepreneur's wealth is w', there are two intersection points, at repayment levels R^* and R'. Of which only R^* solves the contract problem (7.20). To see why, substitute (again) the *PC* into the entrepreneur's objective function, as we have done in order to derive Equation (7.17), we get:

$$\left(y - R^i\right)\pi^i - e^i = \left(\pi^i y - e^i\right) - (1 + r) + w(1 + r). \tag{7.23}$$

[6] Figure 7.6 is plotted so that $\pi^H \underline{R} < \pi^L y$, though this need not be the case.

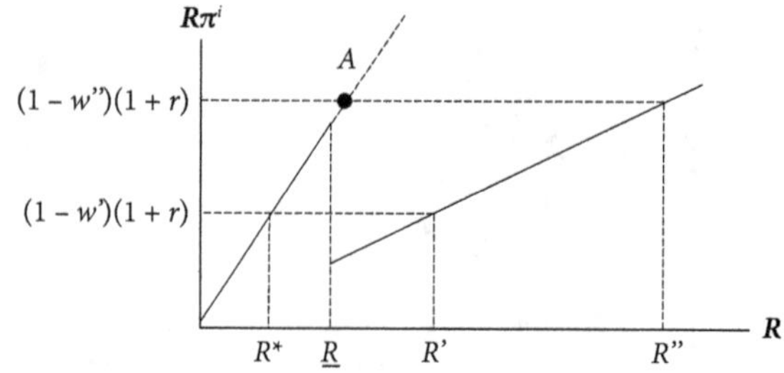

Figure 7.7 The effort decision

Hence, contracting at the H effort level provides the entrepreneur with a higher income relative to the L effort level, while allowing the investor to break even. Hence (H, R^*) is the unique solution to the contract problem (7.20). It also follows from Equation (7.23) that operating the project dominates the money-in-the-bank option.

- When the entrepreneur's has a low level of wealth, w'', no intersection point on the high-effort segment of the Figure 7.6 graph exists. This is in spite of the fact that had effort been observable, a high effort contract would be implemented at point A. Since the project is NPV positive under a low level of effort, funding is available at an R'' repayment, with low level of effort; see Figure 7.7.

The following technical result gives structure to the substantial results below:

Proposition 7.5. *In a maximization problem, a constraint is said to be non-binding if the solution is not affected when the constraint is removed from the problem. A constraint is said to be* binding *if removing it does affect the solution. The effect of a binding constraint on the value of the problem*[7] *is never positive.*

Applied to the discussion above, the IC is non binding when the entrepreneur's wealth is w' but becomes a binding constraint when the entrepreneur's wealth is only w'', driving the entrepreneur towards a low-effort low-value outcome.

The reason for the constraint's negative effect is rooted in the structure of the maximization problem. The intuition is already demonstrated in the analysis of revealed preferences in Chapter 1 (see discussion of Figure 1.4, there). The constraints of a maximization problem define the feasible options from which the problem selects the one that maximizes the objective function. Restricting the set of feasible options cannot increase the value of the problem. It is worth noting that,

[7] To be precise, the value of the problem is derived by substituting the solution into the objective function. In our case, it is the value derived by the entrepreneur once the optimal contract is implemented.

in contrast, imposing a constraint on an equilibrium may have a positive effect on the outcome. Indeed, that is the main message of Chapter 6: an emission tax is Pareto improving. Hence the critical importance of distinguishing equilibrium problems, like adverse selection, from maximization problems, like moral hazard.

7.4.4 Implications

For fluency of presentation, the technical analysis of the contract problem, glossed over some remarkably important observations, highlighted by the following propositions:

Proposition 7.6. *The Modigliani–Miller Theorem does not hold as the composition of funding, internal and external, may affect the choice of effort and, hence, the value of the firm. In particular, a binding* IC *drives the entrepreneur towards the* L *effort and a low valuation of the firm.*

Proposition 7.7. *When, in line with Proposition 7.6, firm value is diminished, the entire loss of value falls on the informed player, i.e. the entrepreneur. Whether the project is operated at the* H *or* L *level of effort, the investor breaks even, earning a market return on the funds that he provides, as implied by the* PC. *To be clear, the loss from information asymmetry always falls on the informed player, as it forces the uninformed player to take precautionary measures, transferring the cost of these measures to the informed player.*

Proposition 7.8. *It follows directly from Proposition 7.7 that being better informed operates to the determent of the informed player. If only he could, he would opt to make his effort observable to the investor (and to the court that would enforce the resulting effort-contingent contract). That would allow him to commit himself to a high level of effort, get a contract with a lower repayment,* R, *and collect the extra surplus that effort generates.*

Proposition 7.9. *Notwithstanding Proposition 7.6, the contract is Constrained Pareto efficient (see definition in Chapter 3). That is, subject to the constraints imposed on the problem by information asymmetry, no Pareto improvements exist. By construction, the contract maximizes the expected payoff to the entrepreneur, subject to a fixed expected payoff to the investor (at the break-even level), at a level of effort compatible with entrepreneur's incentives.*

Proposition 7.10. *Proposition 7.9 does not exclude the possibility of bailouts, namely gifting a low-wealth firm with cash, decreasing its dependence on external* *funding, thereby enabling high-effort contracts. However, such transfers are not a Pareto improvement as the tax payers that fund the gift are worse off.*

7.4.5 Alternative Interpretation of the Hidden Effort Problem

The notion of 'effort' is somewhat abstract. The financial-economics literature mentions several other hidden-action 'stories'. Technically, some of these stories can easily fit into the effort model, above. In that respect, they do not make different theories, only different interpretations of the same model. They are still interesting in providing a stronger motivation and a sense of broader applicability to the effort model.

7.4.5.1 Private Benefits of Control

Consider an entrepreneur who, in addition to cash, derives pleasure from the sense of empowerment or the publicity associated with owning a business. We denote the subjective valuation of such private benefits of control by $b > 0$; see Section 9.2 of Chapter 1 for an earlier discussion. Suppose, also, that indulging in such pleasures comes at the expense of effectively running the business, which decreases the probability of success from π^H to π^L. It is up to the entrepreneur to decide whether to draw private benefits of control—or not. It is assumed that:

$$y\pi^H - (1 + r) > (y + b)\pi^L - (1 + r), \tag{7.24}$$
$$y\pi^H - (1 + r) > 0.$$

Plausibly, drawing private benefits of control is hidden action. Even if it is not, it is hard to see how avoiding them can be included as part of a funding contract. Notice that cash flow, y, is assumed to be identical across the two options, so that even ex post, the firm's success or failure provides no indication of the entrepreneur's decision.

7.4.5.2 Cash Diversion

An even more credible interpretation of the effort model is that b is cash benefits diverted away from external investors, by virtue of the entrepreneur's (or the manager's) control of the business. That is, a certain part of the project's cash flow has sufficiently low visibility that it can be hidden from external investors. Examples of low visibility cash may involve off-shore activities, 'creative accounting' or inflated expenses. Assumption (7.24) implies that cash diversion come at the expense of effective management. Notice that the observable part of the cash flow, y, is the same whether the entrepreneur diverts cash or not, so that the outcome of the project, success or failure, provides no indication of diversion activities.

Readers may find some of the 'stories' above credible and others—less so. Refining the stories is not the main object of this sub-section. Rather, it is to demonstrate the richness of the theoretical framework in terms of its ability to accommodate various interpretations.

7.4.6 Application: Internal and External Funding

One of the strongest prediction of our theory is that an increased reliance on external finance might drive the company towards lower-value production decisions; see Proposition 7.6. In popular discourse, the result is sometimes expressed as follows: effective decisions require that the company's insiders have enough 'skin in the game' so as to align their interests with those of the external investors.

Cutler and Summers (1988) report an innovative way of testing this prediction of the theory, based on a highly unusual event. On 2 January 1984, Pennzoil, an oil company, signed a legally binding contract to buy a substantial minority stake in Getty, another oil company. Within a week, Texaco, a third oil company, acquired Getty, breaching Getty's contract with Penzoil. Penzoil sued Texaco, the new owner of Getty, thereby the bearer of its pre-acquisition liabilities, for breach of contract. On 19 November 1985, a Texas jury awarded Pennzoil damages of $12 billion, starting a series of legal battles through several rounds of appeals all the way up to the Supreme Court of the United States, culminating with Texaco filing for bankruptcy on 12 April 1987. On December 18 1987 the two companies settled for $3 billion of damages. The entire process was widely criticized on both legal and economic grounds. Suffices to mention that the original decision of the Texas jury is, to say the least, puzzling, as the joint value of the two companies was just $10.5 billion.

The Cutler–Summers analysis starts with the observation that under the Modigliani–Miller Theorem, the transfer of wealth, w, from Texaco to Penzoli, does not affect the production decisions of the two companies and, therefore, their joint value. Indeed, a one-unit transfer would increase the value of Penzoil by one unit and decrease the value of Texaco by one unit, leaving the joint value unaffected. That is not the case in a world of asymmetric information. A unit reduction in Texaco's wealth will have a direct one-unit (negative) effect on its value and, possibly, an additional indirect (negative) effect, a result of driving the company towards low productivity decisions; see Equation (7.23). At the same time, gifting Penzoil with one unit is likely to have just a one-unit (positive) effect on its value. Particularly, once this (huge) gift has driven Penzoil to the internal mode of financing, its operation decisions are already optimized, removing the possibility of an additional (positive) indirect effect. It follows that the net effect of the transfer on the joint value of the two companies is likely to be negative. Hence, the (null) hypothesis of zero net effect is consistent with a Modiglian–Miller world but

Table 7.2 Penzoil–Texaco changes in stock-market valuations, $millions

Date	Event	Texaco	Penzoil	joint
19 Nov. 1985	Texas jury rules for Penzoil	−646	296	−351
18 Dec. 1985	Texaco obtains temporary restraining order	446	−127	319
12 Feb. 1987	Court of Appeals upholds judgment	−819	379	−440
6 Apr. 1987	Supreme Court vacates bond ruling	−1000	276	−733

Source: Cutler and Summers (1988).

inconsistent with an asymmetric-information world. Rejecting the null hypothesis is therefore evidence to the presence of asymmetric information, and to an effect in the direction syggested by the theory developed in this chapter.

Notice the analytical convenience of the test, as it does not require an estimation of the magnitude of the transfer, which is affected, along the dispute, by expectations of a revision in legal decisions. Only the joint value is required. Notwithstanding, the joint value can still be affected by factors such as oil prices or stock-market conditions. To separate the effect of the transfer from these factors, the authors use a method known as an *event study*. It measures the price changes relative to the market price of other companies, not involved in the Texaco–Penzoil legal dispute. To increase the robustness of the test, the authors execute the calculations in various manners, which all yield similar results. A sample of the estimations are presented in Table 7.2 (based on Table 1 in the published paper). Accumulated, the changes over the entire sequence of events, the authors summarize their findings as follows: '[while] Texaco's value fell a total of $4.1 billion; Pennzoil's rose only $682 million. Pennzoil gained only 17% of what Texaco lost. Before the litigation was filed, Texaco's value was about $8.5 billion, while Pennzoil's was about $2 billion. The loss thus represents over 32% of the pre-litigation joint value.'

7.4.7 Application: The Savings and Loans Crisis in 1980s US

Massive defaults that engulfed the Savings and Loans (S&L) industry in 1980s US exemplifies the relationship between corporate wealth, w and risk taking. According to White (1992), traditionally 'the S&L industry was a sleepy, (apparently) safe industry' dominated by small banks that were mutualized in the sense that the households from whom they were taking deposits and to whom they were making mortgage loans, were also their shareholders. Safety was supported by both regulation and by historically low default rates. However, the industry had one major weakness: a mismatch between its long-term assets (mortgages) and its short-term liabilities (saving accounts). Viability therefore relied on long-term interest rates being higher relative short-term rates; upwards-sloping *yield curve* in finance lingo.

When, in the late 1970s, the short-term interest rate increased sharply, S&Ls started to lose money. As a result, the industry's capital base (captured by w) was eroded from 5.6% in 1978 to just 0.5% in 1983; see Table II in the published paper. To which government response was to deregulate the industry, hoping that this would result in higher profitability and a build-up of the industry's capital base. Instead, a rapid expansion accompanied by a substantial shift towards an investment in more risky assets, like commercial real estate or equity investment, took place. As low oil prices affected the economy of the south-eastern United States, the industry incurred heavy losses. By 1985, 21% of operators, holding 27% of the industry's assets, were classified as 'soon to fail', this sub-group being more heavily invested in more risky assets; see Table V in the published paper. Losses were estimated at $200 billion, much of it fell on the taxpayer as failed S&Ls were bailed out by the regulator.

7.4.8 Application: The Firm as a Nexus of Contracts

Jensen and Meckling (1976) were among the first to notice the great potential of asymmetric-information theory, to reshape the legal and economic analysis of the modern corporation. Their view can be elegantly summarized by idea that the firm is a *nexus of contracts*, that allocates cash and other rights (for example, control rights or liquidation rights) across the many stakeholders that are active in the company: managers, equity holders, bankers, workers, buyers, and suppliers. The contracts allocate these rights so as to moderate conflicts of interests between the stakeholders, aligning their interests. That is each stakeholder's value is maximized given other stakeholders' ICs are satisfied. To do so, each stakeholder is provided with an incentive to take actions that would benefit not just himself but also other stakeholders.

Both words, 'contract' and 'corporation', are used somewhat more broadly than their legal sense. As for 'contract', any scheme that affects the allocation of rights across stakeholders can be viewed as a contract. For example, the corporation's charter, its article of association, legal precedents that affect the interpretation of clauses in these documents, public or regulatory disclosures that commit management to take a certain action—may all be considered contracts, explicit or implicit. As for the 'corporation', any contract that allocate rights between the stakeholders or, indeed, any other third party, are considered part of the nexus. For example, warranties against goods sold by the company, or an 'outsourced' service agreement are all part of the legal structure that is the corporation. In fact, the corporation has no clear boundaries; it just fuses into the economic environment around it. It is also implied that the distinction between corporations, partnerships, family businesses, alliances are immaterial in the sense that they can all be fitted into the notion of a nexus of contracts.

Neither does the corporation have any clear purpose or objective; not even the maximization of profit or NPV as assumed in the first part of Chapter 6. The corporation is just a web of conflicting interests. It is hoped that profit-seeking emerges out of the contracting process once the stakeholders are successful in resolving their conflicts and aligning their interests. At the same time, non-profit (charitable) objectives can be written in, if stakeholders wish to do so.

It is worth noting the principle of a nexus of contracts does not differ materially from the notion of the firm as a set of jointly owned assets as discussed in Chapter 3. For the rights of the owners are effectively defined by the contracts that they sign with the other stakeholder. The difference between the schools of thought are more in their approach to the analysis of contracts, whether complete or incomplete.

7.4.9 Contracts, Markets, and Credit Rationing

Stiglitz and Weiss (1981) demonstrate how to integrate the analysis of contracts with the analysis of competitive markets. Doing so, they have discovered that one of the most basic properties of a competitive market, that supply meets demand and markets clear, may no longer hold. As a result, a phenomenon of credit rationing may arise: some borrowers would like to borrow at market interest rates but may not be able to find a lender. For a long time, economic theorists were not willing to accept practitioners' claims that such a phenomenon exists. The Stiglitz–Weiss paper resolved the issue.

We modify the assumptions made at the beginning of this section as follows. The risk free rate, r, is no longer a parameter of the model but, rather, an endogenous variable determined by market conditions; see Figure 7.8. Supply of funds is increasing in the riskless rate as investors prefer to consume less and save more at

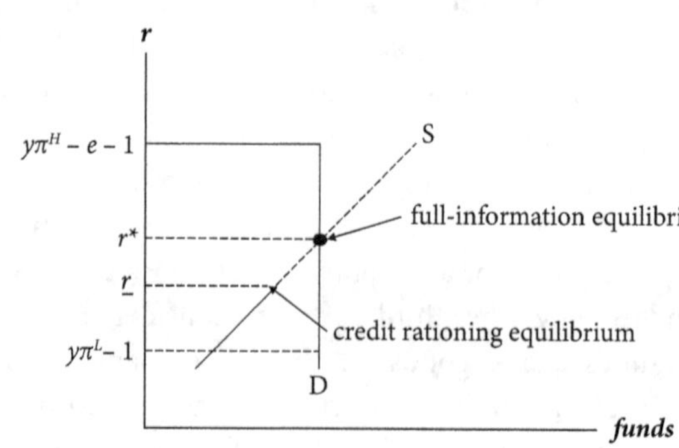

Figure 7.8 Credit rationing

higher riskless rates; see discussion in Section 1.6.1 of Chapter 1. We also assume that entrepreneurship is a scarce resource, so that the demand for funds becomes vertical beyond a certain point. The technological properties of the projects are as before. Under the full-information benchmark, markets clear at r^*, with an H level of effort and $y\pi^H - e > 1 + r^*$. However, at that level of the riskless interest rate, the H level of effort is not incentive compatible, because at $\underline{r} = \underline{R}\pi^H$ entrepreneurs switch to the L level of effort: $\underline{r} < r^*$.

To simplify the analysis, suppose that $w = 0$, so that entrepreneurs have no wealth of their own. It follows that entrepreneurs are eager to borrow at any $R < y$, as they can still make a profit of $\pi^L(y - R) > 0$. However, we also assume that even when R is set equal to y, investors cannot break even as

$$y\pi^L < 1 + \underline{r}.$$

It follows that the riskless rate cannot increase above $\underline{r}$, even if at that level of the riskless rate there is still excess demand for credit. To summarize:

Proposition 7.11. *Consider a market for funds with entrepreneurs' action hidden from investors. Then, there might be a credit-rationing equilibrium where the supply of funds falls short of demand. The entrepreneurs that cannot get funding are identical, in all their characteristics, to those that do get funding. In particular, their projects are NPV positive at $\underline{r}$. And yet, they cannot find investors that would fund them.*

To further motivate the result, consider a more technical explanation: in a 'normal' competitive equilibrium, there are two equations—supply and demand, and two unknowns—price and quantity. 'Normally' there is a combination of price and quantity such that the market clears. In contrast, in a funding market affected by a hidden-action problem, there are three equations—supply, demand, and the *IC*, and still only two variables. It may be impossible to find a combination that satisfies all three.

7.5 Conclusion

This chapter suggests an asymmetric-information modelling to the somewhat vague concept of trading frictions as developed in Chapters 2 and 3. The approach lends itself to rigorous analysis and answers questions that were not fully answered there. For example, in the Hart–Moore modelling of secured debt, where information was observable but not verifiable,[8] the question whether the contract was

[8] That is, the parties to the contract are equally informed but the enforcement agency is not.

constrained efficient had no rigorous answer. The complete-contracts approach of this chapter can answer this question: an optimal contract, derived by solving the contract problem (7.20), is constrained Pareto efficient, and therefore, cannot be Pareto improved upon by regulation. Such results are obviously highly relevant in applied legal-financial analysis of the corporation.

References

[1] Akerlof, George A. (1970). 'The Market for 'q Lemons' : Quality Uncertainty and the Market Mechanism'. *Quarterly Journal of Economics*, Vol. 84, No. 3, pp. 488–500.

[2] Cutler, David M. and Lawrence H. Summers (1988). 'The Costs of Conflict Resolution and Financial Distress: Evidence from the Texaco-Pennzoil Litigation', *RAND Journal of Economics*, Vol. 19, No. 2, pp. 157–172.

[3] Frank, Murray Z. and Vidhan K. Goyal, (2003). 'Testing the Pecking Order Theory of Capital Structure', *Journal of Financial Economics*, Vol. 67, pp. 217– 248.

[4] Jensen, Michael C., and William H. Meckling (1976). 'Theory of the Firm: Managerial Behavior, Agency Costs and Ownership Structure', *Journal of Financial Economics*, Vol. 3, No. 4, pp. 305–360.

[5] Myers, C., Stewart and Nicholas S. Majluf (1984). 'Corporate Financing and Investment Decisions when Firms Have Information that Investors Do Not Have', *Journal of Financial Economics*, Vol. 13, No. 2, pp. 187–221.

[6] Myers, Stewart C. (1984). 'The Capital Structure Puzzle', *Journal of Finance*, Vol. 39, No. 3, 575–592.

[7] Noe, Thomas H. (1988). 'Capital Structure and Signaling Game Equilibria', *Review of Financial Studies*, Vol. 1, No. 4, pp. 331–355.

[8] Mikkelson, Wayne H. and Megan M. Parch (1986). 'Valuation Effects of Security Offerings and the Issuance Process', *Journal of Financial Economics*, Vol. 15, pp. 31–60.

[9] Stiglitz, Joseph E., and Andrew Weiss (1981). 'Credit Rationing in Markets with Imperfect Information', *American Economic Review*, Vol. 71, No. 3, pp. 393–410.

[10] White, Lawrence (1992). *A Cautionary Tale of Deregulation Gone Awry: The S&L Debacle*, Working Papers, New York University, Leonard N. Stern School of Business, Department of Economics.

8
Learning from Trading

8.1 Introduction

Two observations could not have come out more clearly from previous chapters: the first is that information frictions play a pivotal role in finance and, second, that information is a public good. Taking these two observations together may lead the reader to an almost unavoidable conclusion: that competitive markets should play an only limited role to in the financial system. Rather, that the industry should be organized into centralized intermediaries, who generate information by way of monitoring, then manage the distribution of that information, exclusively, to those users who can be charged.

Yet, even a casual observation of the industry reveals that beside large intermediaries, e.g. banks, information-sensitive securities are widely traded in competitive markets. However, a closer look reveals a characteristic that is not captured by Chapter 7 modelling. While many traders may have some exclusive private information, they must be aware of the fact that their information is only a 'small piece of the puzzle', that the information that others have is equally valuable, particularly if all these 'pieces' can, somehow, be collected, processed then combined into a reliable statistic. Hence, as much as players are keen to profit (avoid losses) from trades in which they have superior (inferior) information, they are keen to learn from the trades executed by others. That is, strong complementarities between 'small bits' of widely dispersed information define the problem of this chapter: the economics of *information aggregation* and the formation of *expectations* that are incorporated into a competitive market price.

Information aggregation is critically important to the evaluation of the decentralization. For the purpose of decentralization is not just to avoid the excesses of centralized power. Efficient management of the economy requires collecting and processing large amounts of information and, then, sending operating instructions, coded into short signals in the form of prices, to the operators who supply the information in the first place. Proponents of the market economy argue that no 'machine' has the capacity to execute such a humongous information-processing task. Only the market can do it, somehow; see Hayek (1945). Based on previous-chapters experience, the reader should expect more nuanced conclusions from a careful economic modelling of this problem.

The Economics of Financial Markets and Institutions. Oren Sussman, Oxford University Press. © Oren Sussman (2023).
DOI: 10.1093/oso/9780192869739.003.0009

8.2 Motivation: Learning from Trade

To further motivate the analysis, consider a variation on Chapter 5's case of trade driven by different beliefs. Two players[1] trade event-e contingent Arrow–Debreu Security (ADS). The players have the same coefficient of risk aversion, θ, the same event-e income $y_e^{P1} = y_e^{P2} = \bar{c}$ (no macro risk), but different beliefs about the likelihood of the event. We have demonstrated, there, that such differences in beliefs generate active trade between the players, and that the equilibrium price is in between π_e^{P1} and π_e^{P2}. We did not question the source of belief differentiation, nor did we ask whether $P2$ should change her own beliefs once she learns that $P1$ assigns a higher probability than she does to the event. We do ask these questions now.

To that end, consider the following scenario: initially, $P1$ has the same beliefs as $P2$, namely, π_e^{P2}, which is also the market price; see solid-line demand curves in Figure 8.1. Then, $P1$ gets a *private signal*, some *news* that changes his mind. The information is not entirely reliable, but it carries enough weight for $P1$ to revise his expectations, upwards, to π_e^{P1}, which affects both his own and the market demand for e-contingent ADSs; see broken-line demand curves. As a result, there is a new market price, $p_e > \pi_e^{P2}$. Observing the new price, $P2$ must realize that it must be $P1$ who is bidding up the price, probably upon some news. Moreover, $P2$ should also realize that since she is selling event-e ADSs, $P1$ must be buying them. If so, it must also be the case that the news that $P1$ got was 'good', which justifies an upward revision of her own event-e beliefs, at least up to the level of the new market price, p_e. If so, her new demand curve should be drawn via point A in Figure 8.1, affecting a further upward-shift of the market demand. But then, this argument can be reiterated: if $P1$ is still buying, a conclusion that she draws on her own selling, then his expectations must be higher still, so $P2$ should revise her expectations once again. This process goes on until $P1$ is no longer willing to buy, at the equilibrium price, any amount beyond $\bar{c}$, namely when the market price converges to π_e^{P1}. But,

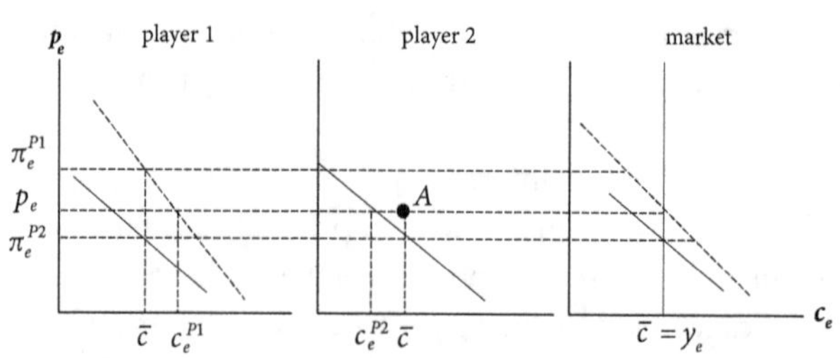

Figure 8.1 $P1$ receives good news and $P2$ learns from prices

[1] As in Chapter 5, we mean a type of atomistic players represented by a single price-taker.

that leads us to a surprising conclusion: all of $P1$'s private information has been dissipated into a market price that is observable to all. Putting it differently, uninformed traders can learn from market prices, draw inferences about information that is private to other traders, leading, eventually, to an equilibrium price that reveals all private information.

Indeed, assuming rationality, we can argue that the convergence to a new market price at π_e^{P1} is immediate. Consider again the first step in the process above, when the market price was p_e. From the fact that $P2$ is selling the amount $\bar{c} - c_e^{P2}$, she can draw the conclusion that $P1$ is buying the same amount. But since $P2$ knows that $P1$'s risk aversion is the same as hers, she can calculate what event-e probability would make him buy that amount:

$$\frac{\pi_e^{P1} - p_e}{\bar{c} - c_e^{P2}} = \theta \pi_e^{P1}$$

(see Figure 8.1), from which she can solve:

$$\pi_e^{P1} = \frac{p_e}{1 - \theta\left(\bar{c} - c_e^{P2}\right)}.$$

Hence, not only that all of $P1$'s private information is revealed; it is revealed instantaneously. Moreover, it is revealed with very little actual trading as $P2$ can infer π_e^{P1} from the very fact that $P1$ is willing to buy the amount $\left(\bar{c} - c_e^{P2}\right)$ at a price of p_e. Once she incorporates this inference into her own beliefs, so that prices adjust and, hence, her demand, prices adjust to π_e^{P1}, which removes any motive for trading.

8.3 Signals and Their Precision

As a first step towards a further development of our analysis we need to define more accurately the notions of 'news' as well as the 'reliability' of that news; we stay with the state-e contingent ADS. Let π be a *prior probability*, namely the probability of event e prior to the arrival of the news.[2] Let a signal be a random variable[3], s, with realizations either g or b, 'good' and 'bad' news, respectively. The signal is informative, but not perfectly informative (hence, commonly called a *noisy signal*). We capture the quality of the information through its precision, namely the probability that the g (b) signal is indeed triggered by a $x = 1$ ($x = 0$) payoff:[4]

$$prob\,(s = g \mid x = 1) = prob\,(s = b \mid x = 0) = \lambda.$$

[2] For brevity, we omit the e subscript.
[3] For brevity, we avoid the $\tilde{s}$ notation for random variables, as we have done in previous chapters.
[4] In general, g and b may have different levels of precision.

Table 8.1 Joint distribution of payoff and signal

		signal	
		g	b
x	1	$\pi\lambda$	$\pi(1-\lambda)$
	0	$(1-\pi)(1-\lambda)$	$(1-\pi)\lambda$

A higher λ implies a higher correlation between the event and the signal and, therefore, a higher quality of the signal. Since the signal is not perfect, there is a positive probability that the news is false:

$$prob\,(s = g \mid x = 0) = 1 - \lambda.$$

The assumption that the false positive probability equals the false-negative probability is made for simplicity of exposition only. The joint distribution of the signal and the payoff is shown in Table 8.1.

Obviously, the recipient of the signal, oblivious of the actual outcome, needs to answer a different question: what difference does the signal make to the perception of event-*e* outcome. Hence, upon observing, say, a g signal, a player should apply Bayes' Law,[5] in order to update (or revise) his prior beliefs to derive x's *posterior probability distribution*:

$$prob\,(x = 1 \mid s = g) = \frac{\pi\lambda}{\pi\lambda + (1-\pi)(1-\lambda)}.$$

Notice that in case $\lambda = \frac{1}{2}$ the revised probability is just π: being uncorrelated with the outcome, the signal contains no information. In contrast, in the $\lambda = 1$ case, the revised probability is one: the signal is perfectly correlated with the outcome so observing the signal is as good as observing the realization of x itself. We shall thus refer to λ as the *precision* of the signal.

8.4 Information Efficiency

Section 8.3 is an exercise probability theory. The object of our investigation is an economic one: how markets, populated by rational players, who understand the

[5] See Section A.3.3 of the Mathematical Appendix.

Table 8.2 The two-signal case, with $\pi = 0.4$, $\lambda = 0.7$ and $\mu = 0.6$

joint distribution		signal			
		(g,g)	(g,b)	(b,g)	(b,b)
x	1	$\pi\lambda\mu$	$\pi\lambda(1-\mu)$	$\pi(1-\lambda)\mu$	$\pi(1-\lambda)(1-\mu)$
	0	$(1-\pi)(1-\lambda)(1-\mu)$	$(1-\pi)(1-\lambda)\mu$	$(1-\pi)\lambda(1-\mu)$	$(1-\pi)\lambda\mu$
$prob(x=1\|\text{signal})$		0.7	0.51	0.3	0.16

theory of Bayesian updating, aggregate information into prices. Since we are also interested in the normative evaluation of the aggregation process, we need to provide a benchmark of performance. Consider the case of two players with private signals: $P1$ has the benefit of a higher-quality (higher precision) signal, λ, compared with the precision of $P2$'s signal, μ; see Table 8.2. The expression (g, b), say, denotes a g realization for $P1$ and a b realization for $P2$. The two signals are independent one of the other: the probability that $P1$'s receives a g signal is λ, regardless of $P2$'s signal. To facilitate the discussion we provide a numerical example: $\pi = 0.4$, $\lambda = 0.7$ and $\mu = 0.6$. Now, what would have happened had the signals been public, observable by all? Then Bayes Law could have been used in much the same way as before; for example

$$prob\,[x = 1 \mid (g, b)] = \frac{\pi\lambda(1-\mu)}{\pi\lambda(1-\mu) + (1-\pi)(1-\lambda)\mu},$$

equal to 0.51 for the case of our numerical example. It makes sense to define such updated probability as a benchmark against which we could measure how well the market aggregates private information. Hence:

Definition 8.1. An equilibrium price is said to be information efficient if all the private information that the players receive are aggregated into the market price 'as if' all the signals were common knowledge and the inference is executed using Bayes Law.

Two points are worth emphasizing. First, we make no use of the dichotomy of strong versus weak information efficiency, popularized by many finance textbooks; we simply measure how close the price is to our benchmark. Second, the notion of information efficiency is often confused with the notion of economic efficiency. Indeed, we shall argue, below, that in some cases markets may be economically inefficient as a direct consequence of them being highly information efficient.

8.5 Competitive Rational-Expectations Equilibria

We carry on with the above example: two players, and $y_e^{P1} = y_e^{P2} = \bar{c}$ (no systemic risk), with prior beliefs of π and two private independent signals of precision $\lambda > \mu$, respectively. The no macro-risk assumption is convenient as the full-information equilibrium price is just the probability that $x = 1$. Though the realizations of the signals are private information, their precision (namely the values of λ and μ) are common knowledge. The players are rational in the sense that they understand how to use Bayes Law and they also understand how the market operates. They know that other players command the same understanding.

Crucially, each player should realize that the market has more information than he has. Therefore, each player should try to extract whatever information she can from the market price and combine it with his own private information, which gives rise to the following definition:

Definition 8.2. A competitive rational-expectations (RE) equilibrium satisfies the following properties: i) the equilibrium price clears the market, ii) each player derives inferences regarding the value of the ADS by combining the information that she extracts from the market price with that of her own signal and, iii) each player adjusts his demand to his revised inference.

To understand how the RE-equilibrium works, suppose that *P*1 got a *g* signal and *P*2 got a *b* signal. The signals are private information, therefore providing each player with only part of the information available to the market as a whole. For example, from his signal alone, *P*1 can safely infer that combination of signals is either (g, g) or (g, b) – see horizontal broken-line rectangle in Table 8.3. But then, the players also learn from market price. Consider a market price: $p = 0.51$. At that price, *P*1 should apply the following line of thinking: 0.51 is consistent with me getting a *g* signal, which is certainly the case, and *P*2 getting a *b* signal, which, I guess, is the case. At a (g, b) realization of signals, both me and the other player should revise our expectations to $prob\,[x = 1 \mid (g, b)] = 0.51$. Hence, at $p = 0.51$ I am not interested in any active trading; nor should *P*2 be interested in active trading. From a market price of $p = 0.51$, it follows that, indeed, *P*2 is not engaged in active trading: since my trade is zero, had *P*2 engaged in active trading, the market would not clear and 0.51 would not be an equilibrium price. That confirms that *P*2 got a *b* signal and is guessing that I got a *g* signal. The other player is also rational and, therefore, follows the same line of thinking as I do, confirming his guess about my *g* signal. If so, all the information that I have is consistent with an equilibrium price of $p = 0.51$.

Though this argument may seem somewhat circular, it is useful to note that for any other price this argument breaks down. For example, a price of 0.7 would conflict, head-on, with the private information that *P*2 has: 0.7 can clear the market

Table 8.3 A *RE* equilibrium with a (g, b) signal

		P2	
		g	b
P1	g	(g,g)	(g,b)
	b	(b,g)	(b,b)

only if both players get a g signals but $P2$ got a b signal. (g, b) is the only combination of signals that is consistent with the private information of both players; see the intersection of the two broken-line rectangles in Table 8.3. Hence, 0.51 is the only price that can clear the market and avoid a clash with the players private information and their understanding about the way that the market works.

Proposition 8.1. *A RE equilibrium is information efficient.*

8.5.1 The 'No-trade' Result

The result, above, that all private information is revealed with no active trade actually taking place is derived for the special case that $y_e^{P1} = y_e^{P2} = \bar{c}$, so that there is no macro risk and no personal exposure to state-e risk. Milgrom and Sokey (1982) have demonstrated that the result applies more generally. (Paul Milgrom is winner of the 2020 Nobel Prize in Economics.) Consider the market for the e-contingent ADS. We now assume that state-e is exposed to macro risk: $y \neq \bar{c}$. There are $j = 1, \ldots, J$ heterogeneous players, differentiated by their risk aversion, θ^j, their a^js and their initial exposure, y_e^j.

Now, suppose that, ex ante, players assign the same prior probability to event e. They trade the ADS and establish an ex-ante equilibrium:

$$p_e^{ex-ante} = \pi_e^{prior}\left(a^j - \theta^j c_e^j\right), j = 1, \ldots, J, \tag{8.1}$$

$$\Sigma_{j=1}^J \left(c_e^j - y_e^j\right) = 0 \quad \Rightarrow \quad \Sigma_{j=1}^J c_e^j = \Sigma_{j=1}^J y_e^j \neq \bar{c}. \tag{8.2}$$

That is, given the ex-ante market price, $p_e^{ex-ante}$, each player selects a level of e-contingent consumption according to $j = 1, \ldots, J$ equations (8.1), from which certain trades, $c_e^j - y_e^j$, positive or negative, buy or sell respectively, follow. Then, the market clears when these trades add up to zero, which can be also written as: market demand for state-e consumption equals the market supply of state-e

income. From the assumption that state e is exposed to macro risk it follows that $p_e^{ex-ante} \neq \pi_e^{prior}$. Notice also that, in all likelihood, equilibrium involves active trading, unless, by sheer coincidence, $c_e^j = y_e^j$ for each and every $j = 1, \ldots, J$.

Next, suppose that ex post, each player receives a private signal. Through a process similar to the one described above, an updated probability, common to all players, $\pi_e^{updated}$, arises. Let

$$\frac{\pi_e^{updated}}{\pi_e^{prior}} = \kappa,$$

κ (the Greek letter kappa) being, simply, the ratio between the prior and the updated probability. Looking for an ex post price, let us try:

$$p_e^{ex-post} = \kappa \times p_e^{ex-ante}.$$

Substituting that price and the updated probability in the J (8.1) equations, we get:

$$p_e^{ex-post} = \kappa \times \pi_e^{prior}\left(a^j - \theta^j c_e^j\right), j = 1, \ldots, J.$$

That is: the same $c_e^1, \ldots, c_e^J$ demands that were preferable at the ex-ante price, are also the demands that are preferable at the κ-product of the ex-ante price. Since these demands clear the market ex ante, they must also clear the market ex post. Conclusion: $\kappa \times p_e^{ex-ante}$ is, indeed, the ex-post equilibrium price. Moreover, since $c_e^1, \ldots, c_e^J$ are already delivered through ex-ante trades, there is no need for any extra (active) trading in order to reach the equilibrium price. This argument is applicable to all $\omega = 1, \ldots, \Omega$ (complete) markets in the economy.

To summarize:

Proposition 8.2. *Following the arrival of news (private signals) to a competitive (complete markets) RE equilibrium, prices adjust to reflect the new information, without any trade actively taking place.*

Technically, the ex-ante trade exhausts all risk-sharing opportunities and puts the economy on a footing similar to the two-player $y_e^{P1} = y_e^{P2} = \bar{c}$ case. Then, new information in the form of private signals arrives, but the aggregation of this information into a new ex-post price requires no active trading. In spite of its common name, the 'no trade' result does not imply that there is no active trading; the various motives for trade explored in Chapter 5 still apply—ex ante. At the same time, the no trade result highlights the conceptual difficulty of explaining information-based trading. Once the 'fundamental' motives for trade have been satisfied, any new private information is incorporated into players' expectations immediately, removing the motive to extra trade; see Bagehot (1971).

8.5.2 Conceptual Problems with the RE Equilibrium

The no-trade result further highlights the circularity in the argument behind Proposition 8.1. Notice, however, that rather than starting with an arbitrary price, then showing how the market *discovers* the equilibrium price (as we have done in Chapter 4), the argument starts with a market price and, then, demonstrates how the players verify that this is, indeed, an equilibrium price. But then, how can 'the market' present that price to the players without collecting their private signals in the first place? And what would happen if the market 'makes a mistake' and starts with none of the four prices in Table 9.2, say 0.59? Clearly, the players will not have any idea about how to proceed from that point onward.

While the above issues can be deemed as 'theoretical niceties', the next concern is clearly a substantial one. Suppose, for the sake of the argument, that the players can start the mental process above to confirm the equilibrium price. But then, if the price actually reveals all the information that they need in order to value of the security, why bother with checking that the market price is consistent with their own signal? Clearly, once traders believe that the market-price is indeed informative, they have no incentive to put any effort into collecting and processing information. Once players under-invest in information, economic efficiency cannot be obtained either. Grossman and Stiglitz (1980) highlight the point in their seminal paper titled: 'On the Impossibility of Informationally Efficient Markets'. Needless to say, the effect is directly related to Chapter 6's discussion regarding the public-good nature of information.

Another implication is that once players believe that the market price already carries all the relevant information, they would be willing to trade upon any market price. At that point the market turns from an information-processing mechanism to a herding mechanism, where convictions about the 'correct' value of assets are adopted for no good reason other than others' convictions. Instead of an information-efficient price, the market generates a 'bubble'.

8.5.3 Empirical Testing

Testing the RE theory is not easy. In most markets, new information keeps on arriving while older private information is still being aggregated. How can we distinguish, empirically, price changes due to information aggregation from price changes due to new information? Another question is against what benchmark should we evaluate the quality of the aggregation process? Remember that most financial markets aggregate information about news that feed into expectations, not actual outcomes; it is not clear what the 'correct expectations' should be used as a benchmark. Often, ingenuity in empirical work is in finding the setting in which difficult questions have 'clean' answers. Such is the test of RE that is suggested by Kandel et al. (1993).

The securities that are selected for this test are Israeli inflation-indexed government bonds, whose price is directly related to the monthly *consumer price index* (CPI), the cost of living as measured by the Central Bureau of Statistics (CBS). As it happens, prices are sampled during the month, processed during the first two weeks of the next month, released on the 15th day of that month. In between, there are 10 days when the market for indexed bonds is open for trading. Hence, the two problems mentioned above do not arise. First, during these 10 trading days, no event is realized that affects the CPI of the previous month (though such events will affect the CPI of the next month).[6] Second, since the event has already been realized (only the information about it still being processed), next-month's CPI announcement provides an exact benchmark against which the quality of the aggregation can be tested. Notice, also, that the traders in the bond market have all the relevant CPI information from their regular shopping. While each one is unlikely to shop for all the items that constitute the CPI, jointly they do buy the entire basket that is used in the calculation of the CPI. In that sense, this is a pure information-aggregation setting.

The main results of the study are presented on Figure 8.2.[7] The market's forecasting error is calculated against the CBS' announcement and against the 10th trading day. Since these forecasting errors may be either positive or negative, averaging them would provide a false impression of precision. Instead, the study computes the standard deviation of the forecasting error. The findings are consistent with

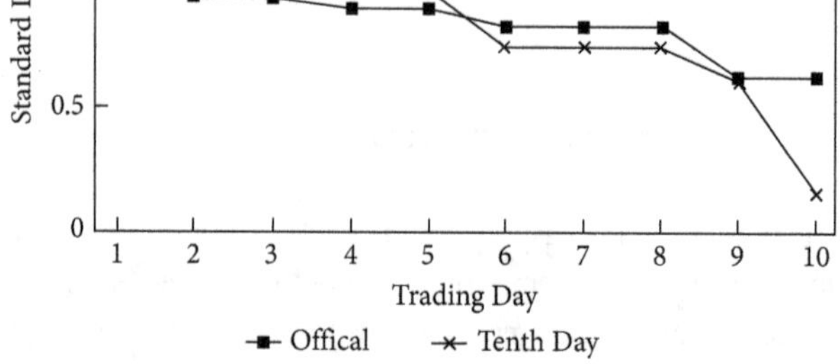

Figure 8.2 Market prices as CPI forecast (SD)

[6] To think separating this-month effect from the next, consider bonds that expired during the month and are therefore not affected by the next-month CPI. The actual calculations in the paper are more complicated.

[7] Reproduced from Kandel et al. (1993), Figure 8.2.

the hypothesis that through active trading, albeit executed in a remarkably short period of time, a significant amount of information is actually being incorporated into the market price, as predicted by the RE theory.

8.6 Sequential Updating and Information Cascades

A possible interpretation of RE is that information has a natural tendency to spread out, a view cleverly articulated by Mark Twain: 'two people can keep a secret if one of them is dead'. Less metaphorically, information is valuable to the extent that it guides action. Unlike the information, action tends to be observable by others. If so, revelation of private information may be a fact of life rather than a RE phenomenon. The theory of information cascades, originally developed by Bikhchandani et al. (1992), shows that this is not the case. In some settings, information is very poorly aggregated.

Consider a *sequence* of $j = 1, \ldots, J$ risk-neutral players. Each, in her own turn, gets the opportunity to invest in a project whose cash flow, x, is not yet known; it may be either 0 or 1, each outcome is equally likely. Whether it is 0 or 1, it is the same for all J players. The project requires an investment of 1/2, so that in absence of additional information, the players are indifferent between investing in the project—or not. Players have sufficient resources to fund the project—internally. To simplify things, we assume that the riskless rate is zero. Prior to investing, each players receives a private signal, $s^j = g, b$, informing her about the quality of the project, 1 or 0, respectively. The signal has $\lambda > 1/2$ precision. To be clear, players are heterogeneous in their information, but not in the properties of their projects. It follows that each new signal contains some additional information about the project's cash flow. Since decisions are sequential, each investor can observe the history of investment decisions by players who moved before her, but not their signal. Other than observing investment decision, there is no communication between the players. The key question is to what extent that information is aggregated as the game progresses and more investment decisions are revealed.

The $j = 1$ problem is simple. To interpret the signal, the player computes the joint distribution of quality and signals (see Table 8.4) and then applies Bayes' Law[8] in the usual manner,

$$prob\left(x = 1 \mid s^1 = g\right) = \lambda, \tag{8.3}$$

$$prob\left(x = 1 \mid s^1 = b\right) = 1 - \lambda. \tag{8.4}$$

[8] See Section A.3.3 of the Mathematical Appendix.

Table 8.4 Joint distribution of income and signals for $j = 1$

		signal	
		g	b
x	1	$\lambda/2$	$(1-\lambda)/2$
	0	$(1-\lambda)/2$	$\lambda/2$

Notice that our model's parametrization has the convenient property that the updated probability that $x = 1$ is also the updated expected gross value of the project, v^1. It follows that the $j = 1$ player faces a simple decision rule: invest upon a g signal and avoid the investment otherwise. Since each signal maps to a different action, a by-stander can map actions to signals in the opposite direction: observing that $I^1 = \frac{1}{2}$ one can infer, with confidence, that $s^1 = g$; a similar argument applies to $I^1 = 0$.

For subsequent players, it is useful to think of a two-step decision process. Firstly, player j, say, values the project on the basis of history, h, of the observed decisions of her $j-1$ predecessors:

$$v^{j-1} = prob\left(x = 1 \mid h^{j-1}\right), \qquad h^{j-1} = \left(I^1, I^2, \ldots, I^{j-1}\right).$$

Secondly, she applies Bayes Law on the joint distribution of the v^{j-1} and her own signal, so as to updated the historical information; see Table 8.5. Let the v_g function map the historical valuation of the g-signal update:

$$v_g\left(v^{j-1}\right) = \frac{\lambda v^{j-1}}{\lambda v^{j-1} + (1-\lambda)(1-v^{j-1})} > v^{j-1}. \tag{8.5}$$

Table 8.5 The joint distribution of x and s_j under a v_{j-1} prior

		signal	
		g	b
x	1	λv^{j-1}	$(1-\lambda)v^{j-1}$
	0	$(1-\lambda)(1-v^{j-1})$	$\lambda(1-v^{j-1})$

Table 8.6 Four possible $j = 2$ combinations of histories and signals

j=1		j=2	
h^1	v^1	s^2	v^2
I^1=1/2	λ	g	$v_g(\lambda) > 1/2$
		b	$v_b(\lambda) = 1/2$
I^1=0	$(1-\lambda)$	g	$v_b(1-\lambda) = 1/2$
		b	$v_b(1-\lambda) < 1/2$

Notice that the v_g function is the same for all players: though they witness different histories, they use the same v_g to update that history upon a g signal. Likewise, we define the v_b function:

$$v_b\left(v^{j-1}\right) = \frac{(1-\lambda)\,v^{j-1}}{(1-\lambda)\,v^{j-1} + \lambda\,(1-v^{j-1})} < v^{j-1}. \tag{8.6}$$

The direction of the inequality signs in Equations (8.5) and (8.6) may be derived algebraically, though the intuition is straightforward: upon a g signal update the historical valuation upwards, and upon a b signal update downwards.

Equipped with the two function, v_g and v_b, we can move on to the decision of $j = 2$. Table 8.6 describes the various combinations of histories and signals. For example, $I^1 = \frac{1}{2}$ fully reveals a g signal and, accordingly a $v^1 = \lambda$ historical valuation; so upon a b signal, the $j = 2$ player updates to $v_b(\lambda)$. A pedantic reader may want to go through some tedious calculations (substitute λ into the g_b function and simplify) in order to demonstrate that

$$v_b(\lambda) = \frac{1}{2},$$

but may also settle for an intuitive explanation: two signals, an historical g and a current b just cancel out, taking the $j = 2$ player back to the prior probability that $x = 1$, namely to $\frac{1}{2}$. For a similar reason, it is also the case that $v_g(1-\lambda) = 1/2$. As for the case of two consecutive g signal, by the direction of the inequality signs in Equation (8.5) it is clear that

$$v_g(\lambda) > \frac{1}{2}.$$

That is, a prior valuation of 1/2 was revised upwards by $j = 1$ upon a g signal and, then, revised upwards again upon a g signal by $j = 2$. For similar reasons, $v_b(1-\lambda) < 1/2$, which completes the description of Table 8.6. The derivation of I^2 follows. For the two cases where $v^2 = 1/2$, where the player is indifferent between investing and avoiding investment, we assume, for simplicity, that she follows her own signal, that is investing upon a g signal and avoiding investment otherwise. It therefore follows that decisions are, still, fully revelling at this stage of the game: for $j = 1, 2$ $I^2 = \frac{1}{2}$ indicates a g signal and $I^2 = 0$ indicates a b signal.

Things become more complicated for the $j = 3$ player. As explained above, two out of the four $j = 2$ histories, $\left(\frac{1}{2}, 0\right)$ and $\left(0, \frac{1}{2}\right)$, contain no information taking the player 'back to square one', so that the $j = 1$ analysis applies. Consider, however, the $j = 2$ history $\left(\frac{1}{2}, \frac{1}{2}\right)$ and a b signal at $j = 3$. Again, the pedantic reader may want to execute the tedious calculation so as to derive the result:

$$\nu_g\left[\nu_g(\lambda)\right] > \nu_b\left[\nu_g(\lambda)\right] = \lambda, \tag{8.7}$$

but resort to intuition otherwise: since, for the sake of statistical inference, the order of the signals does not matter, in a (g, g, b) sequence one b signal 'cancels out' against one g signal, the remaining g signal yields a valuation of λ. The inequality on the left-hand side of Equation (8.7) is straightforward. We have therefore derived a striking result: upon a $\left(\frac{1}{2}, \frac{1}{2}\right)$ history, $I^3 = \frac{1}{2}$, regardless of whether the $j = 3$ player receives a g signal or a b signal. It follows that his investment decision no-longer reveals his signal. By a similar argument, upon a $(0, 0)$ history, $I^3 = 0$, regardless of whether she receives a g or a b signal.

Now comes the critical step in the argument: a $j = 4$ player that observes a $j = 3$ history of $\left(\frac{1}{2}, \frac{1}{2}, \frac{1}{2}\right)$ should realize that the $j = 3$ player just followed the decision of his two predecessors. Hence, the $j = 4$ player finds herself in exactly the same position as the $j = 3$ player. That is:

Proposition 8.3. *Following a draw of (g, g) signals for $j = 1, 2$, all subsequent players, $j \geq 3$, would opt for $I^j = \frac{1}{2}$, regardless of their signals. It follows that no matter how long the history of investment decisions $\left(\frac{1}{2}, \frac{1}{2}, \ldots, \frac{1}{2}\right)$ is, $j \geq 4$ players treat it is just a $\left(\frac{1}{2}, \frac{1}{2}\right)$ history. That is, the game has stopped aggregating information from the $j = 3$ player, onward. Such a property is called information cascade. A similar argument applies following an initial (b, b) draw.*

As for a game that starts with a draw of a (g, b) signal or a (b, g) signal, as noted above, that puts the $j = 3$ player on an equal footing as the $j = 1$ player. It is still possible that a (g, g) draw would occur for players $j = 3, 4$, which would cause a cascade for the $j = 5$ player. In case of another (g, b), say, draw for the $j = 3, 4$ players, there is still a possibility of a $j = 7$ cascade; and so on. It follows that

Proposition 8.4. *In a sequential updating game, as $J \longrightarrow \infty$, the probability of a cascade at some point approaches one.*

Notice, however, that it is not a cascade per se that should worry us but, rather, being locked into the 'wrong' cascade, namely a situation where, say, $x = 1$, but the coincidence of two initial (b, b) signals locks the system into a $I = 0$ cascade. The probability of that happening for the $j = 3$ player is $(1 - \lambda)^2$. The probability of $j = 3$ going back to square one is $2\lambda(1 - \lambda)$ It follows that the probability of a wrong cascade by $j = 5$ is $(1 - \lambda)^2 [2\lambda(1 - \lambda)]$. And so on. The probability of a wrong cascade occurring at some point in a $J \longrightarrow \infty$ game is[9]

$$prob\,(\text{wrong cascade}) = \Sigma_{i=0}^{\infty} (1 - \lambda)^2 [2\lambda(1 - \lambda)]^i = \frac{(1 - \lambda)^2}{1 - 2\lambda(1 - \lambda)}. \tag{8.8}$$

Figure 8.3 plots the probability of a wrong cascade as a function of the precision of the signal. As signal precision increases, the likelihood of a wrong cascade falls, although it vanishes completely only when $\lambda = 1$.

To complete the argument we analyse the likelihood of 'getting it wrong' under efficient information aggregation, say, if all players could send their signals to a central statistical office that would process the data and make the results public. Clearly, the statistical office would have to update its estimates as more information accumulates. In that case, the advice would be to invest if the statistical office observes higher (or equal) than 50% g signals in the population and avoid investment otherwise. Probability theory tells us that as the population size approaches infinity, the likelihood of getting it wrong approaches zero even if the signal is just weakly informative (as long as $\lambda > 0.5$). To get an idea about the rate of converging to the correct inference, and since general calculations are tedious, we satisfy ourselves with a numerical example:[10] given a realized income $x = 1$, the likelihood of more than 50% b signals in small populations for a mildly informative signal of $\lambda = 0.65$ is presented in Table 8.7. Evidently, that convergence rate is quite high.

The standard interpretation of an information cascade is that of herding: players take a certain action for no good reason other than other's doing so before them. While herding is commonly viewed as an instance of stupidity, the important

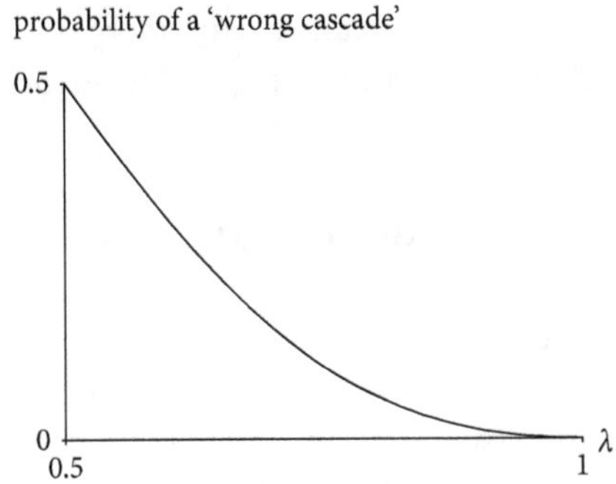

Figure 8.3 The probability of getting it wrong, $\lambda = 0.65$

[9] Equation (8.8)'s $i = 0$ maps to $j = 3$ in the above discussion, $i = 1$ to $j = 5$, and so on.
[10] General formulae for a general binomial distribution can be found in any statistics textbook.

Table 8.7 The probability of getting it wrong, $\lambda = 0.65$

j	$prob\ (\#\mathbf{b} > \mathbf{j}/2 \mid \mathbf{x}{=}1)$
10	24.9%
20	12.2%
30	6.5%
40	3.6%
50	2.1%
60	1.2%
70	0.7%
80	0.4%
90	0.2%
100	0.1%

insight of the cascade analysis is that it can be a result of perfectly rational considerations (in an environment that poorly aggregates information). It is tempting to use the theory of information cascades in order to support the popular belief that financial markets are prone to 'bubbles' or 'fads'. Such interpretation is problematic, however, because there is no market in the setting above: there is no trade between players and, certainly, no market price.

Henrion and Fischhoff (1986) provide evidence consistent with herding among (supposedly) highly rational individuals: physicists conducting a scientific experiment, in this case a measuring the speed of light. Clearly, each experiment is affected by a measurement errors, which should not be correlated over time. The authors plot measurements (reported in academic journals) that show a high degree of correlation; see Figure 8.4.[11] That is, conditional on the publication of a result containing a positive measurement error, there is a high probability that the next published result would also contain a positive error.

8.7 Sequential Markets

Section 8.6 analyses a setting where players make decisions but there is no trade and no market price. Could the information cascade be eliminated by the introduction of market prices? Glostein and Milgrom (1985) suggest an amendment of the cascade model with a market, replacing the investment decision with a trading decision: buy or sell a single ADS with a $x = 1, 0$ cash flow, each outcome with a

[11] Figure 8.1 in Henrion and Fischhoff (1986).

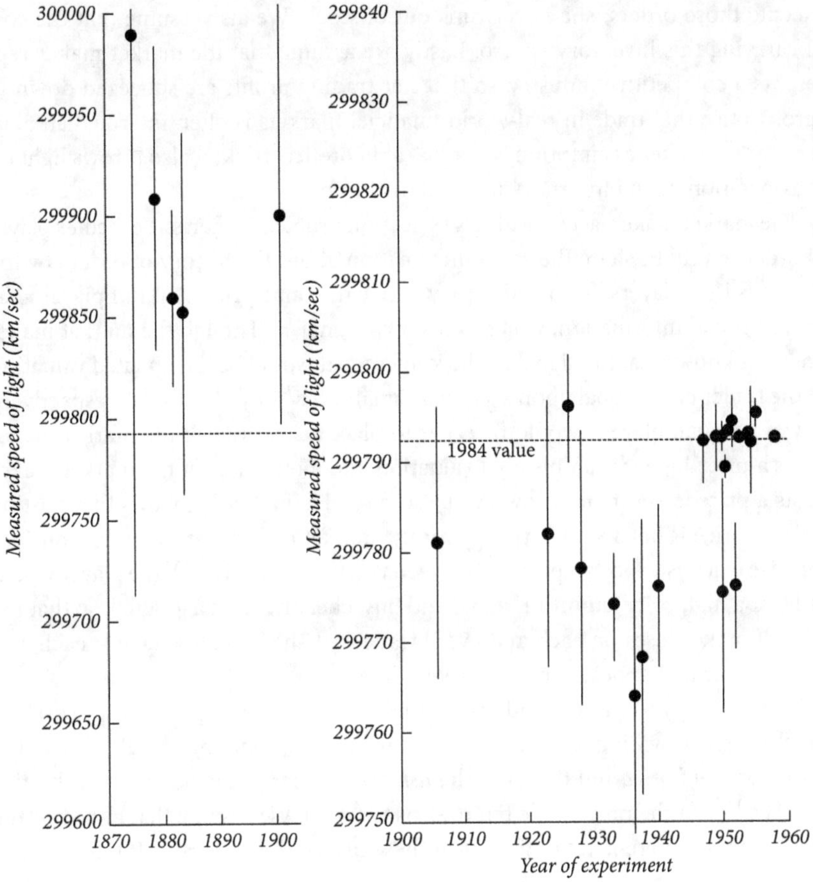

Figure 8.4 Over-time correlation in a scientific experiment

probability of 1/2. (If the player does not have the security, he can still sell short, as described in Section 5.9.3.2 of Chapter 5.) We keep the information structure the same as in Section 8.6; that is g and b signals of λ precision are private, trading is sequential and observable. But how can players trade if they are sequenced, so that each player arrives in the market only after the previous player has already left and before the next player is yet to arrive? We do so by introducing an intermediary, a *market maker* (or just 'the market') who stays in the market and trade with the one player that is present there at each round. Trading proceeds as follows: first the market maker posts a price (or prices), then the player submits a (single) buy or sell order, that the intermediary is committed to execute. The risk-neutral market maker has no information of her own, apart from the history of trades that she, herself, has executed. Since the market maker may face a few consecutive buy orders, say, she must hold an inventory of the security against which she would execute those orders; she never runs out of stock. We also assume that the cost of carrying this inventory is zero. Lastly, we assume that the market maker represents a competitive industry, so that her trading profits are squeezed down to zero. Notice that trade in real-world financial markets is often intermediated, so the market-maker assumption is not just a theoretical trick; it also throws light on the operation of an important financial institution.

The market maker faces an adverse selection problem: when she executes player j's order, say, both share the same information about the history of orders by the previous $j-1$ players, from which they derive the same prior, v_{j-1}. But player j has an additional information, which is his own signal, s^j. Though the market maker does not know what the signal is, she knows what would be the updated valuation of the trader conditional upon a g or a b signal: $v_g\left(v^{j-1}\right)$ and $v_b\left(v^{j-1}\right)$, respectively. Given a signal, player j would be eager to place a sell order if the market maker posts a price higher than his own valuation and a buy order if the market maker posts a price lower than his own valuation; see Figure 8.5. It follows that posting a single price is not a viable strategy for the market maker. For example: consider the case where she posts a price in between $v_b\left(v^{j-1}\right)$ and $v_g\left(v^{j-1}\right)$; the player would sell (for a high price) upon a b signal and buy, cheaply, upon a g signal, so that the market maker loses on each and every trade that she executes, against each and every player that appears on the market.

The only way to sustain trade is for the market maker to post two prices: one in which she is willing to buy, and one in which she is willing to sell. We call the former the *bid price* and the latter the *ask price*. Clearly, the only viable ask price is $v_g\left(v^{j-1}\right)$ and the only viable bid price is $v_b\left(v^{j-1}\right)$. We assume that although the players are indifferent about trading at these prices, they do trade. It follows that:

Proposition 8.5. *There exists fully revealing, information-efficient, equilibrium. For the $j=1$ player, the market maker posts bid and ask prices, $1-\lambda$ and λ, respectively thereby separating players by their signals. Upon a g (b) signal, the*

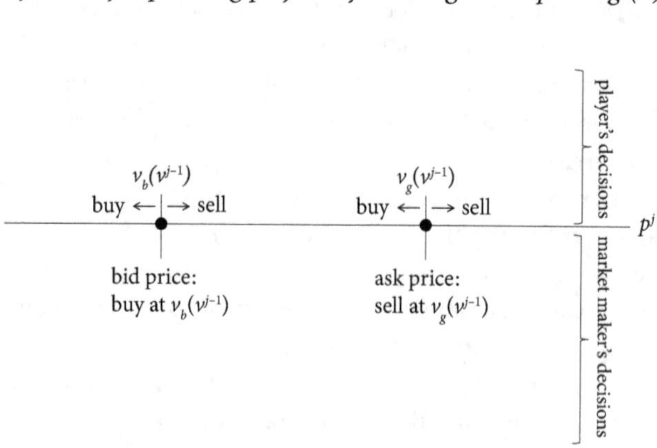

Figure 8.5 Updating in a sequential market

$j = 1$ player submits a buy (sell) order, which the market maker executes, at a zero-profit for both. It follows that a buy (sell) transaction reveals a g (b) signal, setting the transaction price, $p^1 = v^1$, whether the market maker buys or sells from the $j = 1$ player. For $j \geq 2$, the market maker post bid and ask prices, $v_b(p^{j-1})$ and $v_g(p^{j-1})$, respectively. Players submit buy (sell) orders upon g (b) signals, which are being executed. It follows that for any j, the price, $p^j = v^j$ is information efficient, fully revealing, and aggregating, all the private signals that the players received up to the jth round of trading. It also follows that as $J \to \infty$, $p^j \to 1$ if $x = 1$, and $p^j \to 0$ if $x = 0$.

Notice that the equilibrium preserves the simple intuition that buying (selling) activity drives market prices up (down).

8.7.1 Bid-Ask Spreads (I)

Figure 8.6 below simulates the relationship between market prices and the 'spread' between the bid and the ask prices, $v_g(p^{j-1}) - v_b(p^{j-1})$. It has an intuitive interpretation: prices around 1/2 indicate that the market did not accumulate much information about true valuations, either because little trade has occurred so far or because the market had an unlucky draw of roughly equal shares of buy and sell orders, which are not informative. In that region, the bid-ask spread is wide and the information content of the price is low. However, the spreads narrow down as the market accumulates more information and prices move towards either the zero or the unit end, which dilutes the value of any individual private signal. Hence, observable bid-ask spreads offer a good proxy to the severity of the adverse-selection problem in that market and, therefore, the intensity of the information-asymmetry problem.

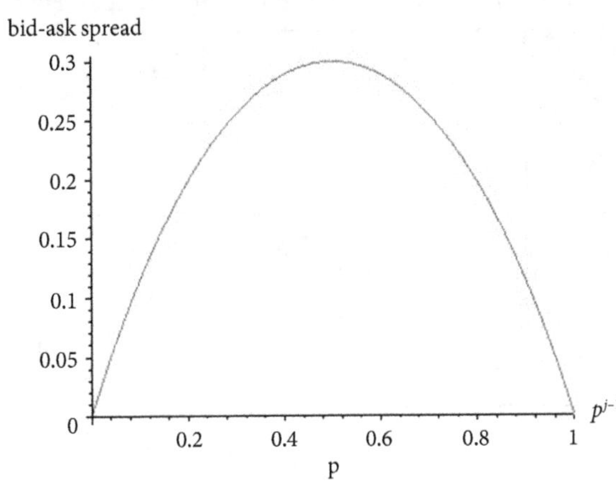

Figure 8.6 Bid-ask spreads and market prices, $\lambda = 0.65$

8.8 Noise Trading

So far, our analysis yields extreme results: either very poor information aggregation (in the cascade model) or a perfect aggregation (in the market maker model) with full revelation of private signals. Noise trading[12] is the extra ingredient that would take us towards the middle grounds of partial revelation. It would also modify another implausible implication of strong information efficiency: that privately informed traders cannot profit from their trades.

The only modification to the previous-section assumptions that each round, there is a probability ϕ that the player that appears on the market is informed with a private signal of precision λ, and $(1 - \phi)$ that he is a 'noise trader' with no private information. Noise traders are motivated by non-financial considerations such as random fluctuations in their consumption. Upon a surge (drop) in his private consumption, the noise trader sells (buys) the security so as to generate (use) the extra cash required (left) by fluctuating income. A noise trader buys or sells one unit of the security with a probability of 1/2; that is, whatever market conditions are, it is equally likely that the noise trader submits a buy or sell order.

Suppose (to be confirmed below) that bid and ask prices are set in such a way that the informed trader buys upon a g signal and sells upon a b signal. In such a case the joint distribution of x and market orders is presented in Table 8.8. It is still the case that p^{j-1} is the probability that $x = 1$, based on the (public) information contained in $j - 1$ rounds of trading. Looking, at the upper-left cell, say, the joint probability that $x = 1$ and the j'th trader is informed is $p^{j-1}\phi$; the joint probability that $x = 1$ and the j'th trader is a noise trader is $p^{j-1}(1 - \phi)$. But, then, there is a $\lambda > 1/2$ probability that the former gets a g signal and submits a buy order, while it is equally likely that the latter submits either a buy or a sell order. Notice, also, that in case the j'th trader is informed, the inference that he draws from the history

Table 8.8 Joint distribution of orders and income at the j'th round of trading

		orders	
		buy	*sell*
x	1	$p^{j-1}\left[\phi\lambda + \frac{(1-\phi)}{2}\right]$	$p^{j-1}\left[\phi(1-\lambda) + \frac{(1-\phi)}{2}\right]$
	0	$(1-p^{j-1})\left[\phi(1-\lambda) + \frac{(1-\phi)}{2}\right]$	$(1-p^{j-1})\left[\phi\lambda + \frac{(1-\phi)}{2}\right]$

[12] See Black (1986).

of the game is the same as the market maker, as both are equally ignorant about the type of traders in the previous rounds, whether they are noise or informed traders; obviously, the j'th player is perfectly informed about his own type.

The market maker therefore applies Bayes Law in the usual manner:

$$v_{g\text{-}noise}\left(p^{j-1}\right) = \frac{p^{j-1}\left[\lambda + \frac{1-\phi}{2\phi}\right]}{\left[p^{j-1}\lambda + \left(1-p^{j-1}\right)(1-\lambda)\right] + \frac{1-\phi}{2\phi}}, \tag{8.9}$$

$$v_{b\text{-}noise}\left(p^{j-1}\right) = \frac{p^{j-1}\left[(1-\lambda) + \frac{1-\phi}{2\phi}\right]}{\left[p^{j-1}(1-\lambda) + \left(1-p^{j-1}\right)\lambda\right] + \frac{1-\phi}{2\phi}}. \tag{8.10}$$

The $g - noise$ subscript indicates that although the market maker infers a g signal upon a submitted buy order, she cannot be confident that the order is based on a signal. Notice, however, that in case that the j'th trader is informed, he uses the $v_g\left(p^{j-1}\right)$ and the $v_b\left(p^{j-1}\right)$ functions, as he obviously knows that he is not a noise traders. With a bit of algebra, it is possible to establish that, for any price p^{j-1}, the following inequalities hold:

$$v_g\left(p^{j-1}\right) > v_{g\text{-}noise}\left(p^{j-1}\right), \tag{8.11}$$

$$v_b\left(p^{j-1}\right) < v_{b\text{-}noise}\left(p^{j-1}\right). \tag{8.12}$$

The inequalities in (8.11) and (8.12) are economically intuitive. The noise weakens the information content of the trade. Since the market maker doubts that the order is based on information, she revises her expectations more moderately in comparison to the case where she know for sure that the order is driven by private information. Figure 8.7 provides a diagrammatic exposition of the inequalities (8.11) and (8.12).

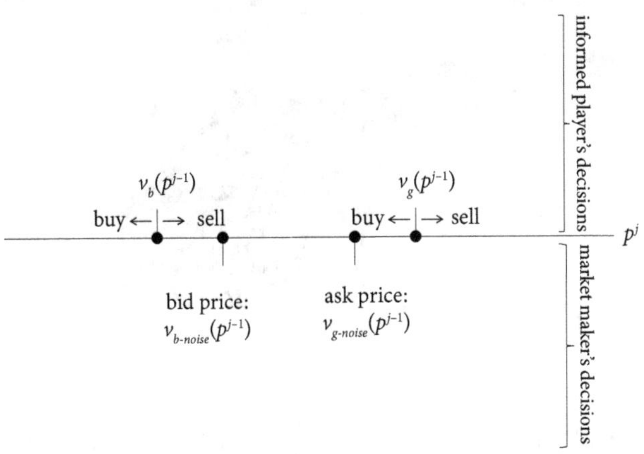

Figure 8.7 Updated valuation, informed player, and the market

Evidently, upon a g (b) signal, an informed player buys (sells) the security at the ask (bid) price, which is lower (higher) than his own valuation of the security. That is, whether he is buying or selling the security, he profits on the private information that he has. Intuitively, the presence of noise traders allows the informed players to hide the fact that they are trading on information and, that way, make a profit. Notice, however, that hiding is partial, for it is still the case that a buy (sell) order indicates a g (b) signal—in probability. The implication may be less dramatic than might seem on first glance:

Proposition 8.6. *With noise traders present, the equilibrium is only partially revealing in the sense that a jth round buy (sell) order adds a g(b) signal to the history of the game, but only with a probability smaller than one. The weaker information content of the price allows the informed traders to profit on their trade. At the same time, it is still the case that as* $J \to \infty$, $p^j \to 1$ *if* $x = 1$, *and* $p^j \to 0$ *if* $x = 0$, *only with slower convergence to that outcome.*

8.8.1 Bid-Ask Spreads (II)

To better appreciate the effect of noise trading, Figure 8.8 below reproduces Figure 8.6 with an extra dimension: the intensity of noise trading. Clearly, the more intense noise trading, the flatter is the bid-ask-spread curve over the zero-one price range. It is, therefore, still the case that the bid-ask spread is a proxi for the intensity of the asymmetric information problem.

Who gains from information asymmetry? Obviously the informed traders, but not the market maker who, by assumption, makes a zero profits—in expectations.

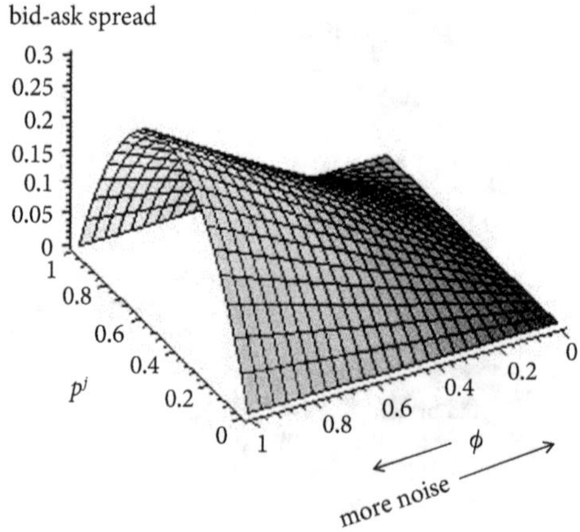

Figure 8.8 Bid-ask spreads as a function of prior beliefs and the incidence of noise trading; $\lambda = 0.65$

It must be at the expense of the noise traders who bear the cost, in the sense that the wider is the spread, the more they are 'punished' for being 'suspected' by the market for trading on private information although, by definition, they have none. In that sense, the bid-ask spread is a measure of market liquidity. At the same time a flat curve also creates more opportunities for the informed traders. (In terms of Figure 8.7, the curve flattens as $v_{g-noise}$ and $v_{b-noise}$ move closer, with no effect on v_g and v_b.) Intuitively, with more noise traders to hide behind, the value of private information increases.

The notion of liquidity was already twice mentioned in this book: in Chapter 4's (Section 4.7.3) discussion of fire sales, and in Chapter 6's (Section 6.3.4) discussion of the Diamond-Dybvig model. In all three cases, the word is inversely related to the cost that a trader has to bear when recovering the value of a commodity, in terms of cash or consumption goods, at a short notice. The motives of noise traders, as explained in this chapter, are actually quite similar to those of the Diamond-Dybvig consumers. Notice, however, that the opportunity costs of liquid inventories was assumed to be significant in the Diamond-Dybvig model, but zero in this chapter.

8.9 The Martingale Property

In the last two sections we have provided (for the first time in this book) an idea about how market prices evolve over time, and how the market discovers the 'true' value through the trading process. (Remember that the absence of a *price-discovery process* was a major weakness in the competitive rational-expectations analysis of Section 8.5.) Models with dynamic pricing commonly have a property called a 'Martingale', which implies that since the current price already captures all the information that was revealed to the market so far, the best prediction of a future price is just the current price. Formally,

$$E\left(p^{j+1} \mid p^{j}\right) = p^{j}. \tag{8.13}$$

We derive the result for the simpler case, without noise. Remember that next period the market will execute either a buy or sell order, the former revealing a g signal, the later revealing a b signal, after which the price will be updated accordingly. The probability of a g signal is λ if $x = 1$ and $(1 - \lambda)$ if $x = 0$. But, then, the probability that $x = 1$ is, simply, p^j, while the probability that $x = 0$ is $\left(1 - p^j\right)$. With similar considerations about a b signal, It follows that

$$\begin{aligned} E\left(p^{j+1} \mid p^{j}\right) &= p^{j}\left[\lambda v_g\left(p^{j}\right) + (1-\lambda) v_b\left(p^{j}\right)\right] \\ &\quad + \left(1-p^{j}\right)\left[(1-\lambda) v_g\left(p^{j}\right) + \lambda v_b\left(p^{j}\right)\right] \\ &= \left[\lambda p^{j} + (1-\lambda)\left(1-p^{j}\right)\right] v_g\left(p^{j}\right) + \left[(1-\lambda) p^{j} + \lambda\left(1-p^{j}\right)\right] v_b\left(p^{j}\right). \end{aligned}$$

Using the v_g and v_b as specified in Equations (8.5) and (8.6), the Martingale result follows. The case with noise trading follows a similar logic.

Proposition 8.7. *Equilibrium prices in a sequential market, with or without noise trading, have the Martingale property: the best predictor of future prices is just the current price.*

The Martingale property has attracted a huge amount of empirical work if only because it is readily testable by running the regression

$$P_j = a + bP_{j-1} + \varepsilon_j,$$

not rejecting the Martingale hypothesis if $a = 0$ and $b = 1$.

8.10 Herding and Bubbles

The question above, whether information cascades vanish once a market price is introduced into the analysis was answered in the affirmative. Even with noise trading, which slows down the information-aggregation process, the market does converge to the 'correct' price in the long run.

Though this result is quite general, it is worth mentioning that certain short-term herding would appear in settings similar to those of Section (8.8) but with few additional sources of noise; see Avery and Zemsky (1998). The argument is way too complicated to be reproduced here. For completeness, we present in Figure 8.9 (Figure 1 in Avery and Zemsky (1998)) one of their simulations. Notice that although herding created a 'bubble' in the short run, a 'bubble burst' took place, eventually.

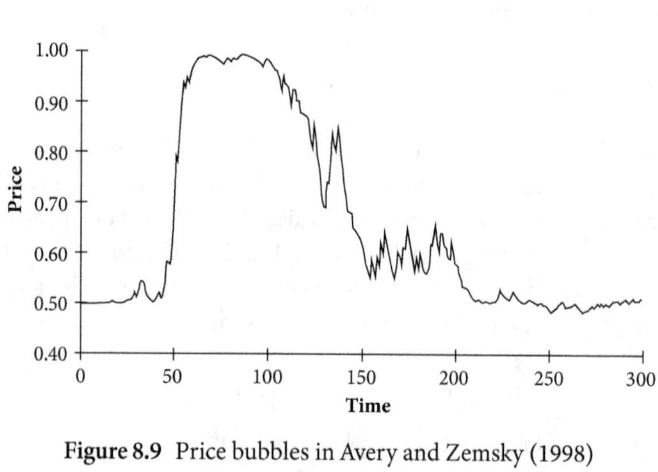

Figure 8.9 Price bubbles in Avery and Zemsky (1998)

8.11 Information Efficiency and Economic Efficiency

Not only that information efficiency and economic efficiency are distinct concepts, in some cases they stand in direct conflict. As already hinted in Section 8.5, above, a market that is too efficient in aggregating information robs participants of the ability to profit on information and, hence, the incentive to generate it. Grossman and Hart (1980), provide a classic example.

In fact, Grossman and Hart expose the weakness in a commonly used argument. Consider a listed company with a widely dispersed ownership, with small shareholders lacking a sufficient incentive to monitor and discipline the managers, who may be more interested in drawing out private benefits than in managing the company. In such companies, where control is separated from ownership, the market for corporate ownership can provide an alternative governance mechanism. Under-performing companies can be *taken over* by *raiders* who buy their shares on the stock market, replace the managers, improve performance and, then, sell the restructured company for a profit. The weakness in this argument, according to Grossman and Hart, is that the share price would respond so strongly to the news about the takeover that it would rob the raiders from the incentive to launch the takeover. There is ample empirical evidence that prices, indeed respond in that way to news about takeover bids.

The Grossman–Hart argument goes as follows. Suppose the current price of the mismanaged company is v, but could go up to $v + \Delta, \Delta > 0$ following a restructuring. The raider places in the market a *conditional tender offer* to buy the company at a price $v + p$, where $0 < p \leq \Delta$. The word 'conditional' means that transaction would be executed only if the shareholders tender the offer in sufficient numbers to grant the raider control.[13] A small (risk-neutral) shareholder's incentive to tender the offer depends on the take over's probability of success. We denote that probability by λ. By tendering the offer, a small shareholder would get his own ownership share of the entire corporate value of

$$\text{profit from tendering} = \lambda\,(v + p) + (1 - \lambda)\,v.$$

By not tendering the offer, a small shareholder would get his own ownership fraction of

$$\text{profit from not tendering} = \lambda(v + \Delta) + (1 - \lambda)\,v.$$

The critical point is that by not tendering, a small shareholder could still benefit from a successful takeover, by collecting his share of the value created by the restructuring, Δ. In fact, regardless of λ, the best response to the offer is not to

[13] Typically, the raider gains control upon buying 50% of the voting rights.

tender if $p < \Delta$. It follows that the takeover can only succeed is if the raider offers a full price, that is

$$p = \Delta.$$

But then, the raider would have to pay out the entire value of the extra productivity to the current shareholders.

It worth noting the role of competition in the above argument. Small shareholders may not tender exactly because, individually, they are too small to have a material effect on the outcome of the takeover bid. As competitive players, they are price takers and, in addition, take the probability of success as given though, obviously, jointly they determine the outcome of the takeover bid. Notice that if only they were holders of significant stakes in the company, a transfer price would be negotiated through a bargaining process which, by the Coase Theorem, would end in a successful transfer of ownership and a following restructuring, to the mutual benefit of the old owners and the raider.

Clearly, the problem would be somewhat less severe if the raider is allowed to build up a certain stake in the company before revealing his intention to takeover the company. Doing so, he would be able to capture a fraction of Δ, proportional to his early position. In fact, in many countries regulators allow the buildup of a certain position so as to facilitate take-over activity. Notice, however, that this policy would work only to the extent that the marker is not 'too information efficient', revealing the raider's position on an early stage of the build-up. In other work, the market has to be liquid enough, with enough noise traders that the raider can 'hide behind' while building up his position.

8.12 Concluding Remarks

What have we learned from the eight chapters of this manuscript?

By and large, financial markets trade title to commodities rather than commodities proper. In Chapter 5 we abstract from the factors that differentiate the title from its underlying commodity in order to derive elegant pricing formulas. Some of these formulas are widely used by financial practitioners. In Chapters 3, 6, or 7 we have focus the analysis on factors that differentiate titles from underlying contingent commodities: a default to deliver the commodity as promised, a difficulty in describing the commodity, missing markets for trading the titles. We have used the word 'frictions' widely across this book, without giving it a precise or general definition; we did, however, provide a more rigorous analysis of some special cases of such frictions; Chapter 7's analysis of information asymmetry is probably the best example. We suspect that 'frictions' may be responsible for the Mehra–Prescott equity-premium puzzle.

Frictionless trade, either in the form of bilateral bargaining (Chapter 2) or in a competitive complete-markets economy (Chapters 4 and 5) deliver economically efficient outcomes. When frictionless trade fails, more complicated mechanisms may be instituted so as to recover, as much as possible, trading opportunities that, otherwise, would be lost to the friction. Because financial markets are information intensive, and since information is a public good (Chapter 6), they present a wide spectrum of such institutions. The three models of debt presented in this manuscript, the Hart–Moore model of security interests, the Diamond–Townsend model of costly state verification and the Myers–Majluf model of information-insensitive debt are good examples. The institution of the modern corporation may just be a nexus of contracts that operates to resolve conflicts of interests among the company's stakeholders. Financial intermediaries also play an important role; for example, Diamond's theory of banking as delegate monitors; Glosten–Milgrom's market maker is another example.

That information is a public good does not call in the regulators, automatically. It is widely agreed that the state plays an important role in the enforcement of contracts. The Diamond–Dybvig analysis of liquidity (Chapter 6) demonstrates that liquidity may be a public good, under provided in a competitive, incomplete markets, equilibrium. Much of the activity of central banks can be understood as liquidity provision. Chapter-4's analysis of the fire-sale market may strengthen the argument. Some contracts create externalities and should, therefore, be banned; for example, insurance companies should be prohibited from discriminating on grounds of diagnostic tests of genetic conditions; see the Hirshleifer effect on Chapter 6. A more controversial case is the role of courts in repairing faulty contracts, as in the case of a creditors' run caused by the failure to prioritize a multitude of creditors; see Chapter 2.

Policy dilemmas are intensified by gaps in the analysis. By and large, titles to future, uncertain cash flows are priced on expectations. Expectations (even about uncertain events) may still be consensual, in which case the competitive, frictionless model applies (Chapter 5). In fact, the competitive model applies even where expectations are non-consensual, as long as the differences in beliefs do not originate in information asymmetries. Chapter 8 exposed a certain fragility in the structure of the competitive equilibrium once traders contribute their private information to market prices but, at the same time, also adjust their expectation to market prices. As we have seen, the circularity in this argument may turn an information-aggregation process into a herding process. The response of economic policy to the possible existence of 'bubbles' is still debated, among academics as well as policy makers.

The eight chapters of this book may seem conceptually detached one from the other, at least upon a first reading. It is hoped that a closer look would reveal a continuity, in terms of both method and substance. Unfortunately, the chapters do not add up to a single 'canonical model', a unified model based on just a few axioms.

This is a reflection of the present understanding of financial markets, rather than the introductory nature of this manuscript. The self-imposed restriction of using only 'simple maths' dictates a gross simplification of the analysis, in some cases even a sacrifice of analytical rigour. Readers are encouraged to 'dig deeper' into the arguments, equipped with sharper analytical tools. While such readers are guaranteed to find a deeper understanding as well as more rigour, they are unlikely to find the unifying principle; perhaps the opposite.

References

[1] Avery, Christopher and Peter Zemsky (1998). 'Multidimensional Uncertainty and Herd Behavior in Financial Markets', *American Economic Review*, Vol. 88, No. 4, pp. 724–748.

[2] Bagehot, Walter (1971). 'The Only Game in Town', *Financial Analysts Journal*, Vol. 27, No. 2, pp. 12–14+22.

[3] Bikhchandani, Sushil, David Hirshleifer, and Ivo Welch (1992). 'A Theory of Fads, Fashion, Custom, and Cultural Change as Informational Cascades'. *Journal of Political Economy*, Vol. 100, No. 5, pp. 992–1026.

[4] Utpal Bhattacharya, Hazem Daouk, Brian Jorgenson, and Carl-Heinrich Kehr, (2000). 'When an Event Is Not an Event: The Curious Case of an Emerging Market', *Journal of Financial Economics*, Vol. 55 (2000) 69–101.

[5] Black, Fischer (1986). 'Noise', *Journal of Finance*, Vol. 41, No. 3, pp. 529–543.

[6] Glostein, Lawrence R. and Paul R. Milgrom (1985). 'Bid, Ask and Transaction Prices in a Specialist Market with Heterogeniously-Informed Traders', *Journal of Financial Economics*, Vol. 14, 71–100.

[7] Grossman Sanford J. and Oliver D. Hart (1980). 'Takeover Bids, The Free-Rider Problem, and the Theory of the Corporation', *Bell Journal of Economics*, Vol. 11, No. 1, pp. 42–64.

[8] Grossman, Sanford J. and Joseph E. Stiglitz (1980). 'On the Impossibility of Informationally Efficient Markets', *American Economic Review*, Vol. 70, No. 3, pp. 393–408.

[9] Hayek, F. A. (1945). 'The Use of Knowledge in Society', *American Economic Review*, Vol. 35, No. 4, 519–530.

[10] Henrion, Max, and Baruch Fischhoff, (1986). 'Assesing Uncertainty in Physical Constants', *American Journal of Physics*, Vol. 54, No. 9, 791–797.

[11] Kandel, Shmuel, Aharon R. Ofer, and Oded Sarig (1993). 'Learning from Trading', *Review of Financial Studies*, Vol. 6, No. 3, pp. 507–526.

[12] Milgrom, Paul, and Nancy Stokey (1982). 'Information, Trade and Common Knowledge', *Journal of Economic Theory*, Vol. 26, No. 1, pp. 17–27.

Mathematical Appendix

Most of the material in this book can be understood with only a basic competence in mathematics, which most students achieve at the age of 16. This appendix presents a few results that might go beyond that level. The presentation does not pretend to be rigorous, general, or comprehensive, only to deliver a level of familiarity with the concepts that are required in order to understand the main body of the text.

A.1 The Sum of an Infinite Geometric Series

A geometric series is obtained by adding, successively, a term that multiplies the previous term by $q < 1$, the first term being q itself. If that goes on 'for ever', then the series is infinite. For example,

$$\frac{1}{2} + \frac{1}{4} + \frac{1}{8} + \frac{1}{16} + \ldots$$

is an infinite geometric series with $q = 1/2$. Although it has an infinite numbers of terms, their sum may be finite. It turns out that an infinite geometric series 'will converge' if $q < 1$, so that the successive terms become, eventually, so small that they 'do not matter any longer'.

Provided that the sum actually exists, finding its magnitude is a simple matter. Denote that sum by V. Then,

$$V = q + q^2 + q^3 + q^4 + \ldots,$$

or using an abbreviated notation

$$V = \Sigma_{i=1}^{\infty} q^i,$$

(the symbol Σ, the Greek capital letter sigma, is used as a summation operator, to be read: sum all q^i elements, from $i = 1$ to $i = \infty$, where ∞ means infinity). Factoring out q for the second term and above, we can write

$$V = q + qV.$$

Solving out for V we get

$$V = \frac{q}{1 - q}.$$

A.2 Functions and Graphs

Economics is largely about magnitudes, say, prices, profits or sales, expressed in numbers. In some cases, it is useful to think of combination of such numbers. Consider a combination of two numbers, (x_1, y_1). Notice that the *variable* x can take on many values, x_1 being just one of them; same goes the variable y and the number y_1. The combination (x_1, y_1) can be represented as a *point* in the (x, y) space, namely a diagram that plots the variable x on the horizontal axis and the variable y on the vertical axis; see Figure A.1.

A function is an operator that maps objects from one set to objects in another set. The former set is called the *domain* of the function and the latter set is called the *destination* of the function. It is common to use the variable x over objects in the domain and the variable y over objects in the destination. Hence, $y = f(x)$ reads: the function f maps every x object to a y object. For example, Figure A.2 plots a graph of a function where both the objects in

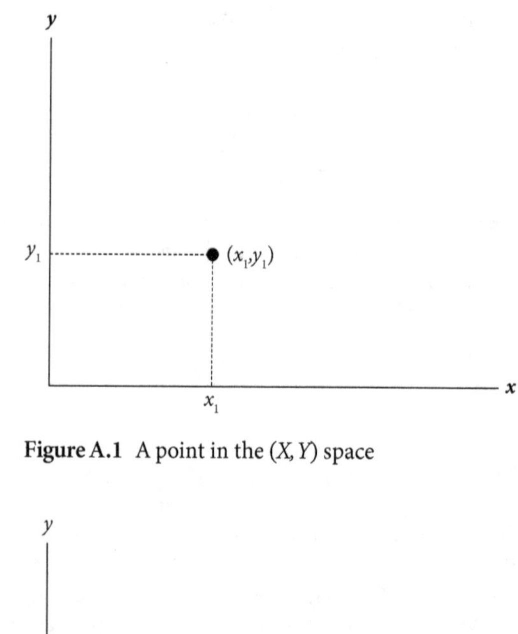

Figure A.1 A point in the (X, Y) space

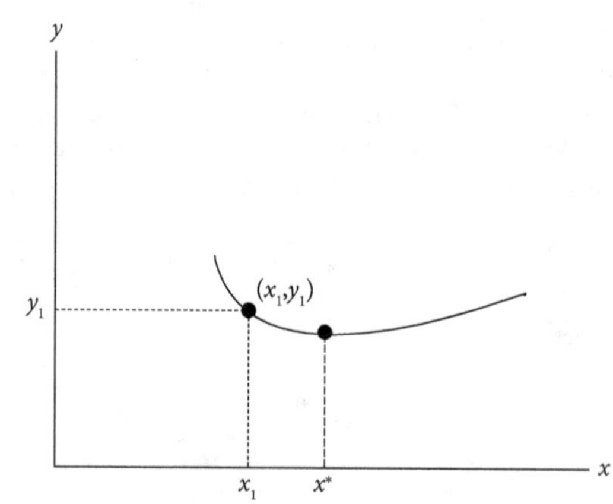

Figure A.2 A convex function

the domain and the destination are numbers. As it happens, it maps the number x_1 to the number y_1 so that point (x_1, y_1) lies on the graph of the function. Alternatively, the graph of the function passes through the point (x_1, y_1).

The function whose graph is plotted in Figure A.2 happens to be convex (with respect to the origin). Convex function may have a point, in this case x^*, such that for any $x \neq x^*$, $f(x^*) < f(x)$; x^* is a minimum. The function f is downwards sloping to the left of x^* and upwards sloping to the right of x^*. Alternatively, f is decreasing in x to the left of x^*; that is, if $x_l < x_h < x^*$, then $f(x_l) > f(x_h)$; f is increasing in x to the right of x^*. Rotating the graph in Figure A.2 'up side down' would result in a concave function, which might have a maximum point.

The formula,

$$y = f^L(x) = a + bx,$$

defines the family of linear functions, differentiated by the parameters a and b. Evidently, $f^L(0) = a$, which defines the point $(0, a)$ at which the graph of f^L intersects with the vertical axis, giving a the common name: *intercept*; see Figure A.3. Then, $f^L(1) = a + b$, $f^L(2) = a + 2b$, $f^L(3) = a + 3b$... which defines a family of triangles with a common vertex at point $(0, a)$ with the property

$$\frac{f^L(x) - a}{x} = b.$$

It follows that: i) the graph of any member of the f^L family is a straight line. ii) The slope of that line is the angle next to the point (0, 1) in Figure A.3; rather than measuring that slope in degrees, we can measure it through the ratio between the sides of the above triangles, namely the number b. It is common to call b, simply, the *slope* of an f^L function.

For any point x, a linear functions has the same slope. For example the function whose graph is presented in Figure A.3 is increasing in x, for any x. An increasing linear function is characterized by a positive b, while a negative b is associated with a function that is decreasing in x. A zero b implies a flat graph, while a vertical graph implies a b that tends to infinity. Notice, also that b has a simple economic interpretation: the change in y per unit-change in x.

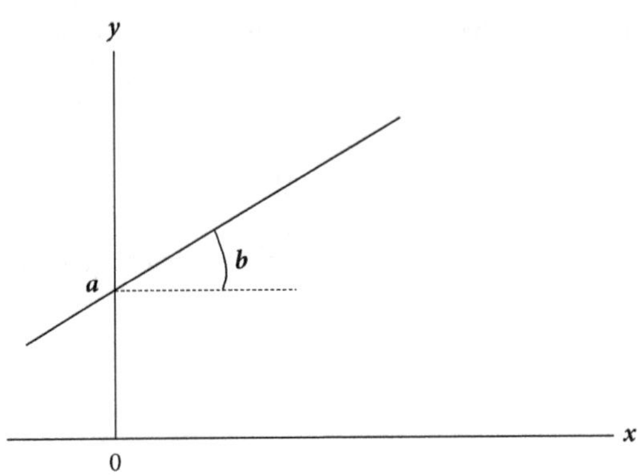

Figure A.3 A linear function

It also follows that any two points mapped by a linear function are sufficient in order to draw the graph of that function. Accordingly, such points are sufficient in order to solve out the intercept and the slope of that function. That is,

$$y_1 = a + bx_2, \qquad y_2 = a + bx_2$$

define two equations in in two unknowns, a and b, which we can solve out:

$$b = \frac{y_2 - y_1}{x_2 - x_1}, \qquad a = \frac{y_1 x_2 - x_1 y_2}{x_2 - x_1}.$$

Linear functions play an important role in economic analysis. Obviously, they are simple to handle. Also, they can 'approximate' some other functions, if not every other function. As we shall see in Section A.5, below, the use of a linear specification in empirical work is, actually, less restrictive than one may imagine.

A.2.1 Notation

There is a tradeoff between precision on the one hand and brevity and simplicity on the other hand. In that tradeoff, we lean, in this book, towards simplicity, even at the cost of inconsistency and, sometimes, imprecision. The policy is, simply, to shorten the notation where it is felt that the reader can follow 'naturally'. For example, we replace the long notation $\Sigma_{j=1}^{J}$ by the shorter notation Σ_j once it is clear that the summation goes from 1 to J. While it is better to denote a variable as, say, x and a value by x_1, say, I drop the subscript 1 where the notation is already too heavy (particularly in Chapter A.5). In diagrams, the variable x is differentiated from a specific of x, by writing the former in bold font. We use ab for 'a times b', but $a \times b$ where the latter might be confused with a constant named 'ab'. We use brackets when there are multiple parentheses just to facilitate the reading, with no added meaning so that

$$a\left[x + b\left(y + z\right)\right] = a\left(x + b\left(y + z\right)\right).$$

As much as we try to unify the notation across the various chapters, the material is too diverse to do so successfully.

A.3 Probability

Probability theory is widely used in financial economics, both in the modelling of risk and in developing statistical methods.

A.3.1 Random Variables

A random variable can yield several outcomes, some more likely than others. For example, tossing a fair coin may yield either 'head' or 'tail', with probability of 0.5—each. Consider a discrete[1] random variable, $\tilde{x}$, with only Ω possible outcomes; we use the tilde symbols above variables in order to separate a random variable from a non-random variable, but drop the tilde where context makes the distinction clear enough. The outcomes are indexed by $\omega = 1, 2, \ldots, \Omega$, so that x_ω is a typical outcome with a probability π_ω. (ω is the Greek letter omega, Ω being capital ω; π is the Greek letter pi.) The probabilities are positive and add-up to one, implying that all the conceivable outcomes of $\tilde{x}$ are accounted for. The probability is a measure of an outcome's likelihood: the higher the probability, the more likely is the outcome. The *probability distribution* of $\tilde{x}$ can be to described by a bar chart like the one in Figure A.4, below. The various values of $\tilde{x}$ are plotted on the horizontal axis and the πs on the vertical axis.

Another way to describe a probability distribution is through its *moments*. The first moment is the *mean*:

$$E(\tilde{x}) = \pi_1 x_1 + \pi_2 x_2 + \ldots + \pi_J x_\Omega,$$

where E is the *mathematical expectations operator*. Using more concise notation:

$$E(\tilde{x}) = \Sigma_{\omega=1}^{\Omega} \pi_\omega x_\omega. \tag{A.1}$$

The mean resembles the average over a set of numbers, only that the mean also applies to theoretical distributions, for which there may be no actual realization. The second moment is the *variance*:

$$Var(\tilde{x}) = \pi_1 [x_1 - E(\tilde{x})]^2 + \pi_2 [x_2 - E(\tilde{x})]^2 + \ldots + \pi_\Omega [x_\Omega - E(\tilde{x})]^2$$

or, in concise notation

$$Var(\tilde{x}) = E[\tilde{x} - E(\tilde{x})]^2. \tag{A.2}$$

Higher moments generalize Equation (A.2) with powers higher than 2, but we shall ignore them here. The variance captures the dispersion of a variable around its mean. For that purpose we measure each outcome's deviation from the mean, square it, and take expectations. The larger the deviations, the larger the variance. It is common to denote

$$Var(\tilde{x}) = \sigma_x^2$$

(σ being the Greek letter sigma). The square root of the variance is the *standard deviation*, σ_x.

The following properties are implied by simple algebra, where k is an arbitrary constant:

$$E(k\tilde{x}) = \Sigma_\omega \pi_\omega (kx_\omega) = k\Sigma_\omega \pi_\omega x_\omega = kE(\tilde{x}),$$

$$Var(\tilde{x} + k) = E[(\tilde{x} + k) - E(\tilde{x} + k)] = Var(\tilde{x}), \tag{A.3}$$

$$Var(k\tilde{x}) = E[kx_\omega - E(k\tilde{x})]^2 = k^2 [x_\omega - E(\tilde{x})]^2 = k^2 Var(\tilde{x}). \tag{A.4}$$

[1] Most of the results, below, also apply to continuous random variables, though the technical machinery may differ substantially.

Notice that k is factored out by virtue of being a constant, i.e. a non-random number, which highlights the importance of using the tilde in order to clearly denote random variables. Notice, also, that while $\tilde{x}$ is a random variable, its mean, $E(\tilde{x})$ is a constant. Hence, the mean can be factored out as in the next result:

$$\begin{aligned} Var(\tilde{x}) &= E[\tilde{x} - E(\tilde{x})]^2 \\ &= E\left[\tilde{x}^2 - 2\tilde{x} \times E(\tilde{x}) + (E(\tilde{x}))^2\right] \\ &= E\left(\tilde{x}^2\right) - 2E(\tilde{x}) \times E(\tilde{x}) + [E(\tilde{x})]^2 \\ &= E\left(\tilde{x}^2\right) - [E(\tilde{x})]^2 . \end{aligned} \tag{A.5}$$

A.3.2 Joint Distributions

The co-incidence of two random variables, $\tilde{x}$ and $\tilde{y}$ is described by their *joint distribution.* Table A.1 provides a simple example. Though both are *binomial* variables, that is variables that have only two possible outcomes, the joint distribution has four possible outcomes, so that π_{00} is the probability that both yield zero, π_{10} is the probability combination $\tilde{x} = 1$ and $\tilde{y} = 0$, and so on.

Consider, first, case A, where $\pi_{00} = \pi_{01} = 0.2$ and $\pi_{10} = \pi_{11} = 0.3$. $\tilde{x}$ is more likely to be realized as 1 than 0, in comparison to $\tilde{y}$ that yields 0 and 1 with equal probabilities. Hence, $E(\tilde{x}) = \pi_{10} + \pi_{11} = 0.6$ and $E(\tilde{y}) = \pi_{01} + \pi_{11} = 0.5$. Notwithstanding, $\tilde{x}$ and $\tilde{y}$ are independent variables, for $\tilde{y}$, say, is equally probable to generate 0 or 1 whether $\tilde{x} = 0$ or $\tilde{x} = 1$. This fact is captured by the key parameter for a joint distribution: the *covariance*, defined as:

$$Cov(\tilde{x}, \tilde{y}) = E([\tilde{x} - E(\tilde{x})][\tilde{y} - E(\tilde{y})]).$$

The reader may verify for the above A case that

$$Cov^A(\tilde{x}, \tilde{y}) = 0.$$

In contrast, consider case B where $\tilde{y}$ tends to be higher when $\tilde{x}$ is higher: $\pi_{00} = 0.3$, $\pi_{01} = 0.1$, $\pi_{10} = 0.2$, $\pi_{11} = 0.4$. For simplicity, the example is constructed so that the

Table A.1 Joint distribution function of two binomial variables

		$\tilde{y}$	
		0	1
$\tilde{x}$	0	π_{00}	π_{01}
	1	π_{10}	π_{11}

means of both $\tilde{x}$ and $\tilde{y}$ are the same as in A-case, 0.6 and 0.5, respectively. The reader may verify that, the more likely coincidence of high outcomes in case B is reflected in a positive covariance, or a positive *correlation*

$$Cov^B(\tilde{x},\tilde{y}) = 0.1.$$

Had $\tilde{y}$ tended to be lower when $\tilde{x}$ is higher, that would reflect in a negative covariance.

The following notation is commonly used:

$$Cov(\tilde{x},\tilde{y}) = \sigma_{xy}.$$

Notice, also, that $Var(\tilde{x}) = Cov(\tilde{x},\tilde{x})$, so that $\sigma_x^2 = \sigma_{xx}$.

Following the similar steps as in the derivation of Equations (A.4) and (A.5), it is easy to see that

$$Cov(k\tilde{x},\tilde{y}) = kCov(\tilde{x},\tilde{y}),$$
$$Cov(k+\tilde{x},\tilde{y}) = Cov(\tilde{x},\tilde{y}),$$

and

$$Cov(\tilde{x},\tilde{y}) = E(\tilde{x}\times\tilde{y}) - E(\tilde{x})\times E(\tilde{y}).$$

Another useful result is:

$$\begin{aligned}
Var(x+y) &= E[(\tilde{x}+\tilde{y}) - E(\tilde{x}+\tilde{y})]^2 \\
&= E[\tilde{x} - E(\tilde{x}) + \tilde{y} - E(\tilde{y})]^2 \\
&= E\left([\tilde{x} - E(\tilde{x})]^2 + 2[\tilde{x} - E(\tilde{x})][\tilde{y} - E(\tilde{y})] + [\tilde{y} - E(\tilde{y})]^2\right) \\
&= Var(\tilde{x}) + Var(\tilde{y}) + 2Cov(\tilde{x},\tilde{y}).
\end{aligned} \tag{A.6}$$

A.3.3 Conditional Means and Bayes Law

A more elegant and more intuitive manner of expressing the observations in Section A.3.2 is by answering the following question: suppose that we are provided with information that $\tilde{x} = 0$. How would that information affect our assessment of the prospects of $\tilde{y}$? Clearly, π_{10} and π_{11} are no longer relevant, for they indicate probabilities of outcomes that did not materialize. The *prior* probabilities, π_{00} and π_{01}, are relevant but require a *revision*, or an *update*, for it is now clear that *posterior* probabilities of outcomes 0, 0 and 0, 1 must add up to one, as these are the only possible outcomes left. At the same time there is no reason to change our assessment of the relative likelihood of events 0, 0 and 0, 1. These considerations are summarized by *Bayes Law*, which tells us how to derive probabilities *conditional* on the information that certain outcomes are no longer relevant. Hence:

$$Prob(\tilde{y} = 0|\tilde{x} = 0) = \frac{\pi_{00}}{\pi_{00} + \pi_{01}}. \tag{A.7}$$

In words: Equation (A.7) derives the probability that $\tilde{y} = 0$, *conditional* on the information that $\tilde{x} = 0$. Conditional means are derived in a similar manner.

We can now use conditional probabilities to characterize cases A and B of Section A.3.2. In the uncorrelated case A,

$$Prob^A(\widetilde{y} = 1|\widetilde{x} = 0) = Prob^A(\widetilde{y} = 1|\widetilde{x} = 1) = 0.5.$$

That is: knowing the outcome of $\widetilde{x}$ requires an updating of the posterior probability of the outcome $\widetilde{y} = 1$, but that made no material difference, as the result was the same as the unconditional probability $\widetilde{y} = 1$:

$$Prob^A(\widetilde{y} = 1) = \pi_{01}^A + \pi_{11}^A = 0.5.$$

In contrast to case B, where

$$Prob^B(\widetilde{y} = 1|\widetilde{x} = 0) = 0.25, \qquad Prob^B(\widetilde{y} = 1|\widetilde{x} = 1) = \frac{2}{3},$$

so that the revised probabilities indicate a more likely $y = 1$ conditional on the information that $x = 1$, in comparison to the, prior, unconditional probability of $\widetilde{y}$,

$$Prob^B(\widetilde{y} = 1) = \pi_{01}^B + \pi_{11}^B = 0.5.$$

A.4 Statistics: Sampling

Statistics is the science of inferring the properties of a *population* from a relatively small amount of data collected from that population—a *sample*. The problem facing the statistician is how to process the data so as to get the most reliable *inference* about the population. Since, in practice, the statistician knows nothing about the population, there is no way she can compare her inferences to the characteristics of the population, thereby assessing the quality of the inference. She can, instead, construct an example of a theoretical population and model a random sampling process. Since, within the example, the properties of the population are known, she can compare the results of the inference to the properties of the population. Once she finds a reliable inference technique, she can apply it to a real sample, hoping that its relationship to the (unknown) population is similar to that which is identified in the example.

Consider an example of a 'large' population generated by a random variable, $\widetilde{x}$ that takes the values 1, 2, and 3, with equal probability, $\pi = \frac{1}{3}$, each. It follows that $E(\widetilde{x}) = 2$, $Var(\widetilde{x}) = \frac{2}{3}$ and $\sigma_x = \sqrt{\frac{2}{3}}$

Suppose that we try to infer the mean of the population, $E(\widetilde{x})$, but, for some reason, we are restricted to a single sample with only two observations. Crucially, the sampling is completely *random*, with each observation drawn out of the population independently of previous draws from the same population.

Obviously, the sample does not give us a precise description of the population. For example, there is a probability of $\frac{1}{3} \times \frac{1}{3}$ that our sample contains observations with values 1 and 2, in which case the sample mean is $1\frac{1}{2}$. However, the reader may verify that averaging across all 9 conceivable samples, the result is 2. That is, studying the mean of a population by looking at a sample's mean gives a correct result 'on average'.

To be more precise, the sample mean, being just a combination of randomly selected variables is, itself, a random variable, call it $\widetilde{m}$. As such, it has its own probability distribution,

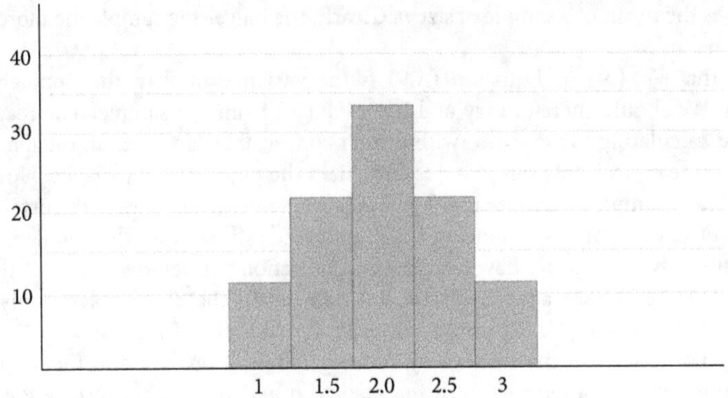

Figure A.4 Probability distribution of the sample mean

which is clearly distinct of the probability distribution of the $\widetilde{x}$ variable. For example, the latter is a *uniform distribution* with only three equal-probability outcomes while the later has five possible outcomes,[2] the central ones being more probable than the extreme ones; see Figure A.4. That both distributions have the same mean, 2, implies, loosely, that 'inferring the mean of a population by calculating the mean of a randomly drawn sample gives the right result, on average'. In fact, a more analytic derivation of this result is an immediate application of equation (A.4) above:

$$E(\widetilde{m}) = E\left(\frac{\widetilde{x}+\widetilde{x}}{2}\right) = \frac{1}{2}E(\widetilde{x}) + \frac{1}{2}E(\widetilde{x}) = E(\widetilde{x}). \quad \text{(A.8)}$$

The result is easily generalized for samples larger than two and populations other than $\widetilde{x}$. An estimator that has Equation (A.8)'s property, namely that its mean equals the population's mean is called an *unbiased estimator.*

Being unbiased implies that the a sample's mean measures the population's mean with an error, which is zero in expectations. Notwithstanding, given a sample, the measurement error can still be sizable. To get a better idea of its magnitude, we should calculate $\widetilde{m}$'s variance, which is just the mean of the squared measurement error. (By definition of 'unbiased', $\widetilde{m}$'s measurement error, which takes both positive and negative values, has a mean of zero.) Using Equation (A.6) above, we calculate:

$$Var(\widetilde{m}) = Var\left(\frac{\widetilde{x}+\widetilde{x}}{2}\right) = Var\left(\frac{\widetilde{x}}{2}\right) + Var\left(\frac{\widetilde{x}}{2}\right) = 2\frac{Var(\widetilde{x})}{4} = \frac{Var(\widetilde{x})}{2}. \quad \text{(A.9)}$$

(Remember that the two observations in the sample are drawn independently one from the other, so their covariance is zero.) The square root of the result in Equation (A.9) is called the *standard error* of the sample mean; in general, it is the stipulated standard deviation of an estimated parameter. Equation (A.9) is easy generalize to a sample of any size, n:

$$Var(\widetilde{m}_n) = \frac{\sigma_x}{\sqrt{n}}, \quad \text{(A.10)}$$

[2] There are 3 × 3 conceivable ordered draws; however, since some, say (1, 3), (3, 1) and (2, 2) yield the same mean, $\widetilde{m}$ has only five conceivable values.

where $\tilde{m}_n$ is the mean of a sample of size n. Clearly, the bigger the sample the more precise is the estimation.

Notice that $Var(\tilde{x})$ in Equation (A.9) is the variance of $\tilde{x}$ in the population—an unknown. We should therefore try and infer $Var(\tilde{x})$ from the sample. The reader may verify that calculating the variance within each conceivable sample and, then, averaging across the nine conceivable samples does not yield the population's variance. However, if instead of each sample's mean we use the population's mean[3] we do get the 'correct result'. In other words, the sample's variance is not an unbiased estimator for the population's variance. Fortunately, statisticians have developed a correction that removes the bias, the detail of which we leave to more advanced texts. It is noteworthy that the problem vanishes in a large sample, as one might grasp, intuitively, from Equation (A.10).

The observations above motivate an important generalization regarding the simplest and most intuitive of estimation methods: the *method of moments.* That is, take the sample moments (mean, variance, covariance, etc.) for the moments of the population. The larger the sample, the more accurate the result is.

A.5 Linear Regression

Regression analysis is the most commonly used statistical tool in empirical economics. Suppose that we have a sample of X and Y pairs, indexed by $i = 1, 2, ..., N$, (X_i, Y_i). Theory tells us that the two variables are related, so we opt to investigate the sample *assuming* that it is a draw from a population where the joint distribution of the variables $\tilde{X}$ and $\tilde{Y}$ can be described by the linear *structure*:

$$\tilde{Y} = \alpha + \beta\tilde{X} + \tilde{\varepsilon}. \tag{A.11}$$

The common terminology *explanatory variable* for $\tilde{X}$ and *dependent variable* for $\tilde{Y}$ hints at some causal interpretation. Such a relationship may be implied by the theory that motivated Equation (A.11) but it plays no role in the statistical analysis that rests, purely, on correlations. We say more about causality at the end of this section. α and β (the Greek letters alpha and beta) are the intercept and the slope, respectively, and they are the main object of interest.

The relationship between $\tilde{X}$ and $\tilde{Y}$ is not a precise one; had it been, just a sample of two, (X_1, Y_1) and (X_2, Y_2) would be sufficient to estimate α and β, accurately; see Section A.2, above. Rather, there are other factors that affect Y in addition to X; hence the *error term*, $\tilde{\varepsilon}$ (the Greek letter varepsilon). However, the crucial assumption is that these other factors do not operate in a systematic manner. Hence, we assume that $\tilde{\varepsilon}$ has a mean of zero; even more importantly, that $\sigma_{X\varepsilon} = 0$, namely $\tilde{\varepsilon}$ and $\tilde{X}$ are uncorrelated. This, is the famous *exogeneity assumption* of regression analysis. It is important to emphasize that exogeneity is an assumed property of the population, not an observation about the sample, where neither α nor β, nor the covariance $\sigma_{X\varepsilon}$ are observed. We denote the variance of $\tilde{\varepsilon}$ by σ_{ε}^2.

It follows form ε's zero mean that

$$E(\tilde{Y}) = \alpha + \beta \times E(\tilde{X}). \tag{A.12}$$

[3] That is, for the (1, 2) sample, $\frac{1}{2}\left[(1-2)^2 + (2-2)^2\right]$ instead of $\frac{1}{2}\left[\left(1-1\frac{1}{2}\right)^2 + \left(2-1\frac{1}{2}\right)^2\right]$.

Subtracting Equation (A.12) from Equation (A.11) we express the structure in terms of $\tilde{y} = \tilde{Y} - E(\tilde{Y})$ and $\tilde{x} = \tilde{X} - E(\tilde{X})$, namely the deviations of $\tilde{X}$ and $\tilde{Y}$ from their respective means:

$$\tilde{y} = \beta\tilde{x} + \tilde{\varepsilon}.$$

It follows from the structure *and* the assumption that $\sigma_{x\varepsilon} = 0$ that[4]

$$\sigma_{xy} = E(\beta\tilde{x} + \tilde{\varepsilon})\tilde{x} = \beta\sigma_x^2, \quad \Rightarrow \quad \beta = \frac{\sigma_{xy}}{\sigma_x^2}. \tag{A.13}$$

Now comes the critical step: suppose that the sample is large enough so that we can use the method of moments and, simply, substitute sample moments s_{xy} and s_x^2, for the population moments, σ_{xy} and σ_x^2 in Equation (A.13) to derive the *ordinary least squares* (OLS) estimator,[5]

$$b = \frac{s_{xy}}{s_x^2}.$$

Notice that b, the sample's estimator for β, is a combination of random variables and is, therefore, itself, a random variable. The exact distribution of b around β, is the business of the science of econometrics. Given b and the sample means of X_i and Y_i, an estimator a, for α, can be solved out of Equation (A.12).

The estimation of *multivariate regressions*, namely structures such as

$$\tilde{Y} = \alpha + \beta^X\tilde{X} + \beta^Z\tilde{Z} + \tilde{\varepsilon}, \tag{A.14}$$

follows the same logical steps as the derivation the *univariate regression* above, though the algebra is somewhat more involved.

A.5.1 Hypothesis Testing

Consider a test of the.

$$H_0: \qquad \beta = 0,$$

hypothesis, namely that $\tilde{Y}$ is unrelated to $\tilde{X}$. Suppose that, on the basis of a certain sample, a relatively low b is estimated, which seems to justify a non-rejection of the null hypothesis. How confident can we be in not rejecting the null hypothesis? The answer depends on b's probability distribution, particularly its standard error. For there is clearly a certain probability that a zero-β population has yielded, by chance, a sample with a low b too distant from 0. The practice is, therefor, to derive a critical value, such that there is only 5% probability, say, that H_0 was rejected by chance. Needless to say, the probability of erroneous

[4] Notice that since x is the deviation of X from its own mean, both variables have the same variance.

[5] For example, for $E(\tilde{X})$ we substitute $\overline{X} = \frac{1}{N}\Sigma_i X_i$, for $Var(\tilde{x})$ we substitute $s_x^2 = \frac{1}{N}\Sigma_i (X_i - \overline{X})^2$, and so on.

inference can never be brought down to zero. Most computerized statistical packages have built-in options to calculate critical values for various levels of required statistical significance. A common rule of thumb is that an estimated two standard errors away should reject the null.

Statistical significance is distinguished from *economic significance*, the actual magnitude of b. Consider, for example, testing the hypothesis that a carbon tax has affects a lower emission of carbon dioxide. A researcher collects a sample of cases where an emission tax was levied and runs a regression where $\widetilde{Y}$ is emission tonnage and $\widetilde{X}$ is the tax levy (per ton). Suppose that a negative coefficient is derived—statistically significant. However, statistical significance is not sufficient to establish that the tax has achieved its goal, namely that the economic magnitude of the change is big enough to resolve the pollution problem.

A.5.2 Dummy Variables

A dummy variable, D receives a value of 1 if a certain condition is satisfied and zero otherwise. Dummy variables are handled like 'normal' variables in a regression analysis. They are particularly useful in financial economics when we try to identify the effect of certain laws or regulations on corporate or market performance. Structures with dummy variables yield predictions such as: the relationship between X and Y changes when a certain condition is satisfied.

Dummy variables can be used in multivariate specifications in order to model 'breaks' in graphs. Construct a dummy variable such that $D = 1$ if $X > \underline{X}$ and zero otherwise. Then, the specification

$$Y_i = a + bX_i + b^{BR}D_i + e_i,$$

(e is the sample's estimated variable ε) implies that $Y_i = a + bX_i + e_i$ to the left of $\underline{X}$ and $Y_i = \left(a + b^{BR}\right) + bX_i + e_i$ to the right of $\underline{X}$. With $b^{BR} > 0$, we get a *piecewise linear* specification; see Figure A.5. It is important *not* to add into the regression another dummy variable,

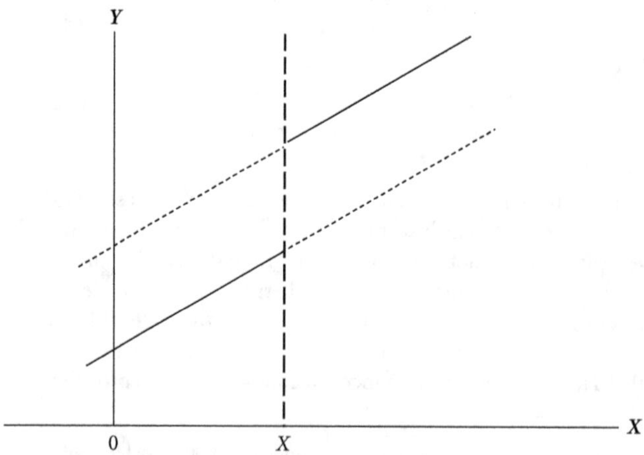

Figure A.5 A piecewise linear specification

$D_{other} = 1$ if $X \leq \underline{X}$, so that any observation in the sample is covered by either D or D_{other}. In such a case, $D + D_{other} = 1$ for each and every observation in the sample, duplicating the regression intercept.

It is worth mentioning that dummy variables can also be used as independent variables, in which case the regression can be interpreted as an estimation of the probability of the dummy's unit outcome. However, such specifications raise many statistical issues that are well beyond the scope of this appendix.

A.5.3 *R*-squared

A regression's *R*-squared (between zero and one) is defined as

$$R^2 = 1 - \frac{s_e^2}{s_y^2}.$$

That is, R^2 is the share of $Y's$ variance that is 'explained' by the regression. It is common to view a high *R*-squared as sign of 'success' in data analysis, which is only partly justified. For, in fact, the purpose of econometric research is to identify a relationship between variables rather than the magnitude of the 'other factors' which are not even specified. Yet, a low R^2 would imply that predictions based on the estimated relationships are likely to deviate, significantly, from prediction implied by the regression, even if 'on average' such deviations are expected to be zero.

A.5.4 Non-linear Specifications

It might seem, at first glance, that assuming a linear specification is restrictive. In fact, one can use the linear specification as a platform on which non-linear specifications can be modelled. For example, adding a squared explanatory variable to a univariate specification:

$$Y_i = a + bX_i + b^{SQ}X_i^2 + e_i$$

with $b^{SQ} > 0$ indicating a convex function. Adding higher powers of would yield *polynomial* specifications that could capture even more complicated shapes. In conjunction with dummy variables, even more irregular shapes can be specified. The reader may already sense, intuitively, that the study of a non-linear relationships requires much more data than the study of a linear relationship. In practice, a limited amount of data leaves little room for such experimentations.

A.5.5 Interpretation of Regression Results

The precise interpretation of a well-specified and well estimated regression model is that

$$E\left(\tilde{Y}|X\right) = a + bX.$$

That is, conditional on X, the mathematical expectation of Y is $a + bX$, admitting, of course, that the error term might take Y significantly away from its expected value. Alternatively, that the slope b, measures the expected change in Y conditional on a unit change in X.

Now consider the emission-tax example above: given that we know that the change in X is instituted by the government in an attempt to curb emission, can we also conclude that there is a causal link between taxation and emission? The answer is: not necessarily.

For three reasons, at least. First, the information that the change in X was a result of government action is external to the statistical analysis. If only for the sake of accuracy in the reporting of research results, we should make a distinction between what we can learn from the data and what we can learn from other sources. Second, government policy must be a result of considerations that are intimately related to emission. The existence of a causal effect from emission to policy implies that Equation (A.8) is not well specified and needs to be amended so as to account for the feedback channel. In general, miss specified models yield biased results. Third, it is possible that the government's new awareness of the environment has motivated it to take some other steps in addition to taxation. Not being specified in the regression, these extra steps are included in the 'all sorts of other factors', namely the error term. The contemporaneous nature of the various policy steps creates a positive correlation between X and the error term, in violation of the exogeneity assumption. In the extreme, it might be the case that the tax has no effect on emission and the negative b just captures the impact of the other steps, which, by virtue of faulty specification, the regression attributed to the tax.

Evidently, *controlling* for all these factors through the inclusion of additional variables and refining the specification would alleviate some of these concerns. However, a doubt would always linger regarding effects that we could not control for, or did not think about. As explained in Chapter 1, a statistical analysis that finds a correlation between two variables does not 'prove' a theory right. At best, it can provide evidence that are consistent with the theory, thereby not rejecting it—for the time being.

Index

Please note that page references to Figures will be followed by the letter 'f', to Tables by the letter 't'.

The manufacturer's authorised representative in the EU for product safety is Oxford University Press España S.A. of el Parque Empresarial San Fernando de Henares, Avenida de Castilla, 2 – 28830 Madrid (www.oup.es/en or product.safety@oup.com). OUP España S.A. also acts as importer into Spain of products made by the manufacturer.

www.ingramcontent.com/pod-product-compliance
Lightning Source LLC
LaVergne TN
LVHW011819200926
848484LV00005B/1249
* 9 7 8 0 1 9 2 8 6 9 7 3 9 *